Guides to Wines & Top Vine

Tuscany

2022 Edition

Benjamin Lewin MW

Wines of Tuscany

ISBN: 9781980411093

Vendange Press

www.vendangepress.com

Benjamin Lewin MW (USA)

- originally a molecular microbiologist

Preface

This guide to the wines of Tuscany covers the major areas where the focus is on either Sangiovese (Montalcino, Chianti Classico, and Montepulciano) or Bordeaux blends (Bolgheri, Suvereto, Maremma, and Super Tuscans). The first part discusses the region, and explains the character and range of the wines. The second part profiles the producers. There are detailed profiles of the leading producers, showing how each winemaker interprets the local character, and mini-profiles of other important estates.

In the first part, I address the nature of the wines made today and ask how this has changed, how it's driven by tradition or competition, and how styles may evolve in the future. I show how the wines are related to the terroir and to the types of grape varieties that are grown, and I explain the classification system. For each region, I suggest reference wines that illustrate the character and variety of the area.

In the second part, there's no single definition for what constitutes a top producer. Leading producers range from those who are so prominent as to represent the common public face of an appellation to those who demonstrate an unexpected potential on a tiny scale. The producers profiled in the guide represent the best of both tradition and innovation in wine in the region. In each profile, I have tried to give a sense of the producer's aims for his wines, of the personality and philosophy behind them—to meet the person who makes the wine, as it were, as much as to review the wines themselves.

Each profile gives contact information and details of production, followed by a description of the producer and the range of wines. For major producers (rated from 1 to 3 stars), I suggest reference wines that are a good starting point for understanding the style. Most of the producers welcome visits, although some require appointments: details are in the profiles. Profiles are organized geographically, and each group of profiles is preceded by maps showing the locations of producers to help plan itineraries.

The guide is based on visits to Tuscany over recent years. I owe an enormous debt to the many producers who cooperated in this venture by engaging in discussion and opening innumerable bottles for tasting. This guide would not have been possible without them.

Benjamin Lewin

Contents

Tables

Appellation Maps

Producer Maps

Overview of Italy

Is it unfair to say that regulations for producing wine in Italy are in permanent disarray? Wine is divided into three levels. Vino da Tavola is table wine. IGT is the intermediate level of Indicazione Geografica Tipica, now officially renamed as IGP. Quality wine has two levels: DOC (Denominazione di Origine Controllata) and DOCG (a super-DOC category). DOC and DOCG both officially have been replaced by DOP [Denominazione di Origine Protetta], but in true Italian fashion no one is paying much attention to the latest European regulations. But Italy finds itself in the topsy-turvy situation that in some regions its best wines are labeled as IGTs rather than DOCGs.

Long and skinny, extending over 10 degrees of latitude from north to south, Italy offers more diversity of climates than any other European wine producer, from cool climate Trentino-Alto-Adige in the far north, to beating hot Sicily in the far south. Italy also has an unusually high number of indigenous grape varieties. Plantings of black varieties are slightly ahead of white overall. The top red wines come from Nebbiolo in Piedmont and Sangiovese in Tuscany, neither of which is grown successfully anywhere else. It's fair to say that, while Italy has many distinguished red wines, it's relatively hard to find interesting white wines.

Italy plays tag with France for the title of the world's largest wine producer and exporter. The proportion of quality wine has been increasing, up from 13% in 1988 to 30% today, but that still leaves table wine as the major part of wine production. The relative increase in quality wine is mostly due to the fact that table wine production is declining more rapidly than other categories. About two thirds of the DOC(G) regions, and the majority of quality wine production, are in the northern half of the country. Production in the South has declined significantly in the past decade.

There are 74 DOCGs and 334 DOCs. Most of the DOCGs have staked out an identify and are reasonably well known. Without the same imprimatur of quality, DOCs are rather more variable. There are 118 IGTs, which is far too many for wines that should have a broader geographical range and diversity of character. Failure of the DOCGs to keep up with modern trends means that the situation in Tuscany, where many top wines are not part of the DOCG system, has been copied elsewhere.

All regions of Italy produce both red and white wine. The most common varieties in each region are usually indigenous, although international varieties are making some headway here as everywhere else. This is especially true in Tuscany.

The Ranks of Tuscany

Tuscany is Italy's most important wine region in terms of the combination of quality and diversity, offering a range of styles extending from the lively freshness of Sangiovese in Chianti Classico to the sterner character of Sangiovese in Brunello di Montalcino, chocolaty from a modernist, deliciously savory from a traditionalist, to the international styles of Bolgheri based mostly on Bordeaux varieties. And from all these areas as well as others come the completely undefined category of the so-called "super-Tuscans."

Tuscany has about 86,000 ha of vineyards, of which 30,000 are classified as DOC or DOCG. But reality is so far distant from the DOC system that many of the top wines are super-Tuscans—basically wines that may use indigenous varieties or focus on "international" varieties, that may or may not actually meet the criteria for the local DOC, but that are sold under the IGT Toscana label. IGT is nominally lower in the level of classification than DOC(G), but producers often feel compelled to have an IGT Toscana to maintain credibility; except in Montalcino, the top wines are likely to be IGT rather than DOC. Nowhere else in Italy has the system of classification been turned so upside down.

All the regions have a hierarchy within the DOC system, but its nature has been changing. It used to be that the top level was Riserva, requiring longer aging, and most often based on a selection of the best lots. Today it is more likely to represent a single vineyard, and producers often talk about their "Crus," meaning top vineyards that would be classified as Premier or Grand Cru if such a system existed. Sometimes these are described as Vigna or Vi-

Tuscan wine estates usually have olive trees planted next to vineyards.

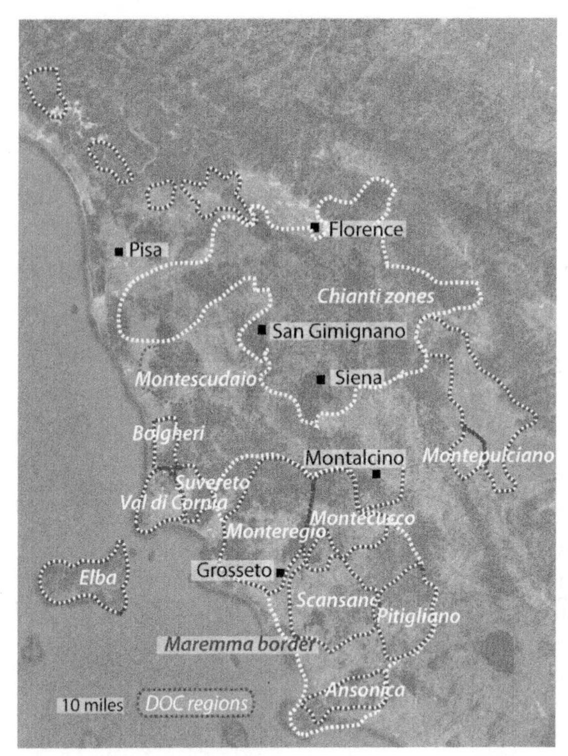

Wine is made over much of Tuscany. There are about 30 DOCs and DOCGs. The most important are named.

gneto followed by the name of the vineyard. Although the wines are often found at the highest classification in the local DOC system, the name has more prominence than the classification.

The hilly terrain of Tuscany is covered in vineyards, olive groves, and forests. Olive groves are usually interspersed with the vineyards. Many wine producers also make olive oil, although I have found scarcely any who will admit to making a profit on the olive oil; it's claimed to be more a traditional accompaniment to wine production than a profit center. It used to be said that vineyards were planted on land that could not be used to grow anything else; and olive trees were planted where you could not even grow grapevines. "Chianti was a survival economy until the 1950s or 60s," says Giuseppe Mazzocolin of Felsina. Most farms practiced polyculture, and the focus on viticulture is really a matter of the past three decades or so.

Except for the coastal regions of Maremma and Bolgheri, most of the best vineyards are on relatively steep and abrupt hillsides. Driving around to visit wineries, you find many located well off the beaten track, often on unpaved roads winding up steep hillsides. The relationships between vineyards are not always obvious. I remember taking a wrong turn on my first visit to Querciabella: more or less at the top of the mountain, I asked a local where it was, and he said, "Just there," pointing across the valley to a more or less equivalent point on the opposite side, several miles back down and then up again. Often built into hillsides or underground, wineries may be much larger than they appear.

Savage Sangiovese

"Sangiovese, Nebbiolo, and Pinot Noir are the three worst grapes in the world—to make the three best wines," says Francesco Ripaccioli at Canalicchio di Sopra in Montalcino. Widely grown, Sangiovese is Italy's most important black grape variety, regarded as a workhouse grape all over the southern part of the country. (It's also grown on Corsica, where it is called Nielluccio.) It is in Tuscany, however, where it can claim to be a noble variety, making great wines that reflect individual terroirs.

The traditional red wines of Tuscany all are based on Sangiovese: the major regions are Brunello di Montalcino, Chianti Classico, and Vino Nobile de Montepulciano. Brunello di Montalcino insists on 100% Sangiovese (of which more later); the other regions allow other varieties to be blended with the Sangiovese. Chianti looms over everything else; altogether it accounts for about half of the DOC(G) vineyards and produces 8 million cases of wine each year. Chianti's best area, Chianti Classico DOCG, is quite distinct, and should not be confused with other Chianti DOCGs. Vino Nobile de Montepulciano (there is no connection with the Montepulciano grape) is roughly comparable in quality to the outlying Chianti DOCs.

Sangiovese is a variety with considerable diversity. For a long time, Brunello di Montalcino was considered to have an advantage over Chianti

The Indigenous Grapes of Tuscany

Sangiovese is a noble variety by any measure. It is relatively light in color, with high natural acidity, and a tendency to savory flavors on the palate.
Canaiolo was important in the nineteenth century, bringing greater body and ripeness (and alcohol) to the blend in Chianti.
Colorino is deeply colored and was used to bring color to Chianti, but is much less used today because of its lack of flavor.
Ciliegiolo gives light red cherry flavors; it has fallen out of favor because it is difficult to grow.
Pugnitello fell out of favor because of its very low yields, but some wineries have reintroduced it for its intense flavor and spiciness.
Mammolo is a somewhat perfumed black variety that is no longer much used in the Chianti blend.
Malvasia Nera is a black variety of Malvasia. It may be the same as Tempranillo, but is not often seen today.
Malvasia is a white grape that is no longer allowed in the Chianti blend, but is used for Vin Santo dessert wine.
Trebbiano is grown in Tuscany (as everywhere in Italy), but is no longer allowed in Chianti Classico, although it can be used for the Vin Santo dessert wine.
Moscadella is a fairly nondescript white variety that is used to make slightly sparking sweet wines.

Sangiovese was traditionally aged in botti (large casks of 20-100 hl) made from Slavonian oak (at back), but barriques (225 liters) or tonneaux (500 liters) of French oak (at front) are now also used to help tame the tannins.

Classico because of the quality of its cultivars. When Sangiovese was introduced into Montalcino, producer Biondi-Santi identified a clone of Sangiovese in his vineyards, which he named Brunello (the little brown one). Sangiovese Grosso is used to describe a family of cultivars that evolved from Biondi-Santi's original clone. Descendants of this strain still are prominent in Montalcino, although Sangiovese develops very extensive clonal variation, and now hundreds of different clones have been identified. The other general strain is called Sangiovese Piccolo, and this was more common in Chianti Classico.

Perhaps the main difference in Chianti Classico over the past twenty years has been the improvement in the quality of Sangiovese. From the 1960s, most plantings used a clone of Sangiovese (R10) that was too productive, giving wines with simple structure and limited aging potential. Since the 1990s, extensive research has led to the development of better clones, leading to higher quality wine with good structure, greater color, and more interesting aromatics. The Chianti Classico 2000 project, supported by the Consorzio, spent 16 years testing clones in experimental vineyards, and several wineries in Montalcino and Chianti Classico have also been developing clones for their particular terroirs. It took 25 years to eliminate the R10 clone, but now much of the Classico region is planted with high quality clones; certainly there is no excuse for poor results.

One interesting result of all this is that the supposed advantage of Montalcino in having higher quality Sangiovese has become no more than a myth; in fact, the best clones in Montalcino, including Biondi-Santi's fabled

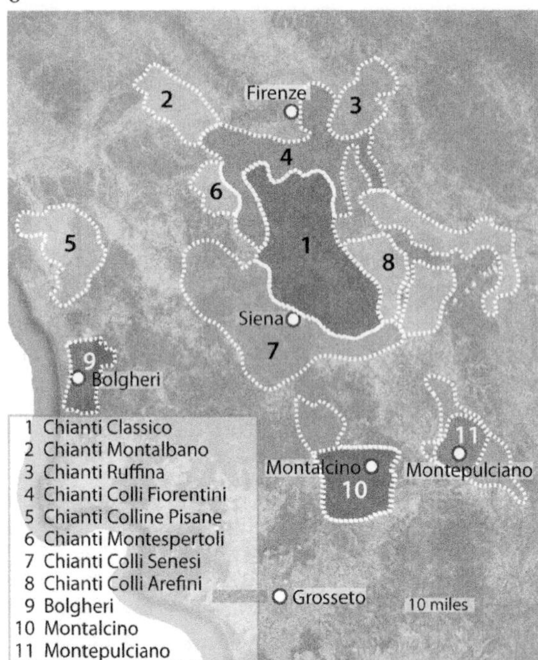

Major DOCs of Tuscany include Chianti Classico (center) and the Chianti sub-areas (surrounding Chianti Classico). The most important region for Sangiovese is Montalcino (farther south). Montepulciano (to the east) also grows Sangiovese. Bolgheri (at the coast) is home to several super-Tuscans.

BBS11, do not necessarily do so well in Chianti Classico. Sangiovese somewhat resembles Riesling in the way its performance reflects terroir. As Guido Orzalesi of the Altesino winery in Montalcino ruefully noted, when they tried propagating vines from their famous Montosoli vineyard in other locations, the results did not give the very special qualities of Montosoli.

Sangiovese is naturally lightly colored; the idea of making more deeply colored wine created an impetus to blend it with other varieties. Increased fruit concentration coming from the new clones takes off some of the pressure to ameliorate the nature of the grape, although Sangiovese is not a variety that benefits from excessive extraction. "Applying the concept of phenolic ripeness to Sangiovese is like the tail wagging the dog," says Francesco Cinzano of Col d'Orcia in Montalcino. The motto for Sangiovese should be "never too much," says Giuseppe Mazzocolin of Fèlsina in Chianti Classico.

The tradition in Tuscany is to age wine in large casks of Slavonian oak. The traditional shape for these botti is oval, but sometimes they are circular. They vary from 30 hl to 100 hl. Sometimes producers change to Austrian or French oak, and, of course, barriques of French oak are now found; as the barrique is 225 liters (or just over 2 hl), its use implies a significantly greater exposure to oak.

In Montalcino, all DOC wine must be 100% Sangiovese, but in Chianti Classico, up to 20% can be other varieties, including international varieties as well as indigenous varieties. It might seem that whether a producer is to be regarded as traditionalist or modernist could be assessed by the use of botti versus barriques and (in Chianti Classico) by whether international varieties are included, but it is not always so simple; although it is true that wines tend to have a smoother impression moving more towards black fruits when barriques are used, and a darker color with more impression of structure when international varieties are used in Chianti Classico.

Sangiovese is a reductive variety, which is to say that its aroma and flavor spectrum are more affected than most by exposure to oxygen. It's not only the tannins that are changed by the aging regime, but also the aromatic profile. The characteristic organoleptic spectrum of Sangiovese, especially as aged in botti, has faintly savage, animal overtones, definitely savory, sometimes a mineral hint of gunflint. Aging in barriques suppresses those savory notes and brings out more direct fruits, perhaps as a result of greater oxidative exposure. So what's the true typicity (or tipicità as they would have it in Italy) of Sangiovese?

The Hills of Chianti

Chianti dominates wine production in Tuscany. Chianti Classico DOCG is the heart of the Chianti region. The Classico area extends between Florence and Siena; this was where Chianti gained its original reputation, and obtained the right to the description Chianti Classico in 1932. There was a protracted legal fight about the right to use "Chianti," which the Chianti Classico producers essentially lost. Surrounding areas also gained the right to use Chianti, with individual zonal descriptions: these are now the seven subzones in the Chianti DOCG. But Chianti Classico is an independent region, not part of the Chianti DOCG.

There is no better demonstration of the vast difference between Chianti Classico and simple Chianti than the recent change in regulations which increased the permitted level of residual sugar in Chianti from the 4 g/l that's standard for dry wines to 9 g/l in order "to meet the preferences of the export markets, especially the Oriental, South American and American ones." In other words, Chianti can now be off-dry. The risk is that people may be confused by this terrible decision into downrating Chianti Classico.

The only one of the other Chiantis with any pretension to the same quality as Chianti Classico is Chianti Rufina, just to the northeast. Rufina is the smallest zone in Chianti, the farthest from the sea, with vineyards mostly above 500m, and has a more Continental climate. Chianti Rufina must have more than 70% Sangiovese, which allows for a lot of variation. The top wines age well—I have had lovely examples more than 25 years old—but the wine can be on the sturdy side when young. It is rarely as refined as Chianti

A pile of straw-covered bottles reflects history, but has little to do with Chianti of today.

Classico. Chianti Colli Senesi might have established a reputation, but it overlaps with Montalcino and Montepulciano, and the best wines always use the better-known DOC name.

Chianti Classico has been struggling to establish its reputation as a quality wine region. The fact that Chianti Classico is not merely one part of "Chianti," but is an independent region is not well understood. It took a long time to recover from the post-second world war image of wine in a straw covered bottle. The bottle was certainly more interesting than the wine. Slowly Chianti became a serious wine. Chianti today is a mix of artisanal and large-scale production. Half of the 600 members of the Chianti Classico Consorzio bottle their own wine; vineyard holdings vary from as little as 1 ha to as much as 200 ha. Antinori, Frescobaldi, Ruffino, and Barone Ricasoli are all major producers. The largest single producer is the cooperative Castelli del Grevepesa, which represents 160 growers.

Although Chianti was one of the better-known wines of Italy a century ago, to the point at which there was a problem with fraudulent imitations, it has developed slowly in the past half century. In the 1960s, it was regarded as uneconomic for wine production because of the hilly terrain. Luca di Napoli at Castello dei Rampolla recollects that making wine was not easy. "People bought sugar and brought in wine from elsewhere–it was a black economy. The role of the oenologue was to be the link to buy the wine from the south."

Chianti's history speaks to the issues in winemaking with Sangiovese. The driving factor has always been the need to tame the tannins, typically accentuated by high acidity, whether this has led to blending with other varieties or the use of barriques instead of botti.

Chianti started as a blended wine. The problem was that the original blend created an issue with quality. Chianti as we know it today had its origins in 1872, when Baron Ricasoli (a future Prime Minister of Italy) recommended a blend of 70% Sangiovese, 15% Canaiolo and 15% Malvasia. This formula was followed when the first DOC regulations came into effect in 1967. The rationale was that Canaiolo (an undistinguished black variety) bulked out the wine

Changing Regulations Have Made Chianti Classico a Quality Wine				
	Sangiovese	*Colorino Canaiolo*	*Malvasia Trebbi-ano*	*Other varieties*
1967	less than 70%	max. 20%	min. 10%	15% grapes permitted from other regions!
1984	min. 75%	max. 10%	min. 2%	10% of international varieties allowed
1996	min. 80% max. 100%		max. 6%	limit increased to 15%
2000				limit increased to 20%
2006			banned	

and improved the color, while including the white Malvasia softened the harsh tannins. Colorino (a grape with colored pulp but little taste) was also used to bump up the color.

Chianti Classico has changed a lot since then. Slowly the requirements for including low quality indigenous varieties, including white grapes, were reduced. International varieties were allowed in small quantities, which were later increased. Finally white grapes were banned, and monovarietal Sangiovese was allowed.

These changes reflect the status of Sangiovese. Improved viticulture gave more reliable ripening, so the inclusion of Colorino, with its dilution of taste, became undesirable. Improvements in vinification gave riper tannins, making it unnecessary to include white grapes. Even so, the over-productive cultivars of the eighties did not have enough structure, so producers decided that they could best improve their Sangiovese by including other varieties, such as Cabernet Sauvignon. Merlot is sometimes used to give a more generous impression. "In the eighties when we understood we had to improve the quality, a lot of wineries felt they had to use international varieties because it was difficult to reliably produce high quality with Sangiovese," says Sergio Zingarelli, president of the Consorzio. Giovanni Manetti at Fontodi thinks that blending Sangiovese with other varieties can be overdone. "It is not a mistake to allow other varieties, but if the official limit is 20%, it should be enforced. The recent from 15% to 20% was a mistake. Some wines have been embarrassing in the past, showing black fruits rather than red fruits."

Finally the Sangiovese reached a quality level at which many producers feel they can make a one hundred percent Sangiovese that has sufficient quality in its aroma and flavor spectrum so as not to need any other grapes. "With Chianti Classico 2000, we found several clones that are high quality. With these changes probably the international grapes will begin to decrease. Twenty years ago some people wanted to increase the international proportion allowed, but now this is anachronistic; people are increasing Sangiovese and indigenous grapes," Sergio Zingarelli explains. "Planting the vineyards with new clones, at higher density, allows us to make 100% Sangiovese without needing any help from other varieties," says Mario Nunzinate, of Colognole in Chianti Rufina.

The change at Fonterutoli over the past decade is typical. "When I started, we and everyone else planted international varieties because we only had poor clones of Sangiovese," says Filippo Mazzei. "It wasn't a fashion, it was necessary. What has changed in ten years is that Sangiovese was dominant, but is now nearly exclusive. The Chiantis are now basically all Sangiovese. We don't have international varieties any more."

There's still some difference between those who believe that the true typicity of Chianti is best brought out by monovarietal Sangiovese and those who believe in keeping Chianti's long tradition of being a blended wine, but by using better quality varieties for the minor part of the blend. As Paolo de Marchi of Isole e Olena says, the real issue is to make the best wine. "Blending should not be used to improve poor results with Sangiovese, but to bring in a variety with complementary qualities that increases complexity... The pressure to make Chianti just from Sangiovese is taking things to excess."

Regulations for the various types of wine in Chianti Classico specify the length. The traditional botti are usually made from Slavonian oak, which comes from Croatia and is milder than French oak. Usually botti are used for about 15 years, so there is little influence from new oak on the wine. In the last thirty years, there's been a move to use barriques of French oak, which produce a softer rounder, more "international" wine, although in the past decade there's been some backing off towards tonneaux, which are larger, and have a less obvious effect.

Types of Wine in Chianti Classico	
Chianti Classico	At least 80% Sangiovese, minimum alcohol 12%, aging for one year (method unspecified).
Riserva	Minimum alcohol 12.5%, aging for 2 years, including 3 months in bottle.
Gran Selezione	Minimum alcohol 13%, aging for 30 months, including 3 months in bottle.
Vigna or Vigneto	The name following Vigna or Vigneto is the name of a single vineyard. Usually used for vineyards that producers consider to be equivalent to Crus, but no legal definition.
Vin Santo	Made from dried Trebbiano and Malvasia grapes: sweet with high alcohol. Aging lasts 3-8 years in very small casks.

The New Chianti

The phenomenon of the super-Tuscans has partially allowed Chianti to bypass the arguments about typicity that have occurred in other regions as modern techniques of viticulture and vinification have changed wine styles. It's easier to make a super-Tuscan than to fight for the soul of Chianti. But what should Chianti taste like? The admission of international varieties diluted the focus on Sangiovese, and many producers believe that the increase to 20% of nontraditional varieties was one step too far. On the other hand, Chianti has always been a blended wine, and it's not surprising that the blend should change over time. Whether or not the wine is blended, the slightly acidic, bright red cherry fruits of the past have generally given way to slightly deeper and darker flavors, following the trend of many other wine regions.

The requirements to include low quality black or white grapes, and the limit on the amount of Sangiovese, forced some quality producers out of the DOC; because they wanted to use 100% Sangiovese or to exclude some other varieties, they labeled their wines as IGT Toscana. Recent revisions of the rules have retroactively validated their response. This has all led to a definite improvement in quality, but the genie is out of the bottle, and the best wines (even those which would qualify for Chianti Classico under the new rules) have usually been labeled as IGT Toscana. When you ask Chianti producers whether they would consider relabeling those super-Tuscans that would now qualify as Chianti, they often shrug and say they would like to help improve the DOCG, but their wine is now universally recognized as a super-Tuscan.

Trying to get away from the impression that Chianti Classico is always second best, the Consorzio introduced a new classification in 2013, adding Gran Selezione as a new top tier (with effect from the 2010 vintage). Previously wines were divided between Chianti Classico as such and the higher level of Riserva. Now there are three levels. Chianti Classico must age for twelve months, Riserva for 24 months, and Gran Selezione for 30 months.

The aging requirements and the other differences in the rules between Riserva and Gran Selezione are not really significant. "People ask, what's the technical difference between Gran Selezione, Riserva, and Chianti Classico," says Filippo Mazzei, "but I say: what's the difference between first growths and fifth growths in Bordeaux—nothing! The only thing that is really important is that all the best production in Chianti Classico should go into the Gran Selezione."

Grapes for Gran Selezione must come from an estate's own vineyards, but the wine can be a blend or selection of lots; the restriction just means that it cannot include purchased grapes. This was clearly a compromise. Sergio Zingarelli gave a big sigh when I asked why the top wine classification doesn't represent special terroirs. There was something of a desire to make Gran Selezione reflect single vineyards, but pressures in the Consorzio were too strong to allow it. As one example, Ruffino's Ducale Oro is a powerful leading brand, formerly a Riserva, which they wanted to move to Gran Selezione. But it doesn't come from a single vineyard, it is a blend from two estates (actually quite close by). "How do you say no to Ruffino," an informant in the Consorzio explained.

There is in fact something of a move towards producing single vineyard wines from what the producers regard as their grand crus. There is a trend for these to be Gran Selezione. "Probably 80-90% of Gran Selezione come from single vineyards," says Sergio Zingarelli. Some producers feel that this isn't the main issue. "The idea that grapes should come from your own vineyards makes no sense. The issue shouldn't be the source, it should be the quality of the grapes," says Giovanna Stianti.

Gran Seleziones must be approved by a committee, which is intended to ensure that they live up to the demands for a top tier, which was not the case with Riserva, and this may very well be the most significant difference. It's secret how many wines are rejected, but it's probably about 15%.

I was sceptical when I tasted the first releases of Gran Selezione: they were very good, but almost all were cuvées that previously had been labeled as Riserva, and they seemed more like a super-set of the old Riservas than anything really different. But since then there has been a significant improvement in quality and interest. The number of Gran Seleziones has increased to more than one hundred; many still come from the same sources as wines previously labeled as Riservas; some are new cuvées (usually from single vineyards), and a few are wines that previously were labeled as IGT Toscana. Producing a Gran Selezione has become the norm instead of the exception. They now represent about 6% of all production of Chianti Classico.

One big question is how competitive Gran Selezione is with the super Tuscans. "The problem is that the top wine is often not labeled as Chianti Classico," says Sergio Zingarelli. "I planted a new vineyard fifteen years ago to be my top wine, but if there wasn't Gran Selezione it would have been an IGT." It would definitely be a mark of success for Gran Selezione if super-Tuscans were relabeled into the new category. There are mixed opinions about this. "One of the intentions of Gran Selezione was to lure back IGTs to the Chianti Classico, but it hasn't worked very well," says Roberto Stucchi at Badia a Coltibuono. "You can't go back," flatly says Giovanna Stianti at Castello di Volpaia.

Riserva and Gran Selezione tend to have a higher proportion of Sangiovese than simple Chianti Classico, perhaps reflecting the fact that they come from riper grapes, so inclusion of other varieties is less necessary. Indeed, there's a tendency to use 100% Sangiovese for Gran Selezione; there was

Reference Wines for Gran Selezione from Single Vineyards	
Producer	*Vineyard*
Barone Ricasoli	Castello di Brolio
Castello d'Albola	Il Solatio
Castello Di Ama	San Lorenzo
Castello Di Volpaia	Il Puro
Fattoria Di Fèlsina	Colonia
Fontodi	Vigna del Sorbo
Rocca Delle Macìe	Sergio Zingarelli

even discussion about making it mandatory, and 2021 the minimum was increased from 80% to 90%, and the other grapes were limited to indigenous varieties. One retrogressive effect is that some top Gran Selezione, such as the wines from Castello di AMa, which included small amounts of international varieties must now either change varieties or become super-Tuscans.

There's a definite move towards producers offering a heirarchy at all levels. In these cases, the Gran Selezione is usually more intense than the Riserva, just as the Riserva is more intense than the Chianti Classico, although the difference between Riserva and Classico has narrowed in recent years due to the general improvement in Chianti Classico.

Perhaps the real message is the improvement of quality all round. Sara Pontemolesi, winemaker at Antinori, summarizes the change in recent years: "We are really defining the style of the wine now, we used to be concerned with the quality, but now we have the quality we can focus on the style of the wine."

Gran Selezione was not universally approved by producers, but it is becoming accepted as the new top tier of Chianti Classico. This may finally make the top Chianti Classicos competitive on the international circuit. But one of the criticisms is that this may drive a change in style. "One of the things I don't like about Gran Selezione is that the tasting panel favors more modern international wines. It sends the message that bigger wines are better," says Roberto Stucchi.

Gran Selezione is turning into a success, but the price is that there has been some dilution of style. At the beginning, the general impression was of a movement from the red fruits of Chianti Classico to black fruits in Gran Selezione. Riservas were more like Chianti Classico than Gran Selezione. The relatively small number of producers making the first Gran Selezione cuvées were determined that they should be the very best Chianti Classico can produce. Now that almost every producer feels compelled to offer a Gran Selezione, many of the wines are less distinctive; they are the best wine the producer makes, but I find them to be more like very good Riservas than to offer something really different. The best Gran Selezione cuvées still show smooth, dense palates, making something of a move towards the style of Brunello di Montalcino.

Some producers feel the real problem now is not so much to improve the top wines, but to tackle the issue of the bottom end. "How can we build the reputation of Chianti Classico," says one producer, "when there are wines in supermarkets at €3.99? And when the Systembolaget monopoly in Sweden puts out a tender for bulk Chianti Classico at €2.99, the Consorzio sends the request to producers," he added in disgust.

Terroirs of Chianti

Chianti is a series of hills and valleys, and vineyards are usually at significant elevations (with the upper limit 100m or more higher than it used to be before global warming). A mountain range marks the eastern border of Chianti Classico, and protects against cold weather. Most vineyards face south or southwest. The major soil types are galestro (highly friable shale coming from compressed clay), alberese (a calcareous marl resembling limestone), and arenaria (sandstone, known locally as macigno).

There are several communes within Chianti Classico, but although producers may be conscious of their locations, so far they have not had much impact for the consumer. There are significant differences in climate (which becomes warmer going from north to south), altitude (with vineyards mostly over 250m, and the highest well up mountains at up to 600m elevation), and of course soil types. There's a tendency for wines from the warmer areas to be richer—Castellina in Chianti or Castelnuova Berardenga, for example—but there's also a tendency for Sangiovese to be planted at higher altitudes than used to be thought desirable, which gives a finer quality.

"The real need here is to clarify Chianti's zones and vineyards, which isn't being done," says Sebastiano Castiglioni of Querciabella a few years back. "We are staying out of Gran Selezione until we are allowed to put subzones on the label," says winemaker Manfred Ing. "The future of Chianti Classico is to understand the individual vineyards." What to do about subzones has been the issue of the day for the past decade.

Finally in 2021 the Conzorzio agreed on 11 subzones. Borders are not based on terroir but on the communal (political) borders, except that Greve in Chianti has three smaller zones within it, some areas at the west are combined into one subzone, and Castelnuovo Berardenga is split into two subzones. The importance of the subzones is limited, however, by a restiction that they can be used only on Gran Selezione.

Climate change contributes to the riper style. As winemaker Sean O'Callaghan, formerly of Riecine and now at Tenuta di Carleone, says, "Twenty nine years ago when I arrived here in Tuscany we would start picking towards the end of October, and we would still have fairly unripe Sangiovese, often not more than 12% alcohol. Now we start picking towards the end of September, fighting to keep the wines under 15% alcohol."

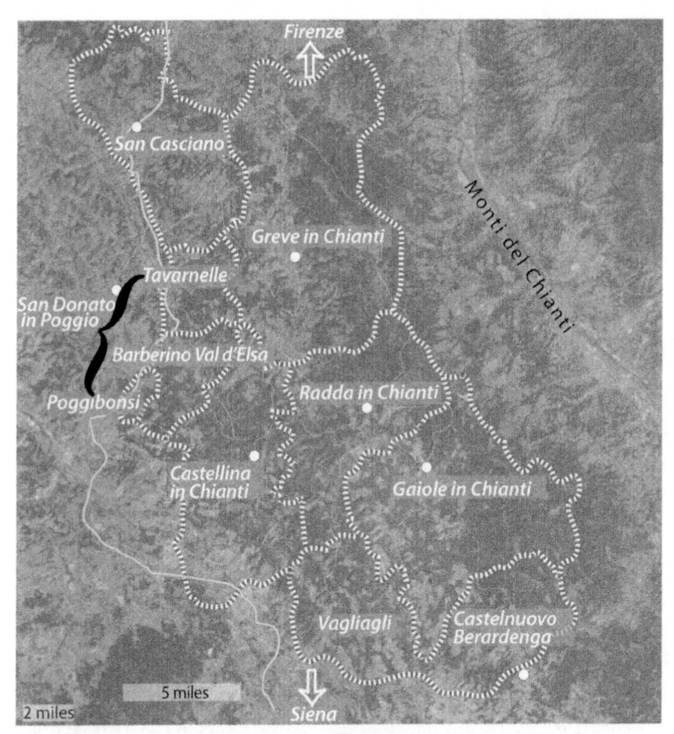

The 9 communes of Chianti Classico are divided into 11 subzones. The subzones follow the communal borders except for San Donato in Poggio (combining Tavarnelle - Poggibonsi), Vagliagli (the western part of Castelnuovo Berardenga) and Panzano, Montefioralle, and Lamole (smaller areas within Greve in Chianti).

Climate change contributes to the riper style. As winemaker Sean O'Callaghan, formerly of Riecine and now at Tenuta di Carleone, says, "Twenty nine years ago when I arrived here in Tuscany we would start picking towards the end of October, and we would still have fairly unripe Sangiovese, often not more than 12% alcohol. Now we start picking towards the end of September, fighting to keep the wines under 15% alcohol."

Almost all Chianti Classico is local. Producers usually have vineyards only in their own communes, often closely around the winery. You might think this would place some emphasis on identifying different subzones, but even aside from political considerations, one of the difficulties in defining subzones is that the geology does not conform with the communal boundaries; for example, the southern part of Radda in Chianti and the northern part of Gaiole in Chianti are both extremely calcareous, with vineyards at 430-600m, but the southern part of Gaiole in Chianti is completely different, with much lower, less rocky vineyards. Greve in Chianti is divided by the Greve river, and soils on the left (west) bank have galestro, while those on the right (east) face the Monti del Chianti and are mostly sandstone and sand.

"Appellation and IGT are the core of the Tuscan problem," says Paolo di Marchi at Isole e Olena. "The wines that have pulled the region up are IGT. Subzones organized by communes (which are basically administrative units) would not make any sense, because they vary so much in size and in the variety of terroirs within each. A classification along Burgundian lines might make sense but would not be politically possible." The issue of subzones is contentious, to say the least, and it seems unlikely they will be introduced at present. "If we divided by soils and geography we would have to have 100 different classifications," says Sergio Zingarelli.

Chianti seems to be evolving towards two extreme styles. I think of them as red fruit and black fruit. What you might call traditional shows lively red fruits with a spectrum in the direction of sour red cherries, with a tang of savory acidity at the end. This tends to dominate the Chianti Classicos *tout court*. The black fruit wines make a more modern impression, with greater density on a softer palate, less obvious acidity, and sometimes tannins evident at the end.

There may be a tendency for the modern class to include more in the way of international varieties, and more often to be matured in barriques, but you can find both 100% Sangiovese and blended wines in either category, and wines matured in the traditional large casks in either category. Gran Selezione tend to show more weight (and more alcohol), with some moving in the direction of the smoothness of Brunello.

I would not say it's a mistake to use barriques or new oak, but the effect is to reduce the typicity of Sangiovese from Chianti, that delicious savory counterpoise to the red fruits. For my taste, it's the wines in the traditional, red fruit category that really express the freshness I expect in Chianti, but there are lovely wines in both categories, and it may well be that the more "modern" wines have greater success in today's market. Some of the modernists are moving to tonneaux, which at 500-600 liter impart less impression of oak than barriques. One modernist has even reversed course and is experimenting with botti.

It's difficult to acquire new vineyards in Chianti Classico, partly because of the physical difficulties of the lie of the land, partly because it has become expensive, and an alternative is to expand into the more affordable region of Maremma, where the focus moves towards international varieties. The grapes can be brought to the winery in Chianti Classico for vinification under the name of the estate there.

With the change in the rules in Chianti Classico, and the introduction of Gran Selezione, the honors for the top monovarietal Sangiovese wines are

Reference Wines for Monovarietal Sangiovese Chianti Classico Gran Selezione
Fattoria Di Fèlsina, Colonia
Fontodi, Vigna del Sorbo
Barone Ricasoli, Colledilà
Castello Di Volpaia, Il Puro
IGT Toscana
Badia A Coltibuono, Sangioveto
Fontodi, Flaccianello della Pieve
Isole E Olena, Cepparello
Montevertine, Le Pergole Torte

split between Gran Selezione and super-Tuscans. The best-known wines are still in the super-Tuscan category, but the gap is narrowing.

The development of top quality monovarietal Sangiovese in the Chianti area gives a chance to compare the character of the variety in different areas. Chianti at its best shows the savory side of Sangiovese while Montalcino shows a richer, more chocolaty side. Montepulciano makes a less refined impression, partly due to more clay in the soil. Perhaps greater density of fruits hides minerality in Montalcino, which is tauter, the fruits are more compact, less acid, less overtly mineral, and the cherry fruits are more black than sour red. The big challenge for Gran Selezione is to equal the quality of Montalcino, but in the style of Chianti Classico.

With the change in the rules in Chianti Classico, and the introduction of Gran Selezione, the honors for the top monovarietal Sangiovese wines are split between Gran Selezione and super-Tuscans. The best-known wines are still in the super-Tuscan category, but the gap is narrowing.

The development of top quality monovarietal Sangiovese in the Chianti area gives a chance to compare the character of the variety in different areas. Chianti at its best shows the savory side of Sangiovese while Montalcino shows a richer, more chocolaty side. Montepulciano makes a less refined impression, partly due to more clay in the soil. Perhaps greater density of fruits hides minerality in Montalcino, which is tauter, the fruits are more compact, less acid, less overtly mineral, and the cherry fruits are more black than sour red. The big challenge for Gran Selezione is to equal the quality of Montalcino, but in the style of Chianti Classico.

Vino Nobile di Montepulciano

Vino Nobile di Montepulciano had a high reputation from the sixteenth through the eighteenth centuries, but then fell into serious disarray. By the nineteenth century, it was more common for the wines to be labeled as Chianti as the area lies within the zone of Chianti Colli Senesi. Recovery did not really begin until after it became a DOCG in 1980. (One impediment to recognition is confusion with Montepulciano d'Abruzzi, made from the Montepulciano variety in the south of Italy; from 2019 Toscana has been

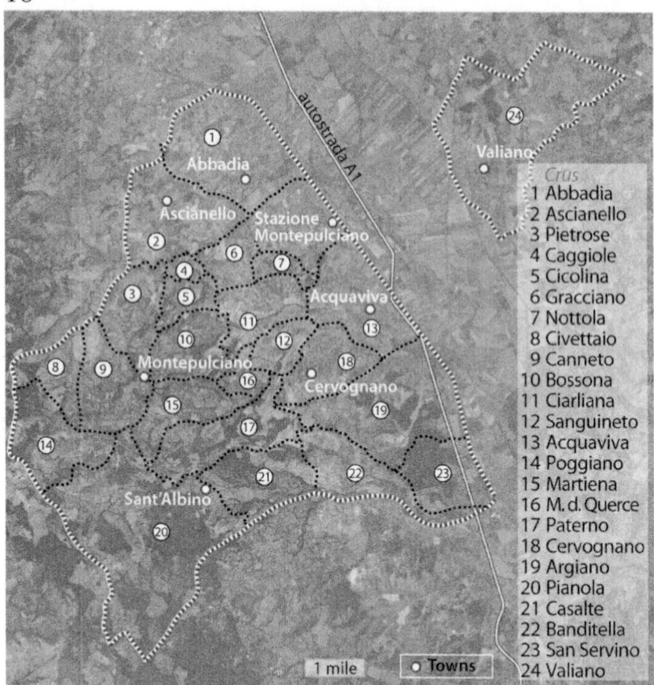

Vino Nobile di Montepulciano DOCG is in two parts. The major crus are marked on the map.

added to the label to emphasize the difference. There's also a move to refer to the wines simply as Nobile.)

Vino Nobile is based on Sangiovese (known locally as Prognolo Gentile). Regulations are still more relaxed than those for the Chianti zones, requiring a minimum of 70% Sangiovese, but allowing any mix of local grapes, including the usual suspects of Canaiola and Colorino to fill the rest. International varieties can also be used. It's nominally possible to include up to 5% of white varieties, such as Malvasia (reduced in 2018 from 10%). There is, however, no maximum limit on Sangiovese, so it is possible for it to comprise 100%.

The area of the DOCG is around and to the east of the town of Montepulciano, a few miles southeast of Siena. There are 1,250 hectares of vineyards, at elevations from restricted to altitudes of 250-500m, but on gentler slopes than the more rugged terrain of Chianti Classico or Brunello di Montalcino. The west and east of the appellation are separated by an area about a mile wide that is around the minimum altitude and more or less flat. The western part has thin soils of calcareous clay, said to produce more concentrated, more structured wines, while Valiano has deeper sandier soils said to produce smoother, silkier wines. The climate is Continental, moderated by the influence of Lake Trasimeno just to the east in Umbria. The appellation is divided into 37 subareas, informally called Crus, although the names are not usually used on labels. The Consorzio has a plan to introduce formal subzones, called Pieve (parishes).

Vino Nobile must age for two years after the harvest before release, including 12 months in oak. Riserva must be held a year longer before release, but does not have to spend any longer in oak. Rosso di Montepulciano has the same rules for the varietal mix, but no requirements for aging; some are aged in oak, some in stainless steel. There is also a Vin Santo (sweet, from dried grapes), which must be at least 50% Sangiovese.

Chianti Classico came out of the doldrums by tightening regulations on grape varieties and focusing more sharply on Sangiovese, with many top wines now 100% varietal. This is not as common in Montepulciano. However, the Alliance Vinum of six leading producers has committed to making a top wine from Sangiovese each year. Perhaps this will lead the way to greater quality.

Brunello di Montalcino

In Montalcino just to the south, no one was paying much attention to red wine, until led by producer Biondi-Santi, Brunello di Montalcino emerged as one of the best red wines of Italy in the 1970s. Today there is no real challenge to Brunello di Montalcino as home of the greatest Sangiovese wines, except perhaps for one or two super-Tuscans.

Sangiovese is the grape that typifies Tuscany, but Brunello di Montalcino stands alone in its history of making wine from 100% Sangiovese. Before the 1880s, Montalcino was known for sweet wines made from the Moscadello grape (a little Moscadello di Montalcino is still made). When the vineyards were attacked by oïdium, they were replanted with Sangiovese (more resistant to oïdium and already used in neighboring Chianti and Montepulciano).

Brunello di Montalcino dates from 1890, but through the 1920s there were only four producers bottling wine under its name; even through the 1950s there were fewer than fifteen producers, because most producers were bottling their wines as Chianti Colli Senesi. Brunello di Montalcino was defined as a DOC in 1966—the Consorzio was created in 1967 with 25 members

Types of Wine in Montalcino	
Rosso di Montalcino	Must age one year, but does not have to be in wood.
Brunello di Montalcino	Must age 2 years in wood, and cannot be released until 5 years old.
Brunello di Montalcino Riserva	Must age 2 years in wood, and cannot be released until 6 years old.

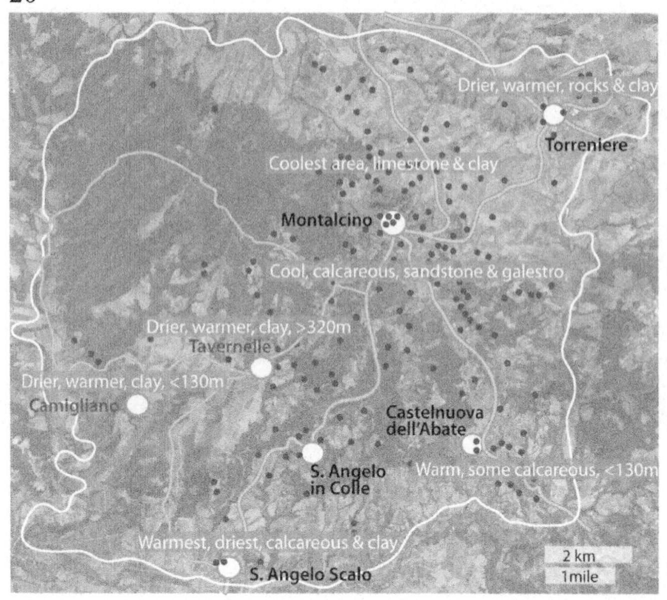

The Montalcino DOCG describes a circle (boundary in white) around the town of Montalcino. Wineries (black circles) extend to the north and south of the town.

cultivating only 80 ha—but really revived only in the 1970s. In 1980, it was the first region in Italy to become a DOCG. Brunello di Montalcino has now far outstripped Chianti on the international market, being the only traditional wine of Tuscany to vie with the price level of the super-Tuscans.

The production area coincides with the communal territory of Montalcino, 25 miles to the south of Siena, more or less a circle with a diameter of 10 miles centered on the old town of Montalcino, at an elevation of about 700m. The area is divided into two parts: to the north is the original region; plantings in the south are more recent. Regions to the north and east are high in clay and volcanic soils, but to the south and west there is a high proportion of calcareous soils. The climate of the northern half resembles Chianti, milder and wetter than the southern part, which is warmer and drier. The rules used to limit plantings for the DOC to below 600m, but because of global warming the limitation has been lifted in the belief that grapes can ripen fully at higher elevations.

The grapes ripen more slowly in the northern and higher altitude vineyards close to the town of Montalcino, and produce aromatic wines of greater finesse than those from the southern slopes, which tend to be fuller and richer. There is about a two-week difference in harvest dates. Roughly one third of the vineyards are in the northern half. (The largest producers are

All roads lead to Montalcino. The town occupies a high point that controls all routes through the appellation.

located at Sant'Angelo, which accordingly accounts for more than a third of Brunello production.)

Producers often have vineyards in both the south and north; has traditionally been regarded as the route to getting the greatest complexity. Stefano Cinelli Colombini of Fattoria dei Barbi expresses the traditional view when he says, "Every year is different and there is no one zone best suited for all weather conditions. When there is abundant rainfall, the galestro-rich zones fare better. In drier vintages, the more humid zones perform better."

Blending has now somewhat given way to single vineyard wines. This has to a continuing debate as to whether Montalcino should be formally divided into zones or should have premier crus. So far there is sufficient support for neither. Partly because variations in altitude are so important, defining zones in terms of circumscribed geographical areas is problematic. And even within each commune there is much variation in terroir.

There are certainly multiple differences between areas. Immediately around Montalcino is the coolest area, with vineyards at 300-350m on soils with strong calcareous content. The most elegant wines come from around the hill of Montosoli in the north, which would certainly be a Cru if they existed in Montalcino. There's also a high concentration of producers just south of the town, which has the most ancient soils. Tavernelle to the west ranges from 320-350m: windy and dry, hang times can be longer here. Sant Angelo at the south is prized for more powerful wines, with the best coming from vineyards above 350m where soils are more calcareous. Castelnuovo dell'Abata has lower vineyards, with the best on calcareous soils or shale, and is regarded as balancing power and elegance. The least favored areas are at the southwestern and northeastern peripheries. Camigliano make broader, more rustic wines. It's been controversial whether Torriniere should be part of the DOC, and vineyards really need to be at high elevation here

The original regulations required long aging in oak (five years for the Riserva), which tamed the tannins, but often introduced oxidation. Changes to encourage a more modern style have reduced the minimum period in oak to two years. The only requirement for Riservas now is that the bottle must be held one year longer before it is released, so there is no distinction in the aging regime, although some producers do still age them for longer in wood. Regulations have also reduced the required minimum level of acidity, encouraging softer wines more in line with international trends.

The origins of Riservas vary. Sometimes they are essentially the same wine aged longer; in the past the wines sometimes did not stand up to the long aging that was required, and the Riservas could seem a bit tired or over-extracted compared to the regular cuvée, but this has ceased to be a problem since the period was reduced to two years. Some Riservas come from barrel selections, but there's an increasing tendency for them to come from old vines or special plots; many Riservas are now single vineyard wines. Riservas, or other single vineyard wines, are made only in top vintages.

Traditionalist

Biondi Santi
Barbi
Salvioni
Case Basse di Soldera
Il Poggione
Camigliano
La Palazzetta
Pertimali
Costanti
Lisini
Caprili

Argiano
Col d'Orcia
Ciacci Piccolomini d'Aragona
Canalicchio di Sopra
Cerbaiona
Donatella Colombini
Paradiso di Frassina
Sassodisole
Poggio Antico
Altesino
Mastrojanni
Villa Poggio Salvi
Casanova di Neri
San Filippo
Carpazo
Castiglion del Bosco
Pian Delle Vigne
Valdicava

Castello Romitorio
Talenti
Val di Suga
Silvio Nardi
Uccelliera
Luce Della Vite
Banfi
Gaja
Siro Pacenti

Modernist

Producers range from those committed to traditional production to modernists, with many in between.

Modernists and Traditionalists

Brunello di Montalcino is traditionally described as having savory aromas and flavors, with notes of tobacco and leather, but (as elsewhere) changes in winemaking have resulted in more forward, fruitier wines that can be drunk much younger than previously. Style is perhaps now more determined by whether the producer is a traditionalist (maturing the wine in large old casks of Slavonian oak) or a modernist (using

Located in the northeast, the Montosoli hill is one of the most prestigious sites in Montalcino. Elevation is about 300m.

small barriques of new French oak). Another view is that while the type of wood treatment used to be the difference between modernists and traditionalists, now it's more a matter of extraction, with modernists going for greater extraction in the international style, while traditionalists go for a more restrained elegance. Is it an exaggeration to say that the traditional wines are about red fruits, but that the modernist style is all about black fruits?

Maturation in barrique certainly smoothens the wine, adding an overlay of vanillin or other oaky notes that calm down that animal pungency. (Blending in other varieties can have a similar effect, although this is not allowed in Montalcino.) In good years, Brunello has no need of this, with the grapes achieving a ripeness that shows as tobacco, leather, even a note of chocolate.

Personally, I find the traditional style wonderfully distinctive from international-style wines, giving wines of real character; while admitting that the best modernists make wines that retain enough of that character to be modern in style yet identifiable as Brunello, I like to see those savory notes of traditional Sangiovese. While wines from modernists can be easier to drink sooner, those from traditionalists may age longer.

Of course, it's not always so simple as to describe producers simply as traditionalists or modernists.; some producers age for one year in botti and one year in barriques, while others may mature some wines in botti, but use barriques for others. If there is a trend, it's to mature the general Brunello cuvée in botti, but to use a proportion of barriques for special cuvées, but there is certainly no fixed rule.

When should you drink Brunello? The modern dilemma is expressed by Stefano Colombini at Fattoria dei Barbi. "Of course, Brunello was made to be drunk old, but now we have to do something difficult, to produce wine that will age but that can be drunk on release, rounder with less aggressive tannins, but capable of long aging. This was technically hard, but we did it."

When the wine is ready depends on the vintage. A lighter vintage such as 2011 may be ready in five years, but a weightier vintage such as 2010 may need eight years or more. Most Riservas take longer and probably will not be ready until, say, close to a decade after the vintage. Of course, this depends on your tolerance for tannins: those accustomed to the more extracted wines of the New World may feel that Brunello's are ready within a couple of years.

Rosso di Montalcino

Reference Wines for Rosso di Montalcino
Altesino
Barbi
Canalicchio di Sopra
Cerbaiona
Ciacci Piccolomini d'Aragona, Rossofonte
Col d'Orcia
Il Poggione
Mastrojanni
Pian Delle Vigne
Poggio di Sotto
Sassodisole
Tenuta di Sesta
Uccelliera
Valdicava
Villa Poggio Salvi
Single Vineyard Rosso di Montalcino
Caparzo, La Caduta
Col d'Orcia, Banditella
Il Poggione, Leopoldo Franceschi
These wines give a good preview of the style of the producer's Brunello.

In addition to Brunello di Montalcino itself, there is a second DOC called Rosso di Montalcino. This can be used as a second label, so producers can declassify wines that don't meet their standard for Brunello itself. Like Brunello, Rosso di Montalcino must be made from 100% Sangiovese, but the aging regime is much shorter, simply requiring one year before release.

The regulations controlling production of Rosso have changed. Originally vineyards were divided into those classified for Brunello (about 2,000 ha) or for Rosso (about 500 ha). Vineyards classified for Brunello could be used to produce either Brunello or Rosso, but vineyards classified as Rosso could be used only to produce Rosso. Assignments were not permanent: a producer could move the classification from one vineyard to another, just as long as the total area of each type stayed the same. Now the system has been replaced by a more direct allocation of a proportion of Brunello versus Rosso for the vineyard total. As before, some Rossos are effectively a separate production, coming from particular plots, whereas others are in effect second wines declassified from Brunello.

There is no general agreement on whether Rosso should be a "baby Brunello" or something different. The range runs from simple entry-level to wines that preview the Brunello. "It's a bad attribute of producers to have played with Rosso to make so many things, there've been years of mistakes," says Giacomo Neri at Casanova di Neri. Some producers regard Rosso as a wine in its own right, although less complex than Brunello, and lots that aren't good enough for Rosso are declassified to become IGT Toscana. Some take Rosso seriously enough to produce single vineyard Rossos.

It's common to use the Rosso classification for young vineyards; when they become older, they are likely to be used for Brunello production. Since total production of Rosso is about three quarters of that of Brunello, a significant amount of wine potentially allowed to make Brunello must in fact be declassified to Rosso. The vintages of 2002 and 2014 were extreme cases in which some producers declassified their whole crop to Rosso (the result being that some Rossos, such as Valdicava or Canalicchio di Sopra, which are always at the top anyway, really show increased quality and character).

The Battle for Sangiovese

One factor in modernizing the region was the arrival of Villa Banfi in 1978. The owners are the American Mariani brothers, whose fortune came from selling Lambrusco (sweet, red, and fizzy) in the American market in the 1970s. They purchased large tracts of land, terraformed the landscape, including constructing six lakes to provide water for irrigation, established a huge modern facility, and started to produce a wide range of wines of all types. With 155 hectares of Brunello, they are the largest producer in Montalcino, but this is dwarfed by their production of more commercial wines from a wide variety of grapes and locations.

Banfi remain controversial: there is acknowledgment that they helped to develop the American market for Brunello, but concern that they changed the landscape to benefit varieties other than Sangiovese. Some see the move towards a more international style as a consequence: "Banfi opened the door to the US market, then the whole Montalcino region started to use the smaller barrels for this reason," one producer says.

Does 100% Sangiovese necessarily make the best wine? It's sometimes felt to be a little hard, and there've always been rumors of blending with other grapes to soften it. These came to a head in the Brunellopoli scandal of 2008 when the Italian news magazine, L'Espresso, reported that 20 producers

Located close to the southern boundary of Montalcino, Castello Banfi has one of the largest wine factories in Europe, where wines from surrounding regions as well as Montalcino are made.

were being investigated under suspicion that they had blended Brunello with other varieties (typically Cabernet Sauvignon to bump up the color and structure). The investigation was supposedly sparked by a producer who was indignant at others' continued flouting of the rules.

Million of bottles were seized by the investigating magistrate to be tested to see whether they included other varieties. After two years, the investigation somewhat fizzled out, with an inconclusive report, and the declassification of some of the seized wines to IGT. Some producers were fined, but the names have never been released. The Consorzio (producers' association) considered the matter, and decided by an overwhelming vote that Brunello should remain 100% Sangiovese. Many producers say that allowing other varieties would diffuse Brunello's identity in the way they believe happened in Chianti when international varieties were admitted.

Superficially the argument has been resolved, but a troubling issue underlies it. Production of Brunello di Montalcino has more or less doubled in a decade. This means that it has almost certainly been extended beyond the sites that are optimum for growing Sangiovese, creating pressure to include other varieties to "help" the Sangiovese. As Antonio Galloni remarks in The Wine Advocate, "Brunello is a wine whose fame is based on the supposedly special qualities of the Sangiovese Grosso clone... Allowing for the use of other grapes is a (not so) tacit admission that perhaps Sangiovese from Montalcino was never all that special in the first place and/or that the grape has been planted in an exorbitant number of places to which it is fundamentally ill-suited." The only way out of the box is to pull back Brunello to the best sites, and to use some other label for wine from other sites (with or without other varieties in the blend).

In addition to Brunello and Rosso di Montalcino, there are two other DOCs in the Montalcino area. Moscadello di Montalcino is a (usually cheap) sparkling wine from Muscat, which is not much more than a remnant of history at this point. Only fifteen estates make Moscadello; styles vary from sweet (by blocking fermentation) to late harvest or sparkling.

Sant'Animo was introduced as a catch-all DOC to allow producers to make wines from other varieties, but it has really failed to make any impact. Those producers in Montalcino who make wines from other varieties usually label them as IGT Toscana, and describe them as super-Tuscans.

Not all producers in Montalcino are necessarily committed to the appellation, at least in the sense that it is their main focus. Although this is the most prestigious appellation in Tuscany, and one of the most prestigious in Italy (second to Barolo), the lure of the super-Tuscans is hard to resist. Smaller producers may make only Brunello and Rosso, but larger producers often have a super-Tuscan, made from varieties other than Sangiovese, at a price level comparable to their Brunello.

Bolgheri

The land used to be marshy but has been drained. (At one time it was famous for its population of malarial mosquitoes.) The soil is stony. The climate is maritime. Dominant varieties are Cabernet Sauvignon, Cabernet Franc, and Merlot. The major producers have large estates. Sounds like Bordeaux? No, it's the area of Bolgheri on the Tuscan coast, where thirty years ago there were virtually no vineyards, but which today produces some of Italy's most famous wines from Bordeaux blends. It is an exaggeration to say that the explosive growth of Bolgheri was due to familial rivalry between the original owners of the Sassicaia and Ornellaia estates, but certainly these two great houses had a great deal to do with the success of the region. (All those wines with "aia" at the end of the name, by the way, identify Tuscan origins, because "aia" is Tuscan dialect meaning "the place of.")

The story of Sassicaia, the original super-Tuscan, perfectly illustrates the contortions of the Italian DOC system. The Marquis Incisa della Rocchetta acquired the Tenuta San Guido estate in the 1930s by marriage. Inspired by a love of Bordeaux, in 1944 he planted a hectare each of Cabernet Sauvignon and Cabernet Franc at the estate; and in 1965 extended the plantings to new vineyards of Cabernet Sauvignon and Cabernet Franc. Initially the wine was consumed only in the family; the first vintage of Sassicaia to be offered on the

Types of Wine in Bolgheri	
Bolgheri (red)	May contain up to 100% Cabernet Sauvignon, Merlot, or Sangiovese.
Bolgheri (white)	Can be Vermentino or blends of Sauvignon Blanc or Trebbiano.
Bolgheri Superiore	Minimum alcohol 12.5%, must age one year in wood, cannot be released until 2 years old.

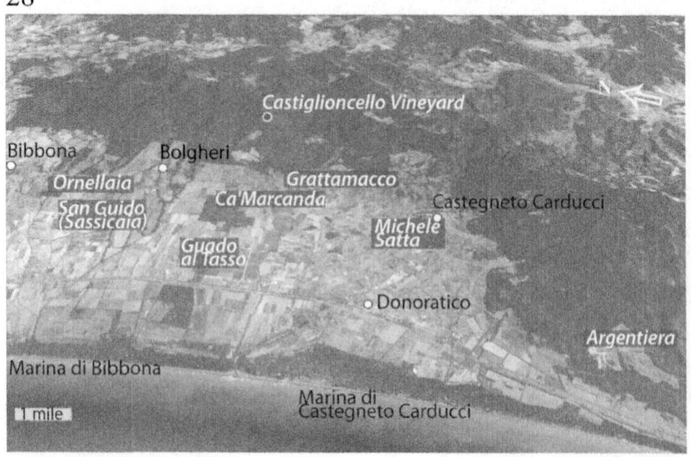

The vineyards of Bolgheri lie in a narrow band between the sea and the mountains. The DOC includes 1,100 ha of vineyards belonging to 40 producers.

open market was the 1968.

There was no precedent in the modern Italian system for producing Cabernet Sauvignon in Tuscany, so the wine was sold only as Vino da Tavola. (However, there is nothing new under the Tuscan sun; a century earlier, a survey of foreign grapes growing in Italy said, "Even the best Tuscan wines improve notably if Cabernet is added in small quantities. Especially worthy of note are the results obtained by blending Cabernet with Sangiovese.")

Although the Marquis was somewhat uncertain about its potential longevity when the wine was launched, Sassicaia rapidly achieved legendary status as a rival to the top wines of Bordeaux. The 1985 is generally reckoned to have been one of the best wines produced in Italy. Sassicaia sparked the whole super-Tuscan phenomenon of exceptional wines that did not fit any DOC, either because they came from outside DOC areas or because they used a blend of grape varieties not permitted in the DOCs. Eventually it became untenable for one of Italy's top wines to be merely a Vino da Tavola, and a special DOC was created in 1994, Bolgheri Sassicaia, just for the one wine.

Not to be outdone in the family, Marquis Lodovico Antinori, a cousin of Sassicaia's Nicolò Incisa, created Tenuta Dell'Ornellaia in 1981 with vineyards adjacent to those of Sassicaia. Perhaps partly driven by a wish to be distinct from Sassicaia, the vineyards were planted with Cabernet Sauvignon and Merlot. The first vintage was harvested in 1985, and the winery was constructed in 1987. Among the vineyards are the 7 ha Masseto hill (about 120m high), where the clay is several meters deep, and the Merlot gave such extraordinary results that it was diverted to a separate wine.

Ornellaia itself actually did not contain much Merlot until the subsequent purchase and planting of the Bellaria vineyard a little to the north of Bol-

Sassicaia was originally made at the vineyard in the hills at Castiglioncello, but when it became a commercial operation, the winery was built close to the coast near the village of Bolgheri.

gheri. More recently, the Merlot has been decreasing to make room for a little Cabernet Franc. But the ownership has undergone a complete change. The Mondavi winery of California took a minority interest in the estate in 1999, then went into partnership with the Frescobaldi family; and then Frescobaldi purchased the estate outright after Constellation Brands took over Mondavi.

Following the lead of Sassicaia and Ornellaia, Bolgheri remains devoted to Bordeaux varieties, with blends resembling the Médoc; in addition there is a small amount of Syrah and an even smaller amount of Sangiovese. "Bolgheri is not a suitable area for Sangiovese, it does not do well here," says Sebastiano Rosso, winemaker at Sassicaia. Perhaps that is why Bolgheri's fame had to wait until the Bordeaux varieties were tried. How far have producers in Bolgheri followed Sassicaia's example? "I think they are doing something different, because when they came out the style of wine was being influenced by the New World and everyone started to look for a lot of extraction and alcohol," comments Marquis Nicolò Incisa.

When the IGT Toscana classification was created, Bolgheri provided its best wines—these were the first super-Tuscans—but a general Bolgheri DOC was created in 1994. It allows a smorgasbord of varieties rather than attempting to impose any uniform style. The original rules required red wines to have at least 10%, and up to a maximum of 80% Cabernet Sauvignon, 70% Merlot, or 70% Sangiovese. Now a change in rules allows 100% of Cabernet Sauvignon, Cabernet Franc, or Merlot. Bolgheri's wines are among Italy's top wines, yet Bolgheri is only a humble DOC; perhaps in due course it will be deemed worthy to join Chianti and others in the DOCG category.

There are two general classifications in Bolgheri: Bolgheri and Bolgheri Superiore. There's a tendency to use Bolgheri Rosso for second labels or lesser wines, and Superiore for those at the top end that started out as super-Tuscans or are equivalent, but the producer's name is far more important. The classification is useful more to distinguish wines within a producer's range than to provide any indication of grape varieties or aging processes.

Some of the original super-Tuscans are now found under the umbrella of the Bolgheri DOC. Some remain in the IGT Toscana classification, such as Masseto, originally excluded because it is 100% Merlot. Wines that started as IGT Toscana and later converted to Bolgheri DOC are still usually regarded as super-Tuscans. And some producers still say that super-Tuscan is the description with recognition in the marketplace, using it for their top wine, while Bolgheri is used for the second wine. Looking forward, winemaker Axel Heinz at Ornellaia thinks that "wine produced for cash flow should be labeled IGT Toscana, but Bolgheri should stand for something more ambitious."

"Bolgheri is a wine of the south," says Axel Heinz. "It's a Mediterranean version of the Bordeaux climate. Bolgheri has a special combination of opulence, ripeness, and freshness, there's an almost exotic ripeness in the nose, but not explosive like young California Cabernet Sauvignon, there is a spiciness, a mintiness, and in the mouth there's sweetness, but compared to the other southern wines they always finish dry and fresh, that's the special feature of this place."

Does Bolgheri have a distinct identity? "In the last twenty years Bolgheri has developed its identity and style," says winemaker Marco Ferrarese at Guado al Tasso. "The blend is similar (to super-Tuscans in the Chianti area). The style is quite different. The wine is warmer with the character more oriented towards red fruit, the acidity is lower, the tannins are sweet and rich. So the wine is ready to drink at two years, but with good longevity. Our ambition is to make wine you can compare with Bordeaux, but we have our identity. It can be difficult to tell whether you have Cabernet or Merlot sometimes. So whatever gives the identity it's not the variety." Fabio Motto at Michele Satta has a similar view: "We feel it in the grapes, we have softness in the tannins, there is always roundness in the mouth, this is the style of Bolgheri."

Although the blend in Bolgheri resembles Bordeaux's left bank, the characteristic softness of the palate more resembles Bordeaux's right bank. It might be fair to say that insofar as Bolgheri resembles Bordeaux (and I'm not sure there is that much resemblance), its character lies somewhere between the left and right banks: there is always structure (at least when the wines are based on Cabernet) but there is also that telltale softness or lushness. Perhaps the single word most appropriate to describe the various wines of Bolgheri is *juicy:* there is a rich impression of overt fruits, but remaining distinctly Old World.

Whites can come from three varieties. I have not had interesting Sauvignon Blanc or Trebbiano, but Vermentino can be unusually characterful, relatively aromatic, sometimes with a saline impression. Guado al Tasso has a big commitment to Vermentino, with 70 ha planted, and Campo alla Sughera and Guado al Melo also make interesting varietal Vermentino.

Like Bolgheri, Maremma's reputation was established for powerful reds, from Sangiovese as well as international varieties, although an interesting difference is that by 2020 the white Vermentino was actually the DOC's most bottled variety.

Super-Tuscans

The origins of the super-Tuscan phenomenon go back to the inflexibility of the DOC system, in particular its exclusion of nonindigenous grape varieties, which led to a revolution when some top wines were classified under a generic Vino da Tavola label. Propelled by the incongruity of Sassicaia and other wines achieving great reputation while in the lowly category of vino da Tavolo, the new category of IGT Toscana was created in 1992 for wines that did not conform to DOC(G) regulations but that rose above table wine, but this took off in an unexpected way when the top wines in this category became known as super-Tuscans.

Super-Tuscans aren't easy to define. Axel Heinz points out that Tuscany is a large area, and is amused by the occasional requests for a vintage chart for super-Tuscans. But let's suppose for a moment that there was actually an equivalent for a DOC for the super-Tuscan. What would its regulations be? It would have to allow any proportion of any of the grapes of Cabernet Sauvignon, Cabernet Franc, Merlot, Syrah, or Sangiovese. Perhaps the rule would state that a super-Tuscan could be any red variety or combination of varieties so long as it was aged in barrique for any period of time. It could come from any wine-producing region in Tuscany, so what would the vintage chart say—would it reflect conditions in the mountains of Chianti or at the seaside of Maremma? Perhaps the most sensible unifying regulation in order to stop the riff-raff from making wines labeled IGT Toscana would be to specify that there must be a high minimum price!

The diffuse definition of super-Tuscans makes it difficult to know how much super-Tuscan wine is really produced. Some are produced in tiny amounts, others at more than 100,000 bottles per year. Of Tuscany's annual total production of 40 million cases, about one third is DOC (of which Chianti is almost two thirds). Probably the entire production of super-Tuscans is below 250,000 cases annually, about half of the production of Brunello di Montalcino. But somewhat like garage wines in Bordeaux, the effect of the super-Tuscans has been disproportionate. They have raised the bar for the quality of all production in the region, although it must be admitted that their success has made it all but impossible for some DOCs to compete.

It's moot what you classify as a super-Tuscan now that many wines that were formerly IGT Toscana are DOC Bolgheri or Maremma. At one point a super-Tuscan was regarded as more or less equivalent to a Bordeaux blend, with a few monovarietals or Syrah-based wines included. Bolgheri and Maremma are still very much focused on international varieties, and Bordeaux varieties now account for about half of the IGT Toscana category, ranging from wines based on Cabernet Sauvignon to 100% Merlots. Overall, today more than a third of IGT Toscana are monovarietal wines.

There's also quite a bit of Syrah; sometimes it is included in a blend (usually with Bordeaux varieties, but there are also some 100% Syrah wines). Syrah in Tuscany gives interesting results, brighter and fresher than the wines of southern France, for example, and can be appealing. Merlot, on the other hand, does not always do so well, and is more popular to soften a blend than as a monovarietal. However, the best wines can offer a take of Tuscan freshness on the variety. If you want to understand the typicity of classic French varieties in Bolgheri, it is hard to do better than the varietal wines of Le Macchiole, where Cabernet Franc is all black precision, Syrah has elegant aromatics, and Merlot is surprisingly fresh.

After starting in Bolgheri, the super-Tuscan phenomenon widened to take in other areas. Chianti is now the most common origin for super-Tuscans, following the lead of Tignanello, a Sangiovese-dominated blend with Cabernet Sauvignon. Tignanello is produced on an estate in the Chianti region, but was labeled as a table wine in 1971, and later became part of the new IGT classification. It contained too much Sangiovese, as well as a small proportion of the Cabernets, to be a Chianti originally, but ironically under the new regulations it could now be Chianti Classico. But the trend is now for many Chianti producers to have an IGT Toscana as their most expensive wine.

Other wines that would have brought prestige to Chianti are Montevertine's Le Pergole Torte, Fontodi's Flaccianello, or Isole e Olena's Cepparello, all 100% Sangiovese, made from vineyards in the heart of Chianti Classico—but labeled as IGTs originally because monovarietal Sangiovese was not allowed in Chianti at the time, and now perhaps because there's more prestige in being IGT Toscana than Chianti Classico!

This demonstration of the potential of Sangiovese might never have occurred without the spur of the super-Tuscans. Indeed, Sangiovese has now become the best represented single grape in super-Tuscans. This is a big change from their origin with Bordeaux blends. A handful of super-Tuscans come from Montalcino, but are not made from Sangiovese, which fetches such high prices under the Brunello di Montalcino label that there is no need to declassify to IGT!

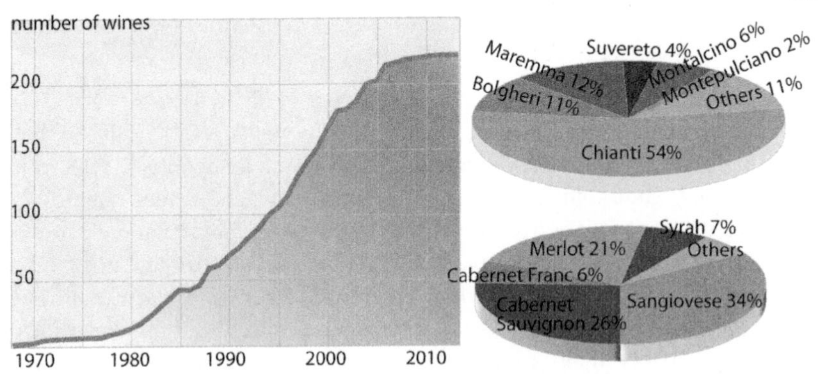

Super Tuscans grew exponentially in the 1990s and leveled off in the 2000s. The pie chart shows the sources of today's super-Tuscans and the overall proportions of grape varieties.

Among Cabernet-based super-Tuscans, there's a difference in the blend from Bolgheri and Chianti. The "average" super-Tuscan in Bolgheri has a distinctly left bank blend: about two thirds Cabernet Sauvignon, with Merlot as the second variety, and a small amount of Cabernet Franc. A Cabernet-dominated super-Tuscan from Chianti is likely to have Sangiovese as the second variety, and sometimes some Merlot. How does a super Tuscan from Chianti differ from one from Bolgheri? "The Cabernet in Solaia [made at the Tignanello estate in Chianti Classico] is more linear, stronger, like stainless steel. Cabernets from Bolgheri are more rounded, more generous," explains Marco Ferrarese.

The super-Tuscans first came to prominence in the 1980s. Some naysayers think the movement has run its course, and that people are now tired of powerful international-style wines, but if so, the news has yet to reach Tuscany. In fact, the number of super-Tuscans continues to increase. Including wines produced in the regions of Bolgheri, Chianti, and Montalcino, there are now well over a hundred super-Tuscans. More than half come from the Chianti region, and of those about half actually could now be classified as Chianti according to current regulations. The most rapidly growing new area is Maremma, just south of Bolgheri. Of course, it's a fine line as to what is a super-Tuscan and what is merely a wine using the IGT Toscana label in the way that was originally intended.

The success of super-Tuscans has led to occasional imitations elsewhere, but for the most part the "super" concept remains confined to Tuscany. The other region of great repute, Piedmont, has not taken up international varieties to any great degree. Perhaps the major importance of super-Tuscans is that they gave a great boost to the confidence of producers in Tuscany that they could produce world-class wines.

Vintages

Recent vintages are exercises in extremes. Generally in Tuscany, 2017 has the same problem as everywhere in Europe, with yields greatly reduced, but high quality. "2017 was a very good vintage for me as an oenologist, the fruit quality is very good, but it is not so good for the owner because quantity is only 30-40%," says Sergio Cantini at Camigliano in Montalcino. There is little precedent for two back-to-back vintages as good as 2016 and 2015. Like 2017, quantity was reduced in 2016, which was generally a warm year, but not as forward as 2015, which was also warm and produced opulent wines. "If you made bad wine in 2015, it would not be worth going on. It's the best year we've ever had," says Giovanna Stianti at Castello di Volpaia.

2014 was more or less a disaster (referring to 2014, "in the past twenty years we've had only one bad vintage," says Michele Scienza in Bolgheri), 2013 was cool ("similar to the vintages of the eighties and nineties, more vertical, more old style," says Riccardo Talenti in Montalcino), 2012 is a good vintage, and depending on location, 2011 or 2010 may be the great year for aging, with the other giving lighter wines for immediate consumption.

Given the variety of grapes and variations in climate, there is no single vintage chart for Tuscany, even though conditions across the region may seem reasonably consistent in any year. Roughly speaking, vintage charts for Bolgheri are likely to represent the success of Cabernet Sauvignon, whereas for Montalcino and Chianti Classico they depend on Sangiovese. Both Sangiovese and Cabernet Sauvignon are late-ripening varieties, but Cabernet is even later, and the gap can make all the difference. "In 1997, Solaia was a great vintage but Tignanello has dusty tannins because of problems in getting to ripeness," says winemaker Renzo Cotarello, describing the Cabernet Sauvignon and Sangiovese-based wines from adjacent vineyards, so super-Tuscans in the Chianti area may not necessarily follow the same rules as Chianti Classico. Even between Chianti Classico and Montalcino, both dependent on Sangiovese, there can be differences; in recent vintages 2010 was the great year in Montalcino, but 2011 was the great year in Chianti Classico.

Vintages in Chianti Classico		
2019	**	Producers are talking about a classic year. Good rain in Spring, cool first half of year, even warm temperatures in summer, regarded as throwback to the 1980s. Very good results all round.
2018	*	Variable across region but relatively better than in Montalcino. Early start, rainy May, relatively dry warm summer, harvest between mid September and mid October.

2017		Very hot dry summer, saved by some rain in September, but lowest yield of last 40 years. Pleasant but longevity is doubtful.
2016	***	Excellent vintage for Chianti, with rich wines. "I have never seen a vintage like this," says Renzo Cotarella of Antinori.
2015	***	Sunny, hot summer—one of the hottest vintages to date—gave well-structured, rich wines. Some producers called it the vintage of the century.
2014	*	Cool, wet summer saved by September; wines range from elegant to green.
2013	*	A tight vintage, ranging from elegant to lean.
2012	**	Well-structured wines generally giving a firm impression.
2011	***	A good start to the decade, ripe and rich.
2010	**	Relatively fresh vintage, early drinking.
2009	*	Rain at start and end of season gave lighter wines.
2008		Average vintage, weakened by rain during season.
2007	***	Best vintage of the decade, aromatic and ripe.
2006	**	Intense wines but over-shadowed by 2007.
2005		Rain during harvest gave lighter wines.
2004	**	A very good vintage, but not as outstanding as in Montalcino.

Vintages in Montalcino		
2018		Difficult year because of rain in June and again in August, but sunny from mid September, with ripe grapes from late harvest. May be like 2013.
2017		Hot, early vintage, with much reduced yields may give concentrated wines.
2016	***	Now described as the best vintage since 2010, with concentrated wines, more reserved and structured than 2015, which it has eclipsed in reputation. At its peak better than 2010, but less consistent.
2015	***	Sunny, hot vintage caused producers to draw parallels with the structured 2010 vintage, but 2015 will be ready (relatively) earlier and shows more obvious fruits.
2014		A poor vintage to point at which a large proportion of Brunello was declassified to Rosso.
2013	*	Tricky summer with wet start and uneven temperatures followed by Indian summer. Wines have a cool climate impression, linear and on lighter side, maturing relatively early.

2012	**	Good vintage but unusually small, with wines that are ready to drink. Very attractive now.
2011	**	Warm year, wines evolving rapidly and good for drinking in short to mid term.
2010	***	This is a great year, with intense, structured wines, but they will not be ready for a few years.
2009	*	Warm summer gave an early drinking vintage.
2008		Cool, wet conditions, but some elegant wines.
2007		Hot, forward vintage.
2006	**	Powerful, well structured wines that need aging.
2005		Rain during harvest spoiled the vintage, but some nice wines for early drinking.
2004	***	A top vintage, stylish and elegant, widely regarded as a classic.

Vintages in Bolgheri		
2018		Rain in July, cool in July, heat didn't start until second week August, so harvest was late, giving lighter wines.
2017		Drought and heat spikes stressed the vines, leading to early harvest of concentrated fruit, with risk of high alcohol.
2016	**	Hot, dry summer until mid-August, then cooler, leading to comparisons with the well-structured 2008 and 2006 vintages. Greater diurnal variation than 2015 may give greater elegance.
2015	***	A very good vintage, as everywhere in Tuscany, uniformly hot.
2014		Wet conditions gave lighter wines and reduced quantities.
2013		Cool rainy start followed by hot dry summer, but good September brought late harvest. Average overall.
2012	*	Hot and dry conditions gave early harvest with intense wines, but not as well balanced as 2011.
2011	**	Dry but not especially hot, very fine wines. A good start to the decade.
2010	*	Inconsistent year due to weather variations in September, but elegant at its best.
2009	*	One of the extremes, hot and dry in July and August, but rain in September; more forceful in style.
2008		Very wet at start, followed by hot, dry conditions; wines are concentrated with higher acidity than usual.
2007	**	Warm at start, then cool in August, but perfect September gave firm fruit expression and more tannic wines.
2006	**	Late, dry vintage gave rich wines and is well regarded.

2005	**	Good conditions in growing season gave wines in fruity style but not as good as 2004.
2004	***	One of the top vintages, ripe but not over-ripe, elegant in style.

Visiting the Region

Bolgheri is quite compact, and all the wineries are within easy reach, many of them concentrated along the Via Bolgherese running parallel to the coast a couple of miles inland. It is easy to visit several in a day from a base in Bolgheri itself or Castegneto Carducci. Bolgheri itself is really no more than a16-31-35 village, with two streets diverging from the tower at the entrance, with several restaurants and food and wine shops. The main tourist centers are the towns on the coast, including Marina di Bibbona and Marina di Castegneto Carducci, offering facilities including accommodation, although they are more focused on beach activities. A new tourist attraction (as of 2017) is MUSEM, a wine museum located in an old farm near Castegneto Carducci. Going farther south, it's an hour or so's easy drive to Suvereto or wineries elsewhere in Maremma.

Montalcino is a small area but governed by the principle that all roads go to Montalcino. So it takes much longer than you expect to go between wineries in the south and the north, as you have to follow the steep roads up to the town of Montalcino and down again. In planning visits, it is best to group wineries by quadrants. Even then, it can take longer than expected from the map to go between wineries, as many roads are unpaved and unmarked. Maps do not distinguish paved and unpaved roads. The locals claim that it is now impossible to pave them because UNESCO has declared Montalcino a World Heritage Site.

Bolgheri is focused on oenotourism.

Chianti Classico is a large area, more or less extending from Florence to Siena, with villages connected by narrow, winding roads that often go up one side of a valley and then down on the other side. It would be ambitious to try to visit the whole region from a single base, and the best schedule is to organize visits to the southern half separately from the northern half. Possible bases for visits are Castel-

The tower in the center of Montalcino is a landmark that's visible from all around the town.

nuova Berardenga at the southern edge, Gaiole or Radda in Chianti in the center, and Tavernelle or Panzano in Chianti for the north. There's an increasing trend for wineries to have accommodation and restaurants.

Some important producers of Chianti Classico occupy medieval castles or monasteries, reflecting a history in which they were the centers of large farming estates, so a visit combines a tour of the winery with a tour of the historic monument. Baron Ricasoli occupies Castello di Brolio, an imposing fortress with extensive grounds, Castello Vicchiomaggio, Castello d'Albola, and Badia a Coltibuono are all historic sites, and Castello di Volpaia occupies an entire fortified medieval village on a hilltop. All are worth seeing

Most producers in Chianti sell wine directly to visitors. The same is true in Montalcino and Bolgheri except for a few producers whose wines are in high demand or on allocation, where you can taste but probably will not be able to buy the top cuvées. An increased focus on oenotourism has made cellar door sales more important to the point where many producers may be disappointed if you do not make a purchase after tasting.

The etiquette of tasting assumes you will spit. A producer will be surprised if you drink the wine. Usually a tasting room or cellar is equipped with spittoons, but ask if you do not see one. Of course, some tourists do enjoy drinking the wines, but producers will take you more seriously if you spit.

The town square makes Greve in Chianti one of the liveliest villages.

Profiles of Producers

Ratings	
***	Excellent producers defining the very best of the appellation
**	Top producers whose wines typify the appellation
*	Very good producers making wines of character that rarely disappoint

Symbols for Producers	
Address	*Tasting room with especially warm welcome*
Phone	*Tastings/visits possible*
Owner/winemaker/contact	*By appointment only*
Email	*No visits*
Website	*Sales directly at producer*
DOC or IGT	*No direct sales*
Red White Sweet Reference wines	*Winery with restaurant*
Grower-producer	*Winery with accommodation*
Negociant (or purchases grapes)	*ha=estate vineyards*
Cooperative	*bottles=annual production*
Conventional viticulture	
Sustainable viticulture	
Organic	
Biodynamic	
Natural Wine	
Wine with No Sulfur	
Vegan Wine	

Chianti Rufina

Profiles of Leading Estates

Marchesi de Frescobaldi *

Castello Nipozzano, Località Nipozzano Fattoria, 50060 Nipozzano	*+39 0552 7141*
info@frescobaldi.it	
www.frescobaldi.it	*[map p. 41]*
1200 ha; 10,000,000 btl	*IGT Toscana, Montesodi*

The Frescobaldis were bankers in medieval Florence, and have been involved with producing wine for seven centuries. Today the wines are produced by Lamberto Frescobaldi. To say that Frescobaldi is a large producer is an understatement: focused on Tuscany, there are six estates: Tenuta Castiglioni (the original estate at Monterspertoli to the west of Chianti Classico, which produces the Giramonte IGT), Castello Nipozzano (Chianti Rufina), Castello Pomino (east of Florence, producing a variety of wines under the Pomino DOC), Tenuta Castelgioconda (in Montalcino and also producing a super-Tuscan), and Rèmole (IGT wines) and Tenuta Ammiraglia (Magiono in Maremma). Their most prestigious holding, however, is Ornellaia, in Bolgheri.

In terms of Sangiovese, the main offerings come from Nipozzano and Castelgioconda. (Chianti Classico is a notable gap in the portfolio.) There's a step up in quality from the Nipozzano Riserva, a Chianti Rufina that includes international varieties but can be a little hard, to the Vecchia Vita, which has only indigenous varieties and comes from the oldest plantings at Nipozzano. Both bring out the classic sour red cherry fruits.

Montesodi is a monovarietal Sangiovese from the named vineyard on the Nipozzano estate that shows its antecedents by bringing out the fresh character of the variety, and then Ripe al Convento is a single-vineyard wine from Castelgioconda, more or less at the same 400m elevation as Montesodi, but giving a riper impression with more fruit intensity. Comparison between Montesodi, which might be considered analogous to a Chianti Classico Gran Selezione, and Ripe al Convento is somewhat indicative of the general difference between Chianti and Brunello di Montalcino. Close to Castelgioconda, but separate from it, the Luce della Vite estate is Frescobaldi's high end in Montalcino (see profile), producing the super-Tuscan Luce, a blend of Sangiovese and Merlot, its second wine, Lucente, and more recently also a Brunello (from 5 of the 77 ha of the estate).

Chianti Classico

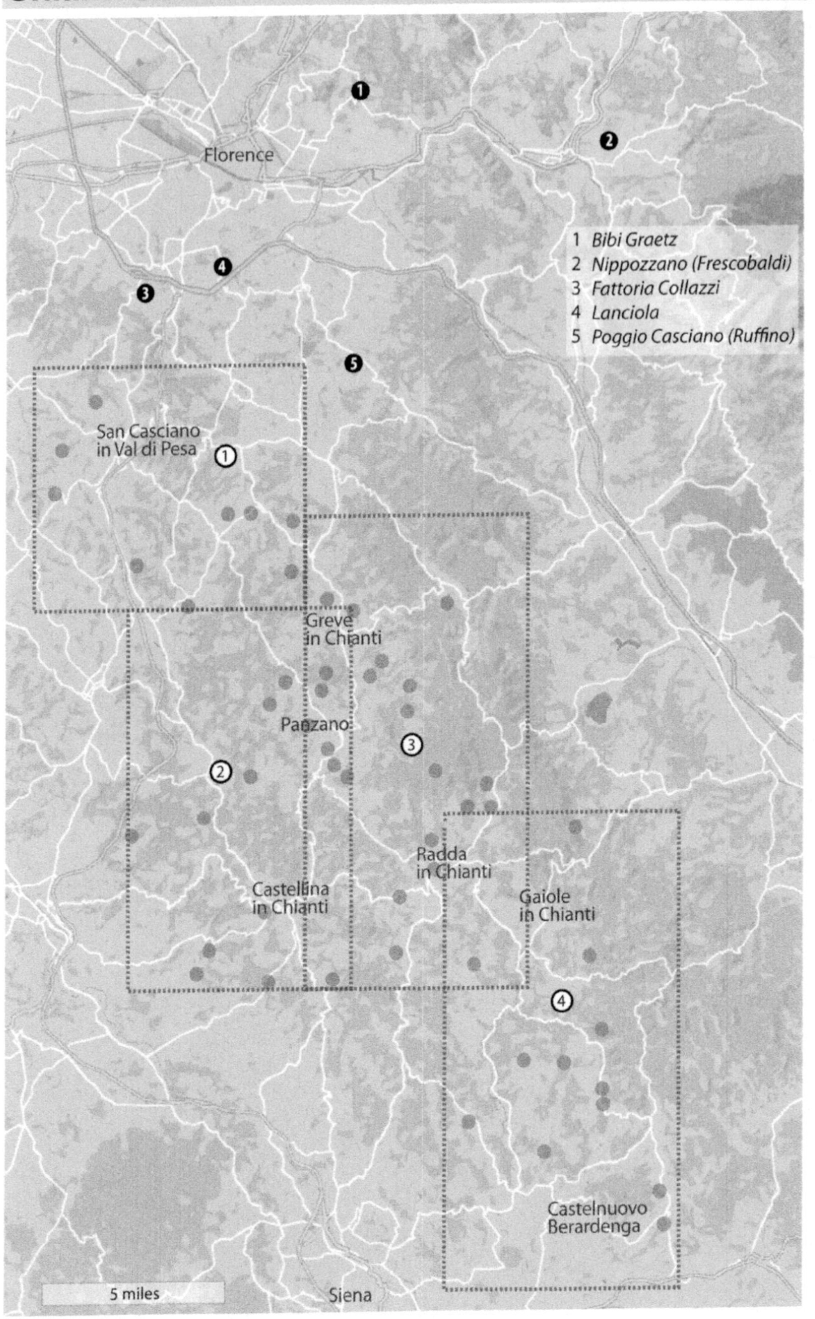

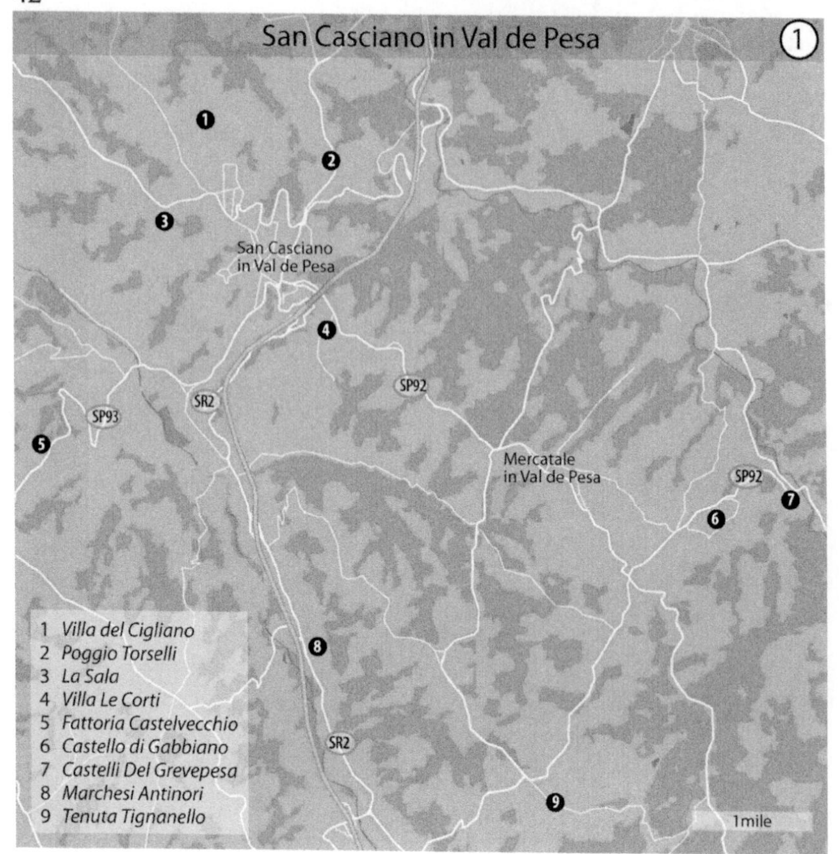
San Casciano in Val de Pesa
1
San Casciano
in Val de Pesa
Mercatale
in Val de Pesa
SP92
SR2
SP93
SP92
SR2
1 Villa del Cigliano
2 Poggio Torselli
3 La Sala
4 Villa Le Corti
5 Fattoria Castelvecchio
6 Castello di Gabbiano
7 Castelli Del Grevepesa
8 Marchesi Antinori
9 Tenuta Tignanello
1mile

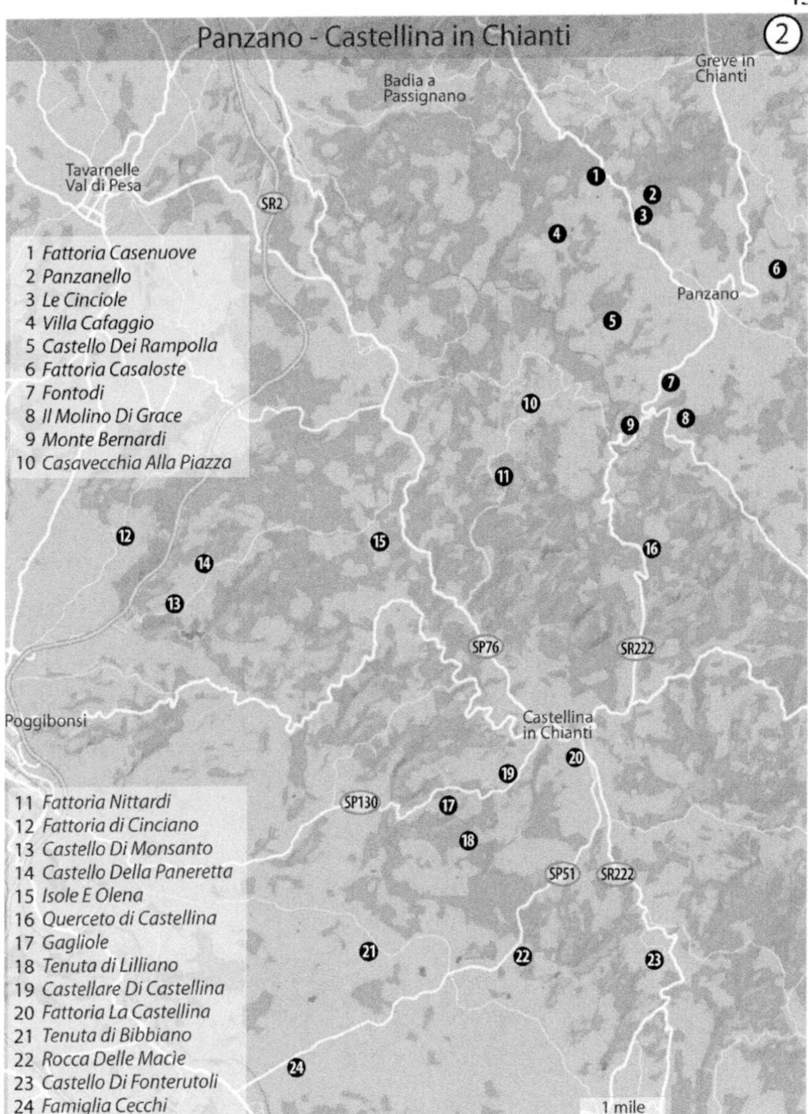

Panzano - Castellina in Chianti
2
Greve in Chianti
Badia a Passignano
Tavarnelle Val di Pesa
SR2
Panzano
SP76
SR222
Poggibonsi
Castellina in Chianti
SP130
SP51
SR222
1 mile
1 Fattoria Casenuove
2 Panzanello
3 Le Cinciole
4 Villa Cafaggio
5 Castello Dei Rampolla
6 Fattoria Casaloste
7 Fontodi
8 Il Molino Di Grace
9 Monte Bernardi
10 Casavecchia Alla Piazza
11 Fattoria Nittardi
12 Fattoria di Cinciano
13 Castello Di Monsanto
14 Castello Della Paneretta
15 Isole E Olena
16 Querceto di Castellina
17 Gagliole
18 Tenuta di Lilliano
19 Castellare Di Castellina
20 Fattoria La Castellina
21 Tenuta di Bibbiano
22 Rocca Delle Macìe
23 Castello Di Fonterutoli
24 Famiglia Cecchi

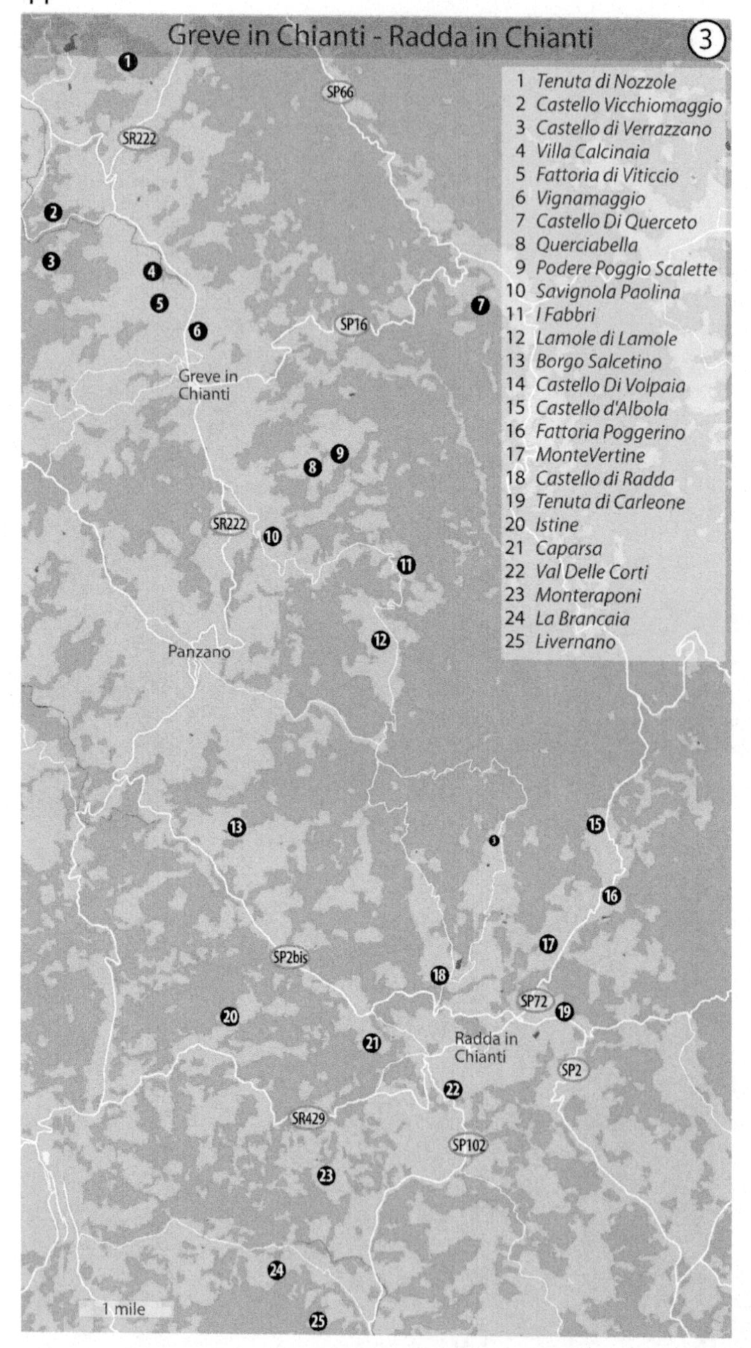
Greve in Chianti - Radda in Chianti
3
1 Tenuta di Nozzole
2 Castello Vicchiomaggio
3 Castello di Verrazzano
4 Villa Calcinaia
5 Fattoria di Viticcio
6 Vignamaggio
7 Castello Di Querceto
8 Querciabella
9 Podere Poggio Scalette
10 Savignola Paolina
11 I Fabbri
12 Lamole di Lamole
13 Borgo Salcetino
14 Castello Di Volpaia
15 Castello d'Albola
16 Fattoria Poggerino
17 MonteVertine
18 Castello di Radda
19 Tenuta di Carleone
20 Istine
21 Caparsa
22 Val Delle Corti
23 Monteraponi
24 La Brancaia
25 Livernano
SP66
SR222
SP16
Greve in Chianti
Panzano
SP2bis
SP72
Radda in Chianti
SP2
SR429
SP102
1 mile

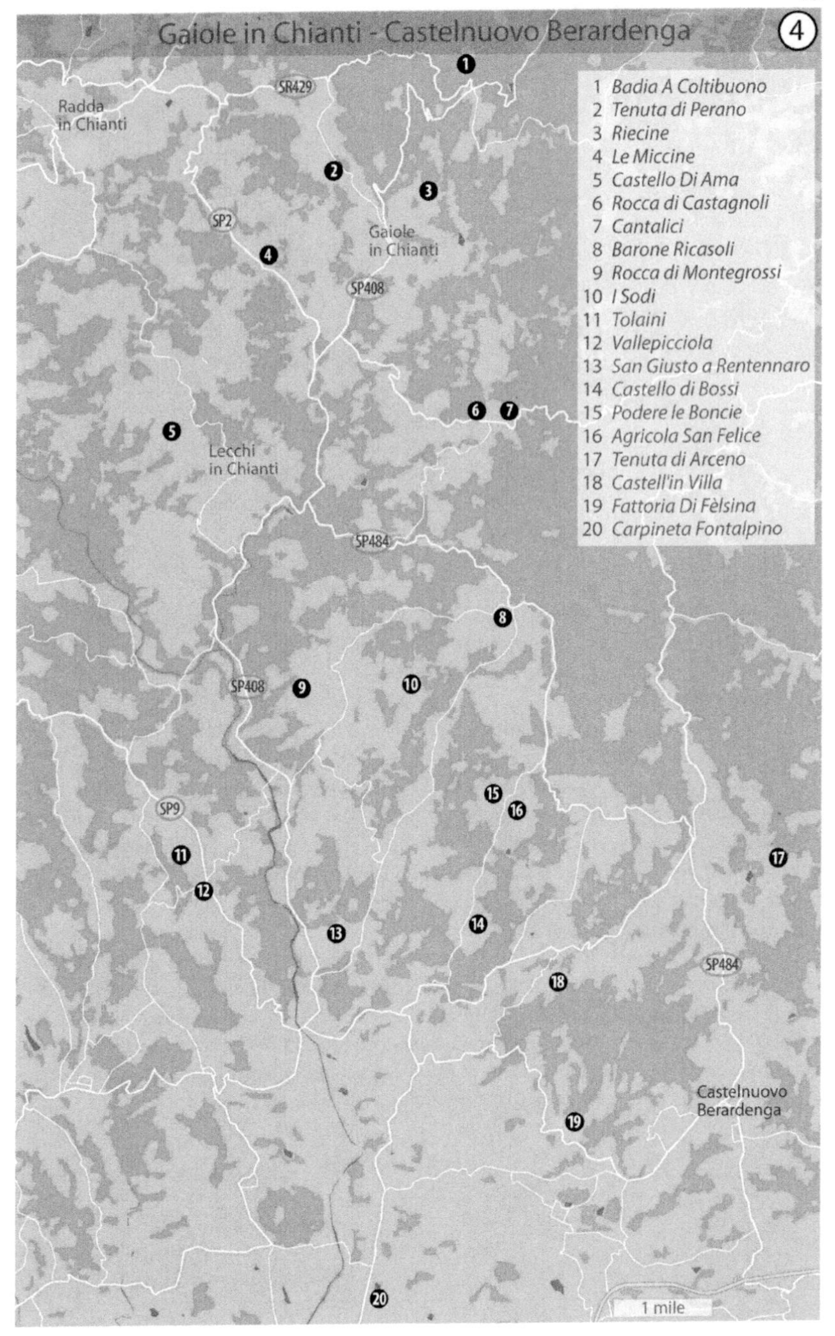
Gaiole in Chianti - Castelnuovo Berardenga
4
1 Badia A Coltibuono
2 Tenuta di Perano
3 Riecine
4 Le Miccine
5 Castello Di Ama
6 Rocca di Castagnoli
7 Cantalici
8 Barone Ricasoli
9 Rocca di Montegrossi
10 I Sodi
11 Tolaini
12 Vallepicciola
13 San Giusto a Rentennaro
14 Castello di Bossi
15 Podere le Boncie
16 Agricola San Felice
17 Tenuta di Arceno
18 Castell'in Villa
19 Fattoria Di Fèlsina
20 Carpineta Fontalpino
Radda in Chianti
SR429
SP2
Gaiole in Chianti
SP408
Lecchi in Chianti
SP484
SP408
SP9
SP484
Castelnuovo Berardenga
1 mile

Profiles of Leading Estates

Castello d'Albola **

Via Pian d'Albola 31, 53017 Radda in Chianti	*+39 0577 738019*
info@albola.it	*Lardori Mazzi Paoletti*
www.albola.it	*[map p. 44]*
	Chianti Classico, Il Solatio
140 ha; 800,000 btl	*Chianti Classico Vin Santo*

The Zonin family comes from Veneto and has been in wine since 1821. They own a variety of estates all over Italy, as well as one in Virginia, USA, and purchased Castello d'Albola in 1979. A former property of the Church, the estate dates from 1010, and the castle was built to fortify the hilltop in the battle between Firenze and Siena around 1100. The original stone structure was extended into other buildings during the Renaissance.

Castello d'Albola has some of the highest vineyards in Tuscany, extending from 300m to 700m, with exposures veering from southwest to southeast. "The size of the estate allows us to produce different expressions of Sangiovese," says Matteo Zonin. "Our style is to focus on the expression of Radda in Chianti. Because of our location, alcohol levels reach only 13 or 13.5%. The wines are not so heavy or alcoholic, that's not our style. In 2013 we switched to 100% Sangiovese for all our wines to keep freshness and character of the grapes. We age our wines much longer than the regulations. We like to sell the wine when it is ready."

Chianti Classico spends 1 year in botti and is released at 2.5 years; Riserva spends 1.5 years in wood, 70% in botti and 30% in 2- and 3-year barriques, and is released at 4 years. It is based on a selection of grapes from the best vineyards. One Gran Selezione is a selection of the best lots from half of a 4 ha plot. The second, Il Solatio, is farther south and higher up, one of the highest vineyards in Tuscany at 600m. It is only 1 ha, "in the middle of nowhere." Both Gran Selezione are produced only in top vintages. The IGT Toscana Acciaiola comes from a plot of old vines near Radda at 400 m.

There's a progression of style along the range. The Chianti Classico is always fresh, even in warm vintages, with moderate alcohol, and shows the bite of Sangiovese. The Riserva has greater depth and smoothness, and moves towards black fruits. Gran Selezione Il Solatio is rounder and smoother, moving towards a richer palate. The IGT Toscana Acciaiola is a blend of Sangiovese and Cabernet Sauvignon, and extends the style further in a more structured direction, but keeping that trademark freshness.

Castello Di Ama ***

Ama Di Gaiole, 53013 Gaiole in Chianti	*+39 0577 746031*
info@castellodiama.com	*Monica Petreni*
www.castellodiama.com	*[map p. 45]*
70 ha; 300,000 btl	*San Lorenzo, Gran Selezione*

At the end of a long approach road, past the Vigneto Bellavista at the summit, Castello di Ama is in the hamlet of Ama. Some houses in the village are used for the restaurant and wine shop, and the winery is just to the side of the hamlet. The estate has 75 ha of vineyards (with 65 ha committed to Chianti Classico) and 35 ha of olive trees. Vineyards are between 390m and 530m altitude. The cellar was built in the eighties, and is full of stainless steel tanks for fermentation, and barriques for aging.

Founded in 1972, Castello di Ama released its first wine later in the decade. Today it is run by Lorenza Sebasti (second generation from one of the founding families) and her husband, winemaker Marco Pallanti. The focus here is on representing Chianti Classico by specific terroirs, all from locations in the vicinity of the winery. "We are in the highest part of the region," says Marco Pallanti. "The wine is different from the rest of Chianti, the altitude gives it freshness and a beautiful aroma. The second difference is the soil, it's rich in calcareous stones, and this gives minerality."

Before 2010, the only estate Chianti Classico was the Riserva, but because vineyards were replanted, production was then split into two: Ama comes from vines under ten years old and basically represents the plantings of a new Sangiovese clone; San Lorenzo is a Gran Selezione that replaced the Riserva, and is a blend of 80% Sangiovese with 13% Merlot and 7% Malvasia Nera. ("Malvasia Nera is a good complement for Sangiovese, it is not so elegant, but it brings some spice.") There are two further Gran Selezione from single vineyards: Vigneto Bellavista (82% Sangiovese and 18% Malvasia Nera) and Vigneto La Casuccia. (about 2 km to the north, less calcareous, with 80% Sangiovese and 20% Merlot; it is produced only in top vintages, eight times in the past twenty years).

The most famous wine here, however, may be the super-Tuscan l'Apparita. In 1982 Merlot was field grafted onto rootstocks in the Bellavista vineyard. "It was planted for blending in the Chianti, but the quality was so outstanding we decided to bottle it. This was the wine that made Ama famous," says Marco. Everything goes into barriques of French oak for 10-15 months. The Ama Chianti Classico goes into second and third year wood, San Lorenzo uses 30% new, and l'Apparita uses 40% new.

The style here goes from freshness in Ama, to weight in San Lorenzo, and elegance in Bellavista, where the lightness of the palate hides the underlying depth and potential for aging. Apparita is more like Bellavista than Bordeaux, with the mineral character of Ama coming right through In addition, Il Chiusa is an unusual blend of Sangiovese and Pinot Noir, which arose from a project to produce Pinot Noir. The latest wine is called Haiku "because it is a simple form but has meaning," Marco explains. It is half Sangiovese, and a quarter each Merlot and Cabernet Franc. It has the flavor spectrum of Sangiovese, but the texture of Bordeaux. An attractive feature of the wines is that all have moderate alcohol, in the range of 13-13.5%.

Marchesi Antinori *

Via Cassia per Firenze 133, Loc. Bargino, 50026 San Casciano In Val di Pesa	*+39 0552 3595*
antinori@antinori.it	*Antinori family*
www.antinori.it	*[map p. 42]*
366 ha; 1,500,000 btl	*Badia a Passignano, Gran Selezione*

The new Antinori winery in Chianti is an impressive building. From a distance, it blends into the hillside as a long, thin line. Close up, it has striking swirls and curves, with a vineyard planted on the roof. Perhaps this is a metaphor for Antinori, one of Italy's most important wine producers, with eleven estates all over Italy. The new winery is the headquarters for administration as well as production. Vast halls are full of stainless steel fermentation tanks and barriques. Opposite the grape reception center on the roof is a restaurant: the Marchesi is anxious that production should be as transparent as possible to visitors. The most important other estates in Tuscany are nearby Tignanello (see profile), Montalcino's Pian delle Vigne (see profile), and Bolgheri's Guado al Tasso (see profile).

There are wines from different estates in Chianti Classico. After the basic Chianti Classico, Villa Antinori presents a traditionally tart view. The Pèppoli cuvée comes from a vineyard close to Tignanello: it shows the classic red cherry fruit spectrum, but with a touch of soft aromatics. The Riserva from Tignanello is smoother and rounder. It used to contain other sources to supplement grapes from Tignanello, but since 2011 has come exclusively from the Tignanello estate. "It matches Tignanello style more than Chianti Classico style," says winemaker Sara Pontemolesi, so today it is labeled as coming from Tenuta Tignanello.

"We consider Badia a Passignano to be our top Chianti Classico," Sara says. Now a Gran Selezione (formerly a Riserva), it comes from a 60 ha estate a few miles to the east, which makes only the Gran Selezione. Smooth and intense, when young it shows the Hungarian oak in which it matures. "We think the French oak is too strong for Sangiovese. The aromatic notes of Hungarian oak are spicy, but do not have so much vanillin. The grain is not as fine as French, so they exchange better with the air. We don't want tannins so much as micro-oxygenation." Entirely Sangiovese, the style of Badia a Passignano is rich and chocolaty, well in the direction of Montalcino; in fact, Antinori's Rosso di Montalcino is smooth and elegant, but has just a touch less intensity than Badia a Passignano.

Outside of Tuscany, Antinori has an important estate in Umbria, Castello della Sala, which produces the IGT Cervara della Sala, a blend of Chardonnay with 10% Greccheto. "This is our top white wine, which started after the Marchesi went to Burgundy and asked why Italy could not produce a wine like Montrachet." The Greccheto brings necessary acidity—the wine does not go through MLF—and increases longevity: the wine has a strong mineral, smoky presence.

Badia A Coltibuono **

Località Badia a Coltibuono, 53013 Gaiole in Chianti	*+39 0557 749498*
info@coltibuono.com	*Roberto Stucchi*
www.coltibuono.com	*[map p. 45]*
	Chianti Classico, Cultus Boni Riserva
63 ha; 240,000 btl	*Chianti Classico Vin Santo*

Badia a Coltibuono was originally a monastery (founded by Benedictine monks in 1051); it expanded until 1810, when the monasteries were secularized. "It has been in our family since 1846," says Roberto Stucchi, who has been managing the estate since 1985. Today it houses a winery, boutique hotel, and restaurant (with a wine shop at the entrance to the access road that winds up to the hilltop at 630m). The buildings surround around a gracious courtyard, with a lovely ornamental garden behind. Wines are aged and stored in the extensive underground cellars, but the winery and vineyards are at Monti in Chianti, a few miles just to the south.

Production focuses on Sangiovese and other indigenous varieties. "I am going in the opposite direction from varietal wines," Roberto says. Chianti Classico and the Riserva are 90% Sangiovese with the other 10% coming from several indigenous varieties; there are no international varieties here. The Riserva is a selection of the best lots, chosen when the Chianti Classico is bottled. They are aged in 25 hl casks of Austrian or French oak. The Cultus Boni Riserva cuts Sangiovese back to 80%, and increases the number of indigenous varieties: it is aged in barriques, including a little new oak. The latest addition to the range is Montebello, an IGT Toscana that is a blend from one barrel each of the various indigenous varieties. This sees more new oak. It comes from a vineyard containing old vines, which were used to provide material for planting the other vineyards. There is one monovarietal wine, Sangioveto, a 100% Sangiovese that comes from the oldest vines, but as though to mark the difference from Chianti Classico, it is labeled as a super-Tuscan.

The style is classic, moving from the fresh Chianti Classico, with bright red cherry fruits, to the Riserva, just a touch smoother, with notes of black as well as red fruits, showing the same focus on purity of fruits. Cultus Boni shows greater roundness and generosity, moving further towards black fruits, and can be stern enough on release to need a couple of years. Sangioveto is the smoothest of the range, really showing the concentration of the old vines. Montebello shows as the most powerful wine. Of course, there's also Vin Santo, olive oils, and grappa. There also a separate range of wines, with the same total production as Badia a Coltibuono, but simply labeled Coltibuono, including Chianti, Chianti Classico, and IGT Toscana, from a negociant activity.

Tenuta di Bibbiano *

Via Bibbiano 76, 53011 Castellina in Chianti	*+39 0577 743065*
info@bibbiano.com	*Tommaso & Federico Marrocchesi Marzi*
www.bibbiano.com	*[map p. 43]*
30 ha; 130,000 btl	*Chianti Classico Riserva*

Located on a plateau at a high point a few miles north of Castellina, the winery identifies something of a strategic high point (it was fought over in the second world war). There's a view right across to San Gimignano, ten miles to the west. The plateau effectively divides the vineyards into two halves: to the south (facing San Gimignano), soils are blue-gray clay, and the vineyards are steeper and warmer; to the north, soils are clays of vari-

ous colors, and the cooler climate means harvest is 10-15 days later. The estate extends over 220 ha, with vineyards just below the plateau at 300m elevation.

The property passed through the hands of the Church and ended up with the Marzi family in 1865. "The boundaries of the estate have not changed since 1760," says Tomasso Marzi. "My grandfather planted the first vineyards in the 1960s." The cellar was built in 1968. Three vineyards on the south side have the Sangiovese Grosso cultivar from Montalcino. Most of the vineyards were planted between 2000 and 2005. Oenologist Julio Gambelli made the wine from 1943 until Stefano Porcinai took over in 2001.

Winemaking is a mix of traditional and modern. The Chianti Classico and the Riserva are blends from vineyards on each side. The Chianti Classico is an example of the traditional style, aged in vat, with a classic fresh, sour red cherry flavor spectrum. The Riserva ages in tonneaux, and is smoother and rounder, with more power and impressions of oak offering some longevity. The Montornello Gran Selezione, coming from a single vineyard in the northern half, has a cool-climate mineral style showing precision, while the Camponinno Gran Selezione comes from the best vineyard to the south, and is warmer and richer, showing greater breadth, with fruits moving towards black. It can be a vin de garde in top vintages. The Chiantis are 100% Sangiovese. The two single vineyards are sufficiently distinctive to make it difficult to define a house style.

The focus here really is on Chianti Classico, but there's also a Sangiovese-Colorino blend as the Bibbianaccio IGT, and the white IGT Listrice from Malvasia. There's a guest house with accommodation.

La Brancaia *

Loc. Poppo 42b, 53017 Radda in Chianti	*+39 0577 742007*
brancaia@brancaia.it	*Barbara Widmer*
www.brancaia.it	*[map p. 44]*
80 ha; 500,000 btl	*Chianti Classico Riserva*

Brancaia is unusual, spanning Chianti to Maremma under one label; you have to look at the back label to see the origin of the wine. It started when Barbara Widmer's parents visited the Chianti region on holiday from Switzerland. They bought the Brancaia estate in Castellina 1980, and started to replant its 7 ha of vineyards. A couple of years later they bought the estate that is now their headquarters, at Poppi, in Radda. (The address is in Radda, but it is easier to get there from Castellina, which is actually closer.) Today there are 40 ha altogether in the Chianti region and another 40 ha at the estate in Maremma, which they bought in 1988. Most wines are IGT Toscana, but there are also Chianti Classico and Riserva.

Vineyards are not dedicated to any particular wine; "lots are assigned to wines depending on quality, so all vineyards are farmed the same," Barbara explains. The entry-level wine, Tre, is a blend from Maremma and Chianti, with 80% Sangiovese and 10% each of Cabernet Sauvignon and Merlot. It ages two thirds in tonneaux and one third in concrete, which was introduced in 2014 to help soften the tannins. Chianti Classico is a step-up in refinement and is now all Sangiovese: it ages in vat, with two thirds in steel and one third in concrete. Chianti Classico Riserva has 20% Merlot; the Sangiovese ages in tonneaux and the Merlot in barriques, with about half new. Oak is evident, and the overall impression is more elegant than the Chianti Classico. The Riserva can be quite stern and structured when young. "With Chianti Classico we want to show flavor, with Riserva we want to show how complex and elegant Chianti Classico can be," Barbara says.

There are three high-level wines under ITG Toscana. All tend to show black fruits with lifted aromatics. Illatria comes from Maremma. Its first vintage was 2002, with a blend of 60% Cabernet Sauvignon, 30% Sangiovese, and 10% Petit Verdot. The blend changed dramatically in 2009 to 40% Cabernet Sauvignon, 40% Petit Verdot, and 20% Cabernet Franc. It spends 18 months in barriques with half new. The Petit Verdot gives it more lifted aromatics than the 100% Cabernet Sauvignon, which is more structured. The flagship is Il Blu, now a blend of 70% Merlot with 25% Sangiovese and 5% Cabernet Sauvignon. It used to have more equal amounts of Merlot and Sangiovese, but "we've increased Merlot and decreased Sangiovese (which goes into the Riserva), and we think it's more complex," Barbara says. It's the most aromatic cuvée, but the densest and finest. "We think this is the best we can do from the Chianti region," Barbara says.

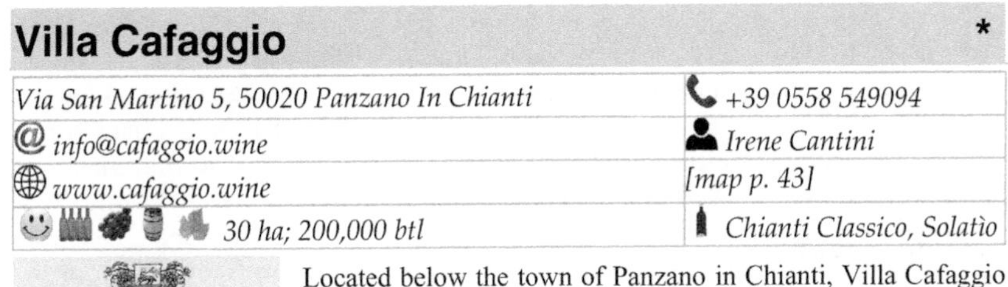

Villa Cafaggio *

Via San Martino 5, 50020 Panzano In Chianti	*+39 0558 549094*
info@cafaggio.wine	*Irene Cantini*
www.cafaggio.wine	*[map p. 43]*
30 ha; 200,000 btl	*Chianti Classico, Solatìo*

Located below the town of Panzano in Chianti, Villa Cafaggio was a Benedictine monastery making wine in the Middle Ages. Its recent history is somewhat chequered. It had fallen into decay by the 1960s, when the Farkas family purchased it. It was restored and replanted, largely with Sangiovese, and in 1986 the first Cabernet vineyard was planted (by field grafting Cabernet over Canaiolo). The estate was sold in 2005 to a co-operative from northern Italy (Cantina La-Vis e Valle di Cembra), and was then sold again in 2016 to the investment bank ISA.

Vineyards are all around, part of the Conca d'Or valley (named for the color of the cereal that used to be grown here). All 21 producers in the valley have agreed to make it entirely organic. The winery has an underground cellar built into the hillside in 1970 on two levels. A new barrel room is close by. The winery is down a steep unpaved road; it would be better not to meet a truck coming the other way.

Chianti Classico comes from the estate and surrounding vineyards. The Riserva is a selection of the best estate grapes. Both are 100% Sangiovese and age in botti of Slavonian oak. There are two single-vineyard wines in Chianti Classico: Solatìo and San Martino. Both are Riservas—"we don't understand Gran Selezione." Solatìo is 100% Sangiovese and ages in botti; San Martino has 85% Sangiovese, 10% Cabernet Sauvignon, and 5% Cabernet Franc, and ages in used barriques. The two "Crus" are IGT Toscana: Basilicata del Cortaccio is Cabernet Sauvignon, and Basilicata del Pruneto is Merlot. Both age in barriques.

The Chianti Classico and Riserva are quite close in style, both somewhat more generous than usual for Chianti, but the Riserva has more weight. Solatìo follows with more intensity, and San Martino marks a transition to a more textured, modern style, somewhat of a halfway house to the international varieties of the IGTs. The vineyards for San Martino and Cortaccio are adjacent, and the wines show a surprising similarity of house style. At Villa Cafaggio they see the wines as developing in parallel, but say that the Sangiovese is a little more delicate, so may age faster if it is not a top year. San Martino's sense of granularity, almost chocolaty, intensifies in Cortaccio and Pruneto, which show a Tuscan take on the international varieties with a soft structure underneath the fruit; Pruneto is more overt than Cortaccio.

Fattoria Di Fèlsina ***

Via del Chianti 101, 53019 Castelnuovo Berardenga	*+39 0577 355117*
info@felsina.it	*Giovanni Poggiali*
www.felsina.it	*[map p. 45]*
74 ha; 500,000 btl	*Chianti Classico Riserva, Rancia*

One of the top properties in Chianti Classico, Fèlsina is located right at the southern border of the appellation. It's an extensive estate of about 150 ha, with olive trees as well as vineyards surrounded by forests. In fact, originally there were more olives than vines, and wine was made only for local consumption. The winery is located just on the edge of the town of Castelnuova Berardenga, and has an enoteca and tasting room. Fèlsina also owns Castello di Farnatella, an estate in Chianti Colli Senesi.

The estate was founded by Domenico Fèlsina in 1966, and today is run by his son-in-law, Giuseppe Mazzocolin, who still shows his origins as a professor of philosophy. Giuseppe believes in Sangiovese. "In 1983 I started to make wine 100% of Sangiovese." In the old vineyards there were Colorino, Trebbiano, and Malvasia, but replanting has used only Sangiovese, all sourced from selection massale with "probably about 30 subvarieties." Giuseppe's motto for production is "never too much," which applies to oak, extract, and so on, and no doubt explains the finesse of the wines. Giuseppe brings the same keen analysis to bear on his production of olive oil as on his Chianti: a visit to Felsina is incomplete without a tasting of the four monovarietal olive oils. "Olives vary with variety, terroir, vintage, but not as much as the grape," Giuseppe says.

The Chianti Classico Berardenga comes from a variety of vineyards in the estate, and is matured in Slavonian oak, with a small percentage in small barrels. The Berardenga Riserva is a selection and uses 30% French barriques. The Rancia Riserva comes from a vineyard at 350m elevation around the old Rancia farmhouse at the northern border of the property, and is matured for 20 months in 2-3-year-old French oak. Fontalloro is labeled as IGT Toscana because it comes from three vineyards, one at a high elevation within the

Chianti Classico part of the estate, two others at lower elevation over the border into Chianti Colli Senesi. It's vinified in a mix of new and one-year French barriques. Colonia is a Chianti Classico from a 2 ha vineyard at the highest point in the property, 400m (planted in 1993). Made only in top years, it started as an IGT in 2006 and 2007, then became Gran Selezione in 2009; when Colonia is not made, the grapes are declassified to Rancia. It is aged for 24 months in barriques, including new oak. I Sistri is a Chardonnay labeled as IGT Toscana. Maestro Raro is a 100% Cabernet Sauvignon, and the most powerful of Fèlsina's wines.

The style here ranges from traditional to modernist. The most traditional wine is the Chianti Classico Berardenga, which shows classic freshness, but is very sophisticated for Classico: I would put it more at the level of other producers' Riservas. Rancia Riserva and Fontalloro place at the same price point in the range, but Fontalloro is more powerful, more chocolaty, than Rancia, which has more of the classic freshness. The same relationship holds through warm and cool vintages, and recently I've found Fontalloro to show too much extraction compared to Rancia's rounded elegance. The Gran Selezione Colonia actually has more oak exposure than Fontalloro, but shows it less obviously. While Fontalloro is an expression of modern Chianti, tending towards the power of (say) Brunello, Colonia is the finest of the cuvées, and has a more traditional typicity, even though it ages in new barriques. Fèlsina makes one of the most elegant Vin Santo's in Chianti Classico.

Castello Di Fonterutoli ***

Via Ottone Iii di Sassonia 5, Loc. Fonterutoli, 53011 Castellina In Chianti	*+39 0577 741385*
mazzei@mazzei.it	*Filippo Mazzei*
www.fonterutoli.it	*[map p. 43]*
117 ha; 800,000 btl	*Chianti Classico Riserva, Ser Lapo*

To reach Fonterutoli, you have to find the right road out of the sixteenth century hamlet huddled just below the main road. The winery is in an amphitheater below the village. The Castello is in the village itself, and offers accommodation and a restaurant. The estate came into the Mazzei family by marriage in 1398. Some 24 generations later, the Mazzei estates include Fonterutoli, Belguardo in Maremma, and Zisola in Sicily.

The estate covers 650 ha, with 120 separate vineyard parcels, at elevations varying from 220-550m. Soils are based on albarese and sandstone, but basically fall into five groups based on elevation and soils. "What we are really looking for here is diversity," says Filippo Mazzei. "We are currently managing 36 clones of Sangiovese plus five other varieties." Half the Sangiovese clones are commercial; the other half come from a program of selection massale on the estate.

Wines become increasingly smooth along the range. The Poggio Badiola IGT Toscana (70% Sangiovese and 30% Merlot) anticipates the fresh style of the Chianti Classico. Called simply Fonterutoli, the Classico is more than 90% Sangiovese, with some Colorino and Malvasia, and gives an impression between traditional and modern. The

Riserva Ser Lapo has a little Merlot. Aged in barriques with no new wood; it is firmer and richer, and moves towards black cherries. The biggest jump in style comes with the Gran Selezione. The first was simply called Castello Fonterutoli as a selection from the best vineyards. It retains the savory character of Classico, and shows an increase in elegance and sophistication rather than greater power. Since 2010, it has been 100% Sangiovese.

In 2017, Fonterutoli changed to offer three Gran Seleziones, each from a different commune with its own identity. Castello remains a selection of the best plots around the winery in Castellina in Chianti. Badiòla comes from high altitude (over 470m) vineyards in Radda in Chianti. It's smooth and silky, slightly nutty, with a savory element, very much its own style. Vicoregio36 started as an IGT, Mix 36, a pure Sangiovese from 36 different clones—"it is an IGT Toscana because it is our research wine," Filippo said at the time—making a smooth and elegant impression, a little livelier than Castello. In 2017 the name changed as it became the third Gran Selezione. Coming from Castelnuovo Berardenga, it's smoother and silkier than Castello with more of a savory tang. All the Gran Selezione age in tonneaux, with 30-50% new oak.

"I'm looking for elegant not opulent wines," Filippo says, and the finesse of the house style carries through to three super-Tuscans with international varieties. Concerto is a blend of 80% Sangiovese with 20% Cabernet Sauvignon; fine and precise, it shows more structure than the Gran Selezione. The single vineyard Siepi is an equal blend of Sangiovese and Merlot, aged in barriques with 70% new oak, balanced between savory and plushness. The 100% Cabernet Sauvignon, Philip, is the most recent cuvée, and retains the fresh character of Tuscany.

Fontodi ***

Località Fontodi San Leolino, 50020 Panzano in Chianti	*+39 0558 52005*
fontodi@fontodi.com	*Giovanni Manetti*
www.fontodi.com	*[map p. 43]*
90 ha; 350,000 btl	*Vigna del Sorbo, Gran Selezione*

Originally involved in producing terracotta tiles in the region, the Manetti family moved into wine production in 1968. The winery sits in a commanding position looking out over the amphitheater of the valley, where the 130 ha estate includes a more or less contiguous array of vineyards and a farm. Agriculture is organic, and largely self-sustaining, with manure from the 25 cows at the farm used for the vineyards, which are in Panzano's celebrated subzone, Conca d'Oro.

The Chiantis have been aged in barriques since 1980. "French oak softens the astringency of Sangiovese; I would prefer to see people using French barriques to soften the wine rather than using 20% international varieties," says Giovanni Manetti. However, Giovanni is experimenting with returning to botti, and also with amphorae, made by his brother at the family tile factory. The Chianti Classico ages in old French barriques. It's relatively dark and structured for Classico, up to the level of most producers' Riservas. Introduced in 2014, the Filetta di Lamole cuvée comes from a vineyard with sandy soils at 600m elevation in Lamole; in the same style as the Classico, it adds complexity to the palate. The Vigna del Sorbo Gran Selezione (formerly Riserva) comes from the del Sorbo vineyard and ages in barriques with 50% new oak.

When Vigna del Sorbo was introduced in 1985, it contained 10% Cabernet Sauvignon; since then the vineyard has been replanted, and a parcel of 45-year-old vines was added in 2009, bringing the Cabernet proportion down to 5%. Today it is 100% Sangiovese. The palate is softer, deeper, blacker, and the style moves towards that of Brunello di Montalcino with chocolaty overtones.

Fontodi's top wine is Flaccianello della Pieve, a selection of 100% Sangiovese from the best vineyards, labeled as Toscana IGT. Other IGTs include the Cabernet Sauvignon Meriggio, the Syrah Casa Via, and the Pinot Noir Case Via. Why is the top wine an IGT when it could be a Chianti Classico? "It's not the right moment yet to go back to the Chianti name. I'd like to see a trade in which the best wines return to Chianti DOC in return for a better classification system that distinguishes the communes."

Castelli Del Grevepesa *

Via Gabbiano 34, 50026 San Casciano In Val di Pesa	*+39 0558 21101*
vinoteca@castellidelgrevepesa.it	
www.castellidelgrevepesa.it	*[map p. 42]*
300 ha	*Chianti Classico Castelgreve, Riserva*

The largest cooperative in the region, Grevepesa was founded in 1965 by 18 winegrowers, and now has 120 members from all over the area. There are three ranges: Castelgreve, Clemente VII, and Castello di Bibbione. Castelgreve starts with a generic Chianti, then presents Chianti Classico, the Fiasco bottling in the old straw-covered bottle, and Riserva. They are 95% Sangiovese, with Merlot or other varieties filling in the rest. The Riserva is definitely a notch up in terms of flavor intensity, adding a faint savory tang and a touch of structure to the obvious red fruits of the Chianti Classico. The top Castelgreve wines are the Gran Seleziones from Lamole and Panzano, both monovarietal Sangiovese. All age in botti. The line also includes cuvées from various other areas. Clemente VII is a range in more modernist style, including Chianti Classico, Riserva, and Gran Selezione, all aged partly in botti and partly in barriques. It's more fruit-driven than Castelgreve. Castello di Bibbione has Chianti Classico, Riserva, and Gran Selezione, all from the Bibbione estate in San Casciano, including 10% Merlot for Classico (aged in botti), and 5% Merlot for Riserva (aged in a mix of botti and barriques) and Gran Selezione (two years in botti and one year in barriques.

I Sodi *

Loc. I Sodi, Frazione Monti, 53013 Gaiole in Chianti	*+39 0577 747012*
info@agrisodi.com	*Andrea Casini*
www.agrisodi.com	*[map p. 45]*
	Chianti Classico Riserva

12 ha; 90,000 btl	Chianti Classico Vin Santo

The name of the estate means hard ground, referring to the stony soil. There's a very long approach from the main road to the somewhat isolated property; from the winery you can see the Castle of Brolio on the hills in the distance. The estate had been more or less abandoned until the Casini family purchased it in 1973 and planted 9 ha of vineyards and 3 ha of olive groves. "My grandfather bought the property from the Church to make wine for the family because he didn't think much of the quality of Chianti at the time," says Andrea Cassini, who manages the estate today. Vineyards surround the property and face south, but although this is a warm spot, it is kept fresh by an underground spring. The cellar built in 1982 was extended with a new cellar in 2007.

The entry-level wine here is an IGT Toscana, Solerto, which has a blend of traditional varieties: Sangiovese, Canaiolo, Malvasia Nera, and Trebbiano. The Chianti Classicos are blends of Sangiovese and Canaiolo, with a big step up from Chianti Classico to the Riserva, which is a selection of the best grapes in the best years, and is not produced every year. Soprasassi is an unusual monovarietal of Canaiolo, which shows a surprising sense of completeness, in the typical savory flavor spectrum of the region. The top wine is Vigna Farsina, a monovarietal Sangiovese. Why is it an IGT and not Chianti Classico? "Because the volume is very small. We already have a Riserva. We could have made a Gran Selezione, but I think many Gran Seleziones are Riserva relabeled, we wanted to do something new." With an impression of umami and gunflint, it is in fact the very model of a modern Chianti Classico.

The Chianti Classico ages in Slavonian botti; the Riserva, Soprasassi and Farsina age in barriques. The style here is modern and elegant, although eschewing international varieties. Going from the Riserva to the Vigna Farsina, there's an increasingly silky sheen, which shows even in the monovarietal Canaiolo. The Vin Santo—"we produce a true Vin Santo," says Andrea—comes from grapes that dry for 3-4 months in a loft, and the wine ages for 6 years in 50-150 liter casks. It has a delicious sweet/sour balance with a mineral edge, and indeed is the real thing.

Isole E Olena ***

Loc. Isole 1, 50021 Barberino Val d'Elsa	+39 0558 072763
info@esseweb.eu	Marta De Marchi
www.isoleolena.it	[map p. 43]
	IGT Toscana, Cepparello
50 ha; 250,000 btl	Chianti Classico Vin Santo

Perched at the end of a path half way up a mountain, Isole is where the winery is located, and below is the hamlet of Olena, whose occupants used to survive by sharecropping the land. The estate was formed when Paolo de Marchi's father combined two properties in 1956, one in Isole and one in Olena. The soils are galestro. He was thinking of selling it when Paolo came from Piedmont in 1976 and decided to create the vineyards. (Paolo now makes a Nebbiolo from the old family vineyards in Lessona under the name of Proprietà Sperino.) Production is increasing now that a replanting program has been completed. "I am happy this is finished, I want to have an eternal vineyard in which we only replace individual vines, but the old vineyards needed to be replanted because they were old clones and the varieties were all mixed up," Paolo says. He's planning to expand the winery underground. "I want to have more space for aging in order to be able to offer older vintages."

The Chianti Classico is a blend of 80% Sangiovese with Canaiolo and (sometimes) Syrah. "The pressure to make Chianti just from Sangiovese is taking things to excess. Chianti has always been a blend, of course the nature of that blend will change with time. I will never abandon Canaiolo because I think it gives a little spice to young Chianti." The Chianti Classico shows as completely ripe, but true to Chianti's traditional freshness, and is well up to the quality of most producers' Riservas. In fact, its aged as long as Riservas in a mixture of small and large casks. "This represents my style, soft tannins and ripeness," Paolo says. "I did have a Riserva in the early 1980s but in 1985 I stopped to focus on these two styles, the Chianti Classico that drinks well young, and Cepparello that ages long term."

Paolo is a forceful character who bubbles over with ideas and goes his own way. Explaining why his top wine, Cepparello remains an IGT Toscana although it is 100% Sangiovese, he says, "Wine of origin to me is not anymore in the appellation. Everything in the appellation works for brands and not for the real origin. They certify the provenance but that is not enough." Cepparello is a selection of the best lots of Sangiovese and is aged in French barriques with one third new. It is always an elegant demonstration of his style in balancing tannins and lacy acidity—Paolo hates over-extraction. It balances the richness of the palate (with some spicy, smoky notes when young) against the savory tang of Sangiovese. In recent vintages 2015 is a knockout, 2014 is a success for the year, and 2013 shows a lighter, elegant style.

The Gran Selezione was originally created as a special cuvée from the 2006 vintage for the family to celebrate the fiftieth anniversary of the winery. A blend with around 10% of Cabernet Franc and a little Syrah and Petit Verdot, it makes a sturdier impression than Cepparello; but although it's richer, there is always an edge of minerality. In top vintages, I find Cepparello more elegant, but the international varieties in the Gran Selezione may give it an advantage in weaker vintages. However, the price of the Gran Selezione is disproportionate compared to Cepparello. I suspect this may reflect Paolo's disdain for the internationalization of Chianti Classico. "I put the Gran Selezione on the market at a very high price but my flagship is still Cepparello," Paolo says.

The Isole e Olena label is used for traditional wines based on Sangiovese, while Collezione De Marchi is used for other varieties and includes Chardonnay, Syrah, and Cabernet Sauvignon. The elegant house style shows right through to the Syrah and Cabernet Sauvignon. The Chardonnay started as blend in an attempt to improve white wine production, but proved so successful that Paolo started to bottle it separately in 1987. "It started as a solution for the excess of white grapes and now it is a good solution for the estate, because I can plant it in locations where Sangiovese won't ripen," Paolo explains. It's the most important variety in the Collezione, showing its new oak rather obviously when released.

Il Molino Di Grace *

Località Il Volano, Panzano in Chianti	*+39 0558 561010*
@ *info@ilmolinodigrace.it*	*Daniel Grace*
www.ilmolinodigrace.com	*[map p. 43]*
20 ha; 15,000 btl	*Chianti Classico Riserva*

There have been vineyards here for three centuries. The name refers to both an old windmill (Molino) on the property, and the current owners, the Grace family. Frank Grace came from Ohio and purchased the 62 ha property in 1995; today his sons Tim and Daniel run the estate. Grapes had previously been sold to local producers, but an abandoned nineteenth century ruin was renovated to become the winery, and the first vintage was 1999.

There are three Chianti Classicos: the Classico, Classico Riserva, and Gran Selezione. All are 100% Sangiovese, the first two matured in a mix of botti of Slavonian oak, and barriques and tonneaux from French oak, the Gran Selezione in barriques and tonneaux with some new oak. It's not a criticism of the Riserva to say that it shows only a touch more depth than the Classico *tout court* , but is rather a comment on the unusual smoothness and ripeness of the simple Chianti Classico. The Gran Selezione retains the freshness of Chianti. Recent vintages have shown more obvious impressions of oak.

Coming from a single parcel of old (more than 60-year) vines on galestro soils at 580m altitude, IGT Toscana Gratius is more traditional in its grape varieties than the Chiantis, with 5% of Canaiolo and Colorino as well as Sangiovese, but aged in new and 1-year barriques and tonneaux, it shows a more international character along the lines of the super-Tuscans. Another IGT, Il Volano, is three quarters Sangiovese and a quarter Merlot, and ages in stainless steel.

The estate is nominally open for tastings, but the gates at the entrance are often locked, so it's wise not to count on being able to visit or buy wine.

MonteVertine ***

Loc. Monte Vertine, 53017 Radda in Chianti	*+39 0577 738009*
@ *info@montevertine.it*	*Martino Manetti*
www.montevertine.it	*[map p. 44]*
19 ha; 85,000 btl	*IGT Toscana, Montevertine*

Located in the hills of Radda in Chianti, Montevertine is a famous producer who actually produces no Chianti Classico. The three wines are the eponymous Montevertine, Pian del Ciampolo, and Le Pergole Torte, all labeled as IGT Toscana. Sergio Manetti acquired Montevertine in 1967 as a vacation. He planted a small vineyard in order to make some wine for the family, but this was so successful soon he became a full time wine producer. Because he would not use Trebbiano in his blend, he was refused the Chianti Classico label. The irony is that Montevertine is a rare producer in the area who has never taken up the international varieties, but has stayed true to Chianti's traditions.

Today the estate is run by Sergio's son, Martino. "My father always wanted to focus on Sangiovese without planting international grapes. I promised my father never to return to the Consorzio," he says. The winery is a cluster of small buildings perched on top of a hill at the end of a narrow, precipitous approach road. It's very hands-on: Martino was in the cellars pumping-over several tanks when I visited. Production has increased a little from a new vineyard, but will not increase any more. "I have no more room in the cellar. Going over 100,000 bottles would change everything radically, I want to go on doing everything without outside help."

The vineyards, with 11 ha on the hill around the winery and another 7 ha a few miles away in the same valley, are dedicated exclusively to Sangiovese, Colorino, and Canaiolo. "There are only three red wines, they are different but they can be considered as brothers," says Martino. Pian del Ciampolo is effectively a second wine to Montevertine, which is the first selection. Both are around 90% Sangiovese, and age in the traditional large casks of Slavonian oak, Ciampolo for one year and Montevertine for two years.

Exclusively Sangiovese, the prestige cuvée Le Pergole Torte comes from the first vineyard that Sergio planted, just at the entrance to the property. The vineyard has been extended a bit, but 60% of the vines are the original stock. "It was the first 100% Sangiovese made in this area, I remember many people coming to taste, they were surprised to find something new in Chianti," Martino recollects. It ages in French barriques (10-15% new). (There used to be a fourth wine, Il Sodaccio, but this ceased production when the vineyard had to be replanted.) Part of the elegance is the moderate alcohol. "This is the coolest area in all Chianti Classico, we're high up, sometimes it's hard to get 12%, the most we ever had was 14% in 2011," Martino says. Always running through the wines here, there is a savory acidity, with a sense of minerality, reaching its peak in Le Pergole Torte, which is regarded by many as the epitome of Sangiovese. Montevertine and Le Pergole Torte age beautifully, becoming increasingly subtle with time.

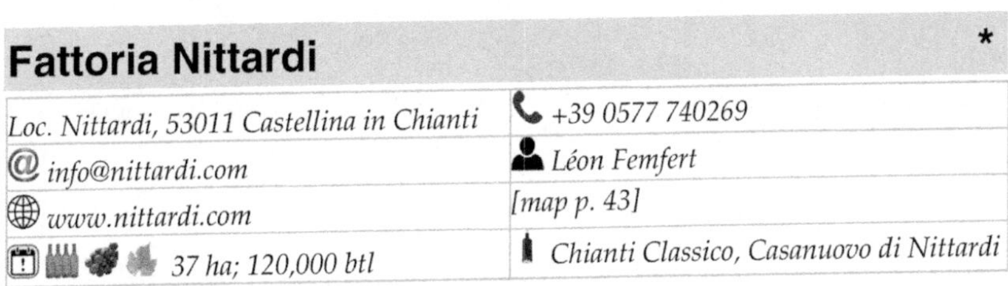

Fattoria Nittardi *

Loc. Nittardi, 53011 Castellina in Chianti	*+39 0577 740269*
info@nittardi.com	*Léon Femfert*
www.nittardi.com	*[map p. 43]*
37 ha; 120,000 btl	*Chianti Classico, Casanuovo di Nittardi*

The name is a contraction of Nectar Dei, the name of a fortification at the border between Siena and Florence in the twelfth century. It was purchased and revived in 1982 by Peter Femfert, a publisher from Frankfurt, and his wife Stefania Canalia, a historian from Venice. Carlo Ferrini was brought in as consulting oenologist. Léon Femfert is the owner today. There were only 4 ha in 1982, and a small cellar by the offices. A new winery was built in 1994, 300m down the road below the original cellar; there are plans to expand it from its present capacity to 150,000 bottles.

Most of the vineyards in Chianti Classico are in the 120 ha estate, nestled into the forest along the winding track that leads up from the main road, and there are also 4 ha at lower down, south of Castellina. In addition, 23 ha were planted in Maremma in 1999; the grapes are brought to the winery in Chianti Classico for vinification. In homage to Michelangelo, who owned the estate in the sixteenth century, there are sculptures and paintings all around, coming from contemporary artists who are invited to create a new label for the Casanuovo cuvée each year.

The entry-level Chianti Classico, Belcanto, is a blend from Nittardi and the plot at Castellina (which includes indigenous varieties as well as Sangiovese). Casanuovo di Nittardi is monovarietal Sangiovese from the single vineyard Vigna Doghesa, which lies between the winery and the offices, planted in 2002 with new clones. The Riserva, which includes some Merlot, is made only in top years and comes from the highest altitude vineyards. The approach is modernist, with wines aged in 500 liter French barrels, including 30% new oak for the Riserva, but Belcanto shows the traditional savory character of Sangiovese, Casanuovo is deeper and richer with some black fruits, but still generally on the side of minerality, while the Riserva is rounder and more "international."

From the estate in Maremma there are Ad Astra (a Sangiovese-Bordeaux blend) and Nectar Dei (a super-Tuscan from Bordeaux varieties). They are more forcefully fruity than the Chianti Classicos. The only white is the BEN Vermentino.

Tenuta di Nozzole *

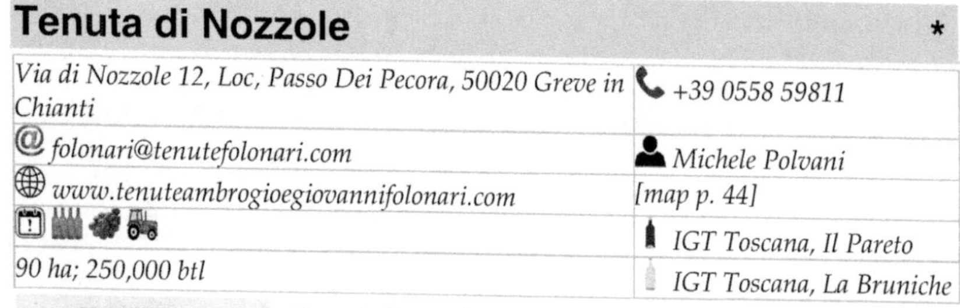

Via di Nozzole 12, Loc, Passo Dei Pecora, 50020 Greve in Chianti	*+39 0558 59811*
folonari@tenutefolonari.com	*Michele Polvani*
www.tenuteambrogioegiovannifolonari.com	*[map p. 44]*
	IGT Toscana, Il Pareto
90 ha; 250,000 btl	*IGT Toscana, La Bruniche*

Nozzole has a slightly chequered history. Located in the northern part of the Chianti area, there have been vineyards here for several hundred years. The Folonaris, who moved into Chianti to make a transition to quality wine at the start of the twentieth century, purchased the estate in 1971. (They owned Ruffino, and introduced the famous Chianti straw flasks). In 2000, the company was divided, and Ambrogio Folonari and his son Giovanni kept Nozzole and Tenute di Cabreo, near Greve in Chianti. They also started Campo al Mare in Bolgheri, as well as La Fuga in Montalcino, Torcalvano in Montepulciano, and Vigne a Porrona in Maremma. Altogether there are five estates in their portfolio.

Nozzole produces Chianti Classico, Le Bruniche Chardonnay, and the Il Pareto monovarietal Cabernet Sauvignon. The style is modern, with the wines aged in barriques, and flavors tending towards fruity rather than savory. "This area gives richer rounder wines than the usual austere Chianti," says winemaker Roberto. The top Chianti Classico is the Riserva—there is no Gran Selezione.

From the Cabreo vineyards there are La Pietra Chardonnay and Il Borgo, a blend of 30% Cabernet Sauvignon with 70% Sangiovese. "The soul of Tuscany, Sangiovese, is fruit driven with high acidity; we wanted to combine it with the power of Cabernet Sauvignon to give structure and longevity," says Roberto. The varietal composition is more determinative of style here than the vineyard characters, since Il Pareto is sandier and lower, while Cabreo has rocky soil at higher altitude; but with 100% Cabernet, Il Pareto is a bigger wine than Cabreo. "But Il Pareto became too powerful, and we eased back around 2008 (using some tonneaux instead of barriques) to look for more elegance," says Roberto. Il Pareto is very much the Chianti-centric view of Cabernet Sauvignon, savory and elegant, a match for food. Il Borgo shows its Cabernet in a sense of structure, but the flavor profile is more dominated by Sangiovese.

Panzanello *

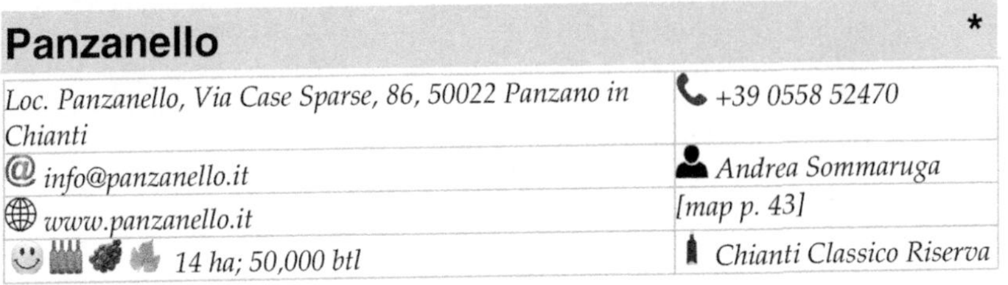

Loc. Panzanello, Via Case Sparse, 86, 50022 Panzano in Chianti	*+39 0558 52470*
info@panzanello.it	*Andrea Sommaruga*
www.panzanello.it	*[map p. 43]*
14 ha; 50,000 btl	*Chianti Classico Riserva*

"I am not a traditionalist, I am not a modernist, I am myself," says Andrea Sommaruga, who came to make wine on this estate in 1994. His grandmother, who lived in Rome and wanted a property in Tuscany, bought this old estate in 1964. "I was previously in finance, I knew nothing about wine. I came here thinking it would be a relaxed business, but in the summer I was here working, and in the winter I had to sell the wine. I started with 8,000 bottles of the 1995 vintage in 1997, 12,000 the year after. But most of the grapes were sold to the coop: my grandmother was one of the founders. I cancelled the contract with the coop in 1998. We bought some more land and planted new vineyards in 1999." The facilities have been expanded with a new cellar and tasting room, and several apartments for accommodation on site. It's a very hands-on operation, with Andrea and Ioletta Sommaruga living in a villa on the 120 ha estate.

There are four wines. The Chianti Classico includes a small proportion of Merlot and is aged used 500 liter barrels. The Riserva is a selection from the best vineyards, has some Cabernet Sauvignon, and is aged in one-year-old oak. The IGT Toscana Il Manuzio is based on a selection of the best lots of Sangiovese and Merlot, and is aged in new barriques. "This is my baby," says Andrea. It's not made every year: first in 2010 and then in 2014. Vindea is Ioletta's project, an equal combination of Sangiovese and Petit Verdot, started in 2006 with the next vintage in 2011. "The IGTs are our top wines, absolutely, but in terms of making Chianti Classico, the Riserva is absolutely the top wine. We don't believe in Gran Selezione, absolutely not."

A powerful house style is evident at once in the deep colors, and the black fruit spectrum of the palates, with the impression of structure increasing as you go along the series; although it remains relatively subtle, fruits become less overt. Chianti Classico shows forward fruits, while the Riserva is deeper, yet more restrained with an impression of minerality. Il Manuzio increases the sense of spicy structure and more reserve to the fruits. Vindea is the most powerful wine and needs time to develop. The olive oil is also quite powerful and peppery.

Castello Di Querceto ***

Via A. François 2, 50020 Greve in Chianti	+39 0558 5921
querceto@castellodiquerceto.it	Alessandro Francoise
www.castellodiquerceto.it	[map p. 44]
60 ha; 600,000 btl	IGT Toscana, Il Querciolaia

The sixteenth century castle of Querceto dominates a small valley of 500 ha where vineyards were first planted in 1897 by Alessandro François's grandfather. Alessandro was an engineer in Milan and moved here to run the vineyards in 1983. Today, Querceto has about 250 ha of vineyards, at elevations of 400-500m; in this slightly cooler climate, harvest is generally a couple of weeks after others in the region. "We have three different areas in the valley, with very different soil types, this is why we decided to produce single-vineyard wines," says Alessandro.

There are four super-Tuscans. La Corte was a single vineyard Sangiovese. "It started as an experiment. One hundred years ago my grandfather planted the first vineyard of 100% Sangiovese. This was the first single-vineyard wine—our first super-Tuscan in 1904," says Alessandro. Il Querciolaia is a blend of Sangiovese and Cabernet Sauvignon ("We tried 50% Cabernet, the Sangiovese disappeared, we tried 10-15% it was not enough, so we decided about 30%"). As you might expect from the blend, the impression lies somewhere between fruity and savory. It's fairly restrained, with the palate driven by black fruits, and a lighter impression than the wines based on Cabernet Sauvignon.

Cignale is a Cabernet Sauvignon with just a softening of 10% Merlot; and Il Sole di Alessandro is a monovarietal Cabernet Sauvignon. Although Cignale has Merlot, it can be more reserved and sterner than Sole di Alessandro, which is driven by the ripeness of the Cabernet Sauvignon. "When we started to produce international varieties our idea was to find the maximum link between the varieties and the terroir," explains Alessandro.

There is also, of course, a Chianti Classico. This is traditional: "I produce Chianti Classico without an international variety because in my opinion it must retain the character of the past." This very proper Chianti Classico offers an excellent representation of the Sangiovese grape that is true to the region. A medium density color, it offers a nose with red fruits and some of the typical animal and leathery aromas of the variety. Bright red fruits are supported by good acidity on the palate, which has medium weight and a nice finish with just a hint of chocolate. Not a blockbuster in the Super Tuscan style, but just what Chianti should be.

There are now two Gran Seleziones. Il Picchio is a selection of the best lots, with 95% Sangiovese and 5% Colorino, aged in barriques for 12 months. It is quite stern and gives the impression that it has some international varieties, although this is not the case. La Corte has changed its label from super-Tuscan, and is now a Gran Selezione. This gives the classy impression I associate with Querceto, smooth on the palate, a savory tang at the end, very much the Gran Selezione interpretation of classic Chianti Classico. Querceto's wines are, in my opinion, among the most elegant of the Chianti Classico region.

Querceto di Castellina *

Località Querceto 9, 53011 Castellina in Chianti	*+39 0577 733590*
info@querceto.com	*Jacopo Di Battista*
www.querceto.com	*[map p. 43]*
12 ha; 50,000 btl	*Chianti Classico, L'Aura*

The 80 hectare property has been in the family since 1945. Initially used for vacations, the land was then leased out for farming, until Laura Di Battista took it back in 1989. She started a cooking school, and developed the farm with olive groves and vineyards. Her son Jacopo began bottling wines after 1998. His brother Filippo joined in 2014 and manages tourism to the estate. Vineyards are in 6 different areas in the estate; Sangiovese is 80% of plantings, and Merlot is most of the rest. There's a small parcel with the white varieties Viognier and Roussanne. Chianti Classico L'Aura was the first wine produced at the estate (only 3,300 bottles in 1998). It's 100% Sangiovese, aged in tonneaux of French oak, and shows a fresh, light, elegant character, a good halfway house between traditional and modern. The range in Chianti Classico then jumps straight to the Gran Selezione, Sei, also 100% Sangiovese, aged for 18 months in tonneaux. It shows more weight than the Classico, with faint impressions of new oak in a modern style, but retains the approach of the house for elegance rather than power. Podalirio is IGT Toscana from 100% Merlot, aged for 18 months in French barriques. The only red blend is Venti, a small production from Sangiovese aged in tonneaux and Merlot aged in barriques. IGT Toscana also includes the rosé Furtivo (Sangiovese) and the white Livia (30% aged in tonneaux, 70% in stainless steel).

Querciabella ***

Via Barbiano 17, 50022 Greve in Chianti	*+39 0558 5927777*
contact@querciabella.com	*Manfred Ing*
www.querciabella.com	*[map p. 44]*
	Chianti Classico
101 ha; 330,000 btl	*IGT Toscana, Batàr*

"What separates us from virtually every other producer in Chianti is that we have grapes from three different subzones," says winemaker Manfred Ing. "Growing conditions are so different in each subzone that we get more complexity by blending." The home estate is in Greve in Chianti, there are 32 ha in Radda in Chianti, and 24 ha of vineyards in Gaiole in Chianti were acquired in 2011.

Querciabella was started as a hobby by businessman Sebastiano Castiglione in 1974 but rapidly became a fully professional producer. Sebastiano has a house on the property, and although he has many diverse interests in technology and art, is very much in control at the winery. He's a committed vegan, which was the impetus for taking Querciabella organic and then biodynamic.

The current project is to produce wines from single vineyards that express each of the subzones. "We've been making Sangiovese from many different sites, we've been following the individual plots for 8 years now, we're beginning to understand," Manfred says. "So far it's undecided which vintages and single vineyards will be released first, but it will probably be as a mixed case, perhaps from the 2011 vintage when the project started." There are only 1,000 bottles of each wine from each vintage.

Chianti Classico has been 100% Sangiovese since 2010: "the Sangiovese has now improved to the point at which is doesn't need the added strength of Cabernet," says Manfred. A blend from all three subzones, it shows red fruits with the savory tang of Sangiovese, but a smoothness that you don't usually find in Chianti Classico until Riserva level. It ages in French oak.

The Riserva stopped being produced in 1999, because the style was too close to the super-Tuscan Camartina at the time, but production resumed in 2011. Smoother and deeper than the Chianti Classico, the style moves towards black fruits. In 2014, there was no Camartina, and the grapes from single vineyards were declassified into the Riserva.

Camartina was one of the early super-Tuscans, with its first year in 1981. It started as a Sangiovese with a little Cabernet Sauvignon and Merlot. Between 1999 and 2003, it made a transition to 70% Cabernet Sauvignon and 30% Sangiovese. It comes from vineyards close to the winery. On release it can be stern, but then the structure shows as a restrained background, and it makes a very Tuscan impression, fresh and elegant, with the smoothness of the house style always in evidence. Production has been declining in recent years.

Batàr is an attempt to produce a World-class Burgundian style white wine in Tuscany. When asked with whom the wine competes, the producers say "Bâtard Montrachet." Indeed, the first vintages (1988-1991) were called Bâtard-Pinot because the wine was a blend of Pinot Blanc and Pinot Gris. The name was changed to Bâtard when Chardonnay was added to the blend, and then changed again in 1995 simply to Batàr. The Current vintages are typically 65% Chardonnay and 35% Pinot Blanc in the belief that the blend gives greater complexity than basing the wine 100% on Chardonnay. Some of the Gouges Pinot Blanc clone from Nuits St. Georges was planted in 2011 and is giving more texture. I remember Batàr from the early years as loaded with new oak. It's barrel fermented with some battonage—"but less now, because the vines are older and the grapes are richer," Manfred says. New oak used to be 100% but has backed off to 20%. Current vintages show a palate poised between stone fruits and mineral impressions, and are more elegant. It begins to show well after about four years, and peaks around eight years.

Palafreno is a monovarietal Merlot, produced in small amounts (and made only in the best vintages). It's plush and smooth, but with a sense of restraint showcasing the elegance of the house style. Mongrana is the entry-level wine, a blend of Sangiovese, Merlot, and Cabernet Sauvignon, coming from a 31 hectare estate at Maremma. Started in 2010, Turpino represents a move in opposite direction from the increasing focus on terroir; it is an IGT blend of Syrah, Cabernet Franc, and Merlot, composed of equal proportions of grapes from Chianti and Maremma. The style here is fresh. As production of Camartina has declined, production of Turpino has increased.

Castello Dei Rampolla **

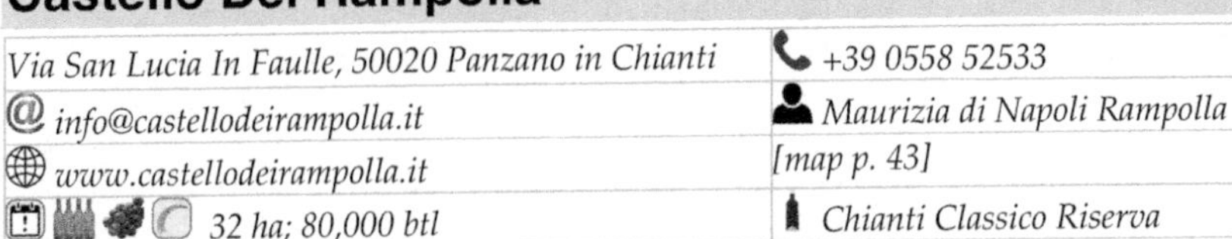

Via San Lucia In Faulle, 50020 Panzano in Chianti	*+39 0558 52533*
info@castellodeirampolla.it	*Maurizia di Napoli Rampolla*
www.castellodeirampolla.it	*[map p. 43]*
32 ha; 80,000 btl	*Chianti Classico Riserva*

This thirteenth century estate has been owned by the Di Napoli family since 1739. During the 1960s the Rampolla estate was mostly olive trees, and Alceo di Napoli sold grapes to Antinori. Today the estate, just below the town of Panzano-in-Chianti, is mostly covered in vineyards. Basically four wines are made here, two based on Sangiovese and two based on Cabernet Sauvignon. "We started planting Cabernet Sauvignon in the late seventies, the intention was to blend it to reinforce the Sangiovese. We took out the Malvasia, Trebbiano, and Canaiolo. We wanted to make a wine that would stand by itself. It was going to be a Chianti, but it wasn't quite legal," recollects Luca di Napoli, who runs the estate together with his sister.

The Chianti Classico includes 5% each of Cabernet Sauvignon and Merlot, but feels more structured than the numbers would suggest. A 100% Sangiovese IGT Toscana, matured in terracotta amphorae without any sulfur, was introduced in 2010. It shows a tendency to red fruits, with less savory impressions than from Sangiovese aged in wood.

The blend for Sammarco, one of the first super-Tuscans, which started with the 1980 vintage, is the opposite of the Chianti, with 80% Cabernet Sauvignon to the minority of Merlot and Sangiovese. It ages in oak for 18-24 months, using Slavonian oak for the Sangiovese and barriques for the Cabernet Sauvignon. It's poised between fruity and savory. Vigna d'Alceo is a blend of 85% Cabernet Sauvignon with 15% Petit Verdot. The two wines are somewhat representative of two styles of super-Tuscan: the first tending towards elegance and almost savory; the second showing more direct fruits and power in a more international style.

Barone Ricasoli **

Cantine Del Castello Di Brolio, 53010 Gaiole in Chianti	*+39 0577 7301*
barone@ricasoli.it	*Simona Brandini*
www.ricasoli.it	*[map p. 45]*
235 ha; 2,000,000 btl	*Colledila, Gran Selezione*

Barone Ricasoli claims to be the oldest winery in Italy, making wine at the Castelo di Brolio since 1141. The eponymous Baron was involved in the establishment of Chianti, and famously devised the first formula for the varietal mix in 1872. The estate has been run since 1993 by Francesco Ricasoli, the 32nd Baron of Brolio, after a somewhat chequered history in the previous decades. As the result of financial difficulties, the winery and brand were sold to Seagrams in 1953, and then Seagrams sold it on to a British businessman in 1986. Seagrams more or less wrecked the business, as it ruined every other wine estate it acquired. The vineyards continued to be owned by the Ricasolis, but could not be well maintained because grapes had to be sold by contract to Seagrams at a low price. In 1993, Francesco was able to buy back the winery and brand name.

The Brolio winery is the largest in Chianti, surrounded by an estate of 1,200 ha that extends from Gaiole in Chianti to Castelnuova Berardenga. It includes 26 ha of olive groves as well as vineyards. Soon after he took over, Francesco replanted the vineyards at higher density, with blocks of each variety replacing the previously intermingled plantings. The cellars were renovated and extended, and now form a vast expanse around and underneath a large courtyard. Basically everything—cellars and vineyards—have been renewed since 1997.

Continuing the tradition of research, Ricasoli has been involved with the development of clones of Sangiovese. "The estate has always been at the front of advancing things in Chianti and we like to feel we can do that today. We are one of the largest estates but we are not comparable to the industrial producers," Francesco says. With such a large estate there are several types of terroir, including sandstone, galestro, and limestone. There is a wide range of wines. The estate Chianti Classico has 5% each of Cabernet and Sauvignon, and the Riserva has 5% Merlot (both used to have 20% Merlot and Cabernet Sauvignon), but Brolio-Bettino pays respect to tradition with a Sangiovese-Colorino blend matured only in large old casks. Two Gran Selezione wines demonstrate the two faces of the company. Colledila is a 100% Sangiovese single-vineyard wine coming from a 7 ha vineyard with calcareous soils, while Castelo di Brolio is based on selection of the best lots of Sangiovese (it now includes 3% Colorino, whereas it used to have small amounts of Cabernet Sauvignon and Petit Verdot). These wines give a modern impression, round and faintly nutty for Classico, deeper and denser for Riserva. Colledila is a chic, elegant version of the savory side of Sangiovese, and Gran Selezione Castelo moves towards the plushness of super-Tuscans without the sheer power. The IGT Toscanas include the 100% Merlot Casalferro (based on selecting the best 4 ha from a 10 ha vineyard with sandstone and limestone soils to give a Tuscan take on Merlot, and the Chardonnay-Sauvignon blend of Terricello. Sangiovese is usually aged in tonneaux—"we like the micro-oxygenation," says winemaker Massimiliano Biagi, and international varieties are aged in barriques.

The trend is now towards showcasing different terroirs: "Sangiovese wines representing different soils are a feature from the 2015 vintage. We started this approach more than ten years ago. If you are 100% Sangiovese, the message comes through more clearly. But we also made a Cru that is pure Merlot, it shows how it can be Tuscan, Chiantified if you like," Francesco says. Ricasoli remains a driving force in Chianti Classico. The castle and is gardens are one of the sights of the region; there's an expansive tasting room, and also a restaurant in the castle.

Rocca Delle Macìe **

Località Le Macìe, 53011 Castellina in Chianti	*+39 0577 732236*
info@roccadellemacie.com	*Sergio Zingarelli*
www.roccadellemacie.com	*[map p. 43]*
207 ha; 1,800,000 btl	*Fizzano, Gran Selezione*

The estate was founded in 1973, when film producer Italo Zingarelli purchased the property with only 2 ha of vines. The buildings around the main courtyard are now residential or used for hospitality; the large modern winery is below on one side. The original cellar from 1973 now houses a dozen botti, and seems awfully small compared with today's operation as one of the largest producers in Chianti Classico. From the original Le Macìe property, production has expanded into other estates, including Sant'Alfonso and Fizzano, also in Chianti Classico, and Campomaccione and Casamaria in Morellino di Scansano. The combined estates include 80 ha of olive trees as well as vineyards. Italo's son Sergio has been in charge since 1985, and has been Chairman of the Consorzio del Chianti Classico.

The range of fourteen wines includes several from Chianti Classico, including a series carrying the Zingarelli name, forming the range Chianti Classico Famiglia Zingarelli, Riserva Famiglia Zingarelli, and most recently Gran Selezione Sergio Zingarelli. "This is a limited production and would have been an IGT Toscana if the Gran Selezione category had not been created," says Sergio. The other estates are represented by Chianti Classico from Sant'Alfonso and Gran Selezione from Fizzano (named the Riserva di Fizzano, this has now become a Gran Selezione). "We like to have wines that come from the individual estates," says marketing manager Thomas Francioni. The Chianti Classico ages in 100 hl Slavonian botti, the Riserva in a 36 hl French casks, and the Gran Seleziones age in a mixture of large and small casks. Besides Chianti, there are several super-Tuscans, including two Sangiovese-Cabernet blends, Roccato and Ser Gioveto, and a Sangiovese-Merlot blend, Rubizzo. Other DOCs in the range include Brunello di Montalcino, Montepulciano, and Bolgheri.

The entry-level Chianti Classico, a blend from all the terroirs, is a modern interpretation of Classico in fresh pungent style; then the rest of the range gives a smooth, rounded impression. "I want elegance, elegance, elegance, not power," says Sergio. Going up the series, that sense of smoothness doesn't change so much as the sense of accompanying texture, although palate weight increases, but there is always a touch of minerality and gunflint at the end to take you back to Sangiovese. The improvement in quality of Classico is shown by the fact that the Riserva is only a little denser. The Gran Selezione has more sense of structure. The super-Tuscans follow the same style, with Sangiovese-dominated Ser Gioveto following the lines of the Gran Selezione, while Roccato moves towards Cabernet and a more Bordeaux-like impression, showing more obvious structure at the expense of opulence.

Rocca di Castagnoli **

Loc. Castagnoli, 53010 Gaiole in Chianti	*+39 0577 731004*
info@roccadicastagnoli.com	*Rolando Bernacchini*
www.roccadicastagnoli.com	*[map p. 45]*
	Chianti Classico Riserva, a'Frati
90 ha; 350,000 btl	*IGT Toscana, Il Buriano*

Wine has been made around the medieval village of Castagnoli for several hundred years. The Castagnoli estate was well known in the eighteenth century, at the end of the nine-

teenth century it passed into the hands of the Ricasolis, in 1981 it was purchased by Calogero Calì, who subsequently purchased several other wine estates, including Tenuta di Capraia in Chianti Classico (whose wines are essentially special cuvées of Castagnoli), Poggio Maestrino-Spiaggiole in Maremma, and Poggio Graffetta in Sicily; the holding company is called Alimenta. Rocca di Castagnoli has an estate of 850 ha, with 15 ha of olive groves as well as the vineyards, and includes a historical house that has been converted into a hotel. After a research program, specific clones of Sangiovese were developed that are now used for planting the vineyards.

The Chianti Classico has a traditional constitution of 90% Sangiovese with 5% each of Colorino and Canaiolo, matured in a mixture of casks and tonneaux, and the Poggio a'Frati Riserva sees some new oak. The Classico is a nice compromise between traditional and modern, with an impression of structure. The Riserva Poggio a'Frati is much in the same style, just a little rounder and also with a more savory impression. The Gran Selezione Stielle is distinctly more modern, deeper and smoother, without going to chocolaty extremes. Capraia has a more modern style than Rocca di Castagnoli, most evident on the Classico, where Capraia is quite nutty compared to the fresher impression of Castagnoli. The Riservas are closer in style, but you see the difference again with the Gran Selezione, where Capraia is just a touch smoother, less savory, more modern.

IGT Toscanas include the international varieties and focus on monovarietals: Le Pratolo is Merlot, Buriano is Cabernet Sauvignon, and Molino delle Balze is Chardonnay. The Stielle IGT was a blend of Sangiovese and Cabernet Sauvignon, from a single vineyard, but became a monovarietal Sangiovese in 2007. "We used to need something stronger to support the Sangiovese, but with our new clone, we don't need that support," says winemaker Rolando Bernacchini. "The drive here is that the market is looking for single varieties and we didn't have a 100% Sangiovese super Tuscan, so we decided to make Stielle 100%," he explains. Stielle was relabeled as Gran Selezione when the category was created. The 2 ha of Cabernet Sauvignon in the Stielle vineyard are now added to the 4 ha plot for Il Buriano. Il Buriano is firm but fresh—"The freshness is the characteristic of the terroir," says Rolando—and ages well.

Rocca di Montegrossi *

Fraz. Monti In Chianti, 53013 Gaiole in Chianti	*+39 0577 747977*
roccadimontegrossi@chianticlassico.com	*Marco Ricasoli-Firidolfi*
www.roccadimontegrossi.it	*[map p. 45]*
	San Marcellino, Gran Selezione
20 ha; 100,000 btl	*Chianti Classico Vin Santo*

This old estate was established in the eighth century and has continued by descent to Marco Ricasoli-Firidolfi. Located on a high point in Monti in Chianti, looking out over the valley from 350m elevation, today its 100 ha include equal areas of vineyards and olive groves. (The thousand olive trees are almost all the Coreggiolo cultivar, so the olive oil can be considered a monovarietal). The wine has been produced on the estate since

Marco restored the buildings in 1999 (previously it was made at another family property).

There are two Chianti Classicos, both including indigenous varieties as well as Sangiovese; the estate wine has Canaiolo and Colorino, and is about half of all production, while Vigneto San Marcellino, now labeled as a Gran Selezione, is produced only in top vintages, and includes some Pugnitello. The IGT Toscana Geremia is a blend of two thirds Merlot to one third Cabernet Sauvignon. The estate Chianti Classico ages in botti for a year and a half, while San Marcellino and Geremia age in a mixture of barriques and tonneaux, including about half new wood, for two and a half years. San Marcellino is much richer than the Chianti Classico, showing the concentration of old vines and its exposure to barriques; it is somewhat reminiscent of Brunello. Geremia shows the Italian take on the Bordeaux blend, with Cabernet structure in the background behind the soft richness of Merlot. There's a split in style between the freshness that balances the fruits of the Chianti Classico, and the richness of the Gran Selezione and the super-Tuscan. The latest cuvée is the IGT Ridolfo, an unusual blend of Cabernet Sauvignon and Pugnitello. A Vin Santo comes from late harvest grapes that are dried on moveable racks in a modern loft, is highly botrytized, and ages for seven years in very small casks of a wood mix of oak, cherry, and mulberry; it's very rich.

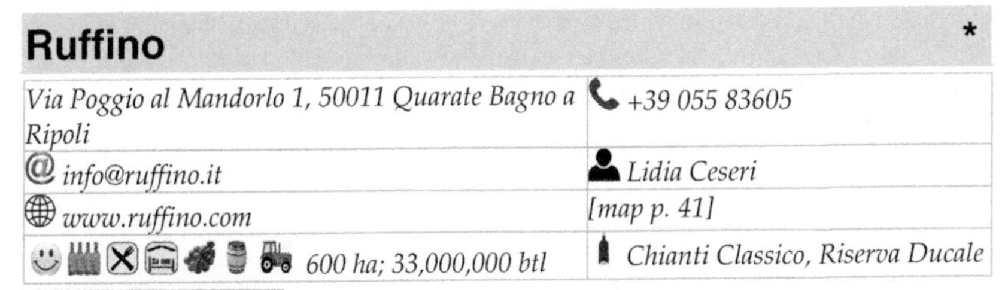

Ruffino *

Via Poggio al Mandorlo 1, 50011 Quarate Bagno a Ripoli	*+39 055 83605*
info@ruffino.it	*Lidia Ceseri*
www.ruffino.com	*[map p. 41]*
600 ha; 33,000,000 btl	*Chianti Classico, Riserva Ducale*

Owned by conglomerate Constellation, Ruffino is one of the largest producers in Chianti. Founded in 1877 as a small producer by the Ruffino cousins, who were traders in wine, Ruffino started in Chianti, and then grew in the second half of the twentieth century by purchasing further estates in Montalcino and Montepulciano as well as Chianti. The Folonari family, who owned Ruffino since 1913, sold a 40% share to Constellation (who had been handling distribution) in 2004, and then in 2011 Constellation took complete ownership. The estate vineyards still belong to the family, but are rented to Constellation on 25-year contracts; they provide about a third of all grapes. The original winery at Pontassieve, close to Florence, is now used for administration and bottling. The Poggio Casciano estate includes a restaurant and resort.

The estates under the Ruffino umbrella include four in the Chianti area: Montemasso, Poggio Casciano, Santedame and Gretole. In addition, there are Greppone Mazzi (in Montalcino), La Solatia (near Siena, which produces white wine), and Lodola Nuova (in Montepulciano). Poggio Casciano sits on the border between Chianti Classico and Chianti Ruffina. Gracious old buildings are set behind a park, with the family residence at one side, surrounded by vineyards; it's the hospitality center for Ruffino. The estates, however, are not always emphasized as the wines are identified by the Ruffino brand. Outside of Chianti Classico, subregions are not used, and the wine is just identified as Chianti. In Chianti Classico, grapes may come from more than one estate.

The style of the Chianti Classicos shows a viscous sheen to the palate, perhaps helped by the common inclusion of Merlot. Santedame could be a Riserva but is not labeled as such in order to emphasize its origins; it's soft and smooth. The flagship Chianti Classicos are the Riserva Ducale and the Riserva Ducale Oro, now a Gran Selezione. These are modern blends of 80% Sangiovese with Cabernet Sauvignon and Merlot, the first coming from Gretole, Santedame, and Montemasso, and the Oro from Gretole and Santedame. With production of more than a million bottles, brand consistency is important for Riserva Ducale, which is aged in Slavonian casks. It's smoother and more elegant than Santedame, with just a touch more structure. The Ducale Oro, which comes only from estate grapes, and is aged in barriques followed by casks, is a little rounder and deeper, its modern style relieved by some savory impressions, and increasing sense of structure. Made only in best vintages since 1947 as a selection from Riserva Ducale, it has a surprising capacity to age: the 1977 was still lively in 2016. The elegant style of the Brunello shows greater purity and precision than the Chianti Classicos. Some of the DOCG wines and super-Tuscans are identified with specific estates, with the Colorino-Merlot blend Romitorio di Santedame coming from the estate. From Poggio Casciano, Modus has more or less equal proportions of Sangiovese, Merlot, and Cabernet Sauvignon, and is a mainstream super-Tuscan, if there is such a thing, while the newest cuvée, Alauda, is a blend of Merlot, Cabernet Franc, and Colorino, and makes a more forceful international impression. There's also a range of white and sparkling wines.

San Felice *

Loc San Felice, 53019 Castelnuovo Berardenga	*+39 0577 3991*
info@sanfelice.com	*Leonardo Bellaccini*
www.agricolasanfelice.it	*[map p. 45]*
150 ha; 1,270,000 btl	*Il Grigio, Gran Selezione*

Located at the southern border of Chianti Classico, San Felice was owned by the Grisaldi Del Taja family, who were influential in establishing the appellation. In 1968, the estate was sold to the industrial group Aesculapius, who put a well known Sangiovese expert, Enzo Morganti, in charge. In 1978, the estate was purchased by an insurance group in Milan which subsequently became part of Allianz Group, a financial conglomerate. The vineyards at San Felice are in a 360 degree circle around the village. (Enzo Morganti's daughter, Giovanna, now has a small property, Le Boncie (see profile) within San Felice.) The estate was expanded first by buying two more properties in Chianti Classico in 1981, Villa Pagliaia and San Vito, and then by buying the 20 ha Campogiovanni estate in Montalcino in 1982, the 60 ha estate of Perolla in Maremma in 1993, and the 7 ha estate of Bell'aja in Bolgheri in 2016. San Felice accounts for about 750,000 bottles of the group's total production.

San Felice has been associated with a significant research program, as Enzo Morganti established an experimental vineyard, known at San Felice as the Vitarium, where clones of Sangiovese were developed; then this was extended into research on Tuscany's other indigenous varieties. The 2 ha vineyard now has 200 grape varieties. One consequence has been the reintroduction of Pugnitello, which is now a significant proportion of some of the estates.

The Chianti Classico is Sangiovese with 10% each of Pugnitello and Colorino; "we look for drinkability more than power, so aging is one year in Slavonian casks," says marketing manager Fabrizio Nencioni. The Il Grigio Riserva is 100% Sangiovese, and the Gran Selezione is 80% Sangiovese (a selection of the best lots) with 20% of five indigenous varieties. The Riserva ages in a mixture of 80% Slavonian casks and 20% French tonneaux (none new), while the Gran Selezione is all tonneaux (one third new). Poggio Rosso is a single vineyard where Enzo Morganti planted selected clones of Sangiovese and Colorino. There is now a single vineyard Gran Selezione from the best lots of Sangiovese.

The super-Tuscan Vigorello has changed its character many times, from 100% Sangiovese in 1968, to a Bordeaux blend in 2006—"It was very good but we felt it was lacking Tuscan typicity"—so since 2011 it has been a blend of Pugnitello with the Bordeaux varieties. "The addition of the Pugnitello obviously changed the style a lot," says Fabrizio. Pugnitello has become something of a specialty: "we performed microvinifications, we liked the results, so in 1997 we planted 12 ha, and it's now the second most important variety here," says Fabrizio. A monovarietal Pugnitello has been produced since the 2003.

There are really two threads here. Chianti Classico and Il Grigio Riserva follow the route of lively fresh red fruits, while Poggio Rosso, Pugnitello, and Vigorello show a more opulent, spicy black fruit style. The estate would describe itself as traditional, and the Chianti Classico and Il Grigio cuvées show the tang of Sangiovese, but Poggio Rosso moves more towards the modernist camp, resembling the Campogiovanni Brunello, which is elegant. The Il Quercione single vineyard Brunello is the most sophisticated. The estate is well into oenotourism; the former hamlet of San Felice is now a hotel in the center of the vineyards.

Tenuta Tignanello ***

50026 San Casciano in val di Pesa	*+39 0552 359700*
antinori@antinori.it	*Pietro Dogliani & Stefano Carpaneto*
www.antinori.it	*[map p. 42]*
127 ha; 744,000 btl	*IGT Toscana, Tignanello*

"In 1966, Antinori bought Cabernet Sauvignon from France and planted it at Tignanello together with Sangiovese. At the time other producers were quite hostile," recollects winemaker Stefano Carpeto. Tignanello actually started as a Chianti in 1970, labeled as Chianti Classico riserva vigneto Tignanello, with a more or less conventional blend of Sangiovese with Canaiolo, Trebbiano, and Malvasia, although it defied convention by aging in French barriques, rather than casks of Slavonian oak. The next vintage it became a Vino da Tavola della Toscana and was just called Tignanello. The white grapes were dropped from the blend, and the Cabernet was introduced. Since 1982 its constitution has

been 85% Sangiovese, 15% Cabernet Sauvignon, and 5% Cabernet Franc (depending on the vintage).

Under the present rules it could be reclassified to Chianti Classico, but "Tignanello has too much quality to be a Chianti Classico," says Stefano. However, "It's a super-Tuscan but you can feel the soul of Chianti," says Sara Pontemolesi, winemaker at Antinori's Chianti Classico winery close by. Indeed, winemaker Renzo Cotarella says, " I have my idea of the super-Tuscans. I think a wine should be considered a super-Tuscan if it is a Sangiovese blend because Sangiovese is the representative of Tuscany. That's why I consider Tignanello to be the *real* super-Tuscan." When asked if it might be relabeled as Chianti Classico, Alessia Antinori says simply, "We believe that Tignanello is Tignanello, so it is still IGT Toscana."

Another super-Tuscan, Solaia, comes from the same estate, from vineyards adjacent to those for Tignanello. Solaia's first vintages in 1978 and 1979 were 80% Cabernet Sauvignon and 20% Cabernet Franc, but since then it has essentially been the inverse of Tignanello, with 80% Cabernet Sauvignon to 20% Sangiovese. "This is our top wine," says Sara Pontemolesi. Personally, I find the savory character of Tignanello more intriguing. (There's a story that Solaia started by accident, because there was too much Cabernet to be used for Tignanello in 1978, but Alessia Antinori says that, "We tasted the Cabernet Sauvignon, and it was so good we decided to vinify it separately.") Solaia ages in 100% new oak, whereas Tignanello has 50% new oak.

The Antinori Marchese Chianti Classico Riserva now also comes from the Tignanello estate (before 2011 it also included other sources), and as a similar blend to Tignanello is sometimes regarded as a mini-Tignanello. However, it is not a second wine; although grapes could in theory be declassified from Tignanello, this does not happen. The vineyards at Tignanello are at an elevation of 200-400m, and the terroir is based on albaresa; in fact, the vineyards now have a white appearance, as the stones were brought up to the surface during replanting and pulverized to create a reflective layer. The elevation helps to explain the taut quality of the wines. For me, Tignanello is a quintessential modern Tuscan wine, with a savory palate reflecting the character of Sangiovese, and the structure brought by Cabernet Sauvignon never overwhelming it; Solaia is more in line with the Cabernet-driven wines of Bolgheri, although taut rather than plush.

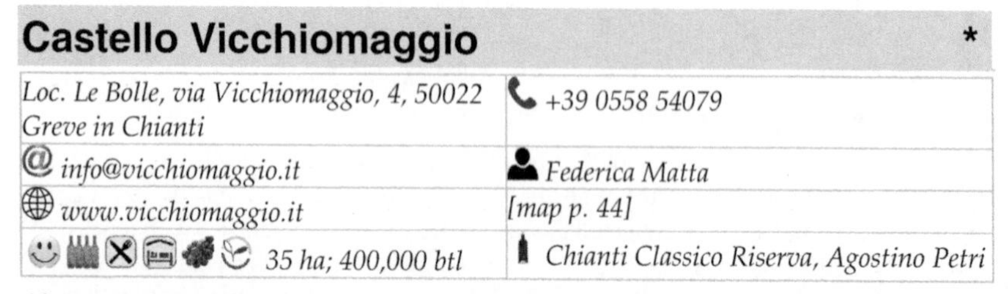

Castello Vicchiomaggio *

Loc. Le Bolle, via Vicchiomaggio, 4, 50022 Greve in Chianti	*+39 0558 54079*
info@vicchiomaggio.it	*Federica Matta*
www.vicchiomaggio.it	*[map p. 44]*
35 ha; 400,000 btl	*Chianti Classico Riserva, Agostino Petri*

Almost at the northern limit of Chianti Classico, the Castello is a historic monument. There's been a castle on the site since the eleventh century; the main building is a Renaissance villa dating from the fifteenth century, but the tower, which contains the aging cellar, dates from about 1100. Today the buildings house the winery, a hotel (with an

additional building given over to apartments), and a restaurant (occupying a gracious room in the villa). There's a wine shop and tasting room just off the main road at the start of the access road that winds up through the south-facing vineyards, rising from 300m to the castle at 500m. The shop offers a wide range of wines, olive oils, and other products.

"Our family has always been in wine and spirits. It was my grandfather who really created the winemaking business here. He was in spirits, in London, and bought Vicchiomaggio when he retired in 1964. My father started making wine here in 1975," says Federica Matta. The estate of 120 ha has 10 ha of olive trees as well as vineyards. The estate was in poor condition, but a steady replanting program and other investments saw the wines begin to gain a reputation in the eighties. There is also a 15 ha property in Maremma, Villa Vallemaggiore; grapes are crushed there, and the juice is transported to Vicchiomaggio for aging.

There are two cuvées of Chianti Classico. San Jacopo used to have 5% Cabernet Sauvignon, but now is pure Sangiovese. It comes from soils with heavy clay and ages in 25 hl or 50 hl botti for 8 months. "We like to be on the new vintage very soon, we like to have it fruity and crisp," Federica says. Introduced in 2015, Guado Alto comes from a specific plot, and ages in botti for 10 months. It shows a rather soft, modern style. The Agostino Petri Riserva continues to have 10% Cabernet Sauvignon. It comes from a single vineyard, and ages first in 2-year barriques, followed by a period in botti. It has greater fruit concentration than the Classico, but also seems intended for consumption relatively soon. The La Prima Gran Selezione comes from a 2 ha plot, and has 10% Merlot. Aged in a mix of new and 12-year barriques for 24 months, it shows the Merlot in a more fruit-driven style.

The IGT Toscana Ripa Della More moves in a more international direction, with an equal blend of Sangiovese to international varieties (Cabernet and Merlot), but Sangiovese remains dominant, albeit with some spice giving a more modern impression. The 100% Merlot of FSM, which comes from a 4 ha plot where the soil is clay-based, shows softness on the palate, but the wine still has the freshness of Tuscany.

Castello Di Volpaia **

Località Volpaia, 53017 Radda in Chianti	*+39 0577 738066*
@ *info@volpaia.com*	*Giovannella Stianti*
www.volpaia.com	*[map p. 44]*
	Chianti Classico Riserva, Coltassala
49 ha; 240,000 btl	*Chianti Classico Vin Santo*

Visiting Volpaia is a completely different experience from the usual winery. There is no single winery, but facilities are spread around various buildings in the mountaintop hamlet of Volpaia, a fortified medieval village. In addition to the buildings that house the winery equipment, there's a hotel, restaurant, and wine shop. One building has fermentation tanks, there are a couple with barrel cellars, there is one with a bottling line—the facilities are spread all around the hamlet. A piping system hidden below the streets moves the wine from upper levels to lower levels by gravity. "This is not a commercial approach, we will never make money in wine, so our philosophy is that we should at least

do something we like," says Giovanna Stianti. Volpaia is unique, we are working in an old place where wine was made two centuries ago; it is absolutely mad. If we had any idea of what would happen, we would never have done this.

Giovannella's father originally bought Volpaia as a hunting reserve, but the government subsequently cancelled all hunting rights, and subsequently gave the gave the estate to Giovannella and her husband, Carlo Mascheroni. The Castello di Volpaia owns about two thirds of the village, which is given over to the winery and associated activities. The road up to the hamlet winds through the vineyards of the 360 ha estate, rising from 450m to 650m. All except one of the vineyards are on this hill, facing south or southwest. The single-vineyard wines come from plots at the higher elevations. "The soil is very particular," Giovannella says, "no one has the same soil, so the wines are very distinctive, you may like them or not."

Well, I do like them. The relatively sandy soils are reflected in the lightness and elegance of the wines. The Chianti Classico is 90% Sangiovese and 10% Merlot. "The Sangiovese is very good, but it needs three years; the Merlot makes the wine approachable a bit sooner," Giovannella says. The three single-vineyard wines are produced most years, but not every year. Because it did not include white grapes, Coltassala was originally labeled as a vino da Tavola in 1980, but after the change of rules in 1998 it became a Chianti Classico Riserva (it has 95% Sangiovese and 5% Mammolo). Il Puro is a monovarietal Sangiovese, and comes from the Casanova vineyard, on the south-facing slope between the Coltassala and Balifico vineyards. It comes from 25 local sub-cultivars of Sangiovese that were propagated from very old vines. Produced in very small amounts, the first vintage was 2006, and it became a Gran Selezione, although "it's more a project than a Gran Selezione." Balifico is the IGT Toscana, with 35% of Cabernet Sauvignon and 65% Sangiovese.

The same style runs through all the wines, smooth and silky. Going from Chianti to the Crus, there is more of that bite of Sangiovese. Coltassala Riserva balances between minerality and more chocolaty notes, and the Il Puro Gran Selezione shows deep concentration. The IGT Toscana, Balifico, moves in a rounder more international direction within the same house style. These are extremely elegant wines. There are also monovarietal wines, Vermentino and Cabernet Sauvignon, from an estate purchased in Maremma in 2007.

Profiles of Important Estates

Tenuta di Arceno

Loc. Arceno, 53010 San Gusmé	*+39 0577 359346*
info@tenutadiarceno.com	*Lawrence Cronin*
www.tenutadiarceno.com	*[map p. 45]*
	92 ha; 250,000 btl

This huge estate, covering 1,000 ha, was founded by American producer Kendall-Jackson in 1994, and produces Chianti Classico at all levels plus three IGTs based on Bordeaux blends. Pierre Saillon, of Verité winery, helped to set it up and remains involved. At the southeast border of the area, vineyards are at altitudes from 300-500m, with a variety of microclimates. Soils vary from sedimentary lower down to sandstone, basalt, and schist higher up. The vineyard is broken up into small blocks, each vinified separately; blending takes place at the end of the process. Chianti Classico is 85% Sangiovese and 15% Merlot, the Riserva is 100% Sangiovese, and the Gran Selezione, Strada al Sasso is 100% Sangiovese from a single parcel, La Porta, planted in 1998. They all age in barriques of French oak. In the IGT range, two Merlot-dominated cuvées come from the areas with most clay in the soil. Il Fauno di Arcanum, is 60% Merlot and 30% Cabernet Franc. Valdorna averages 75% Merlot, 23% Cabernet Franc, and 12% Cabernet Sauvignon, and ages in barriques with 70% new oak. The top IGT, Arcanum, is 73% Cabernet Franc, 17% Merlot, and 10% Cabernet Sauvignon, from sandy-clay soils, aged in barriques with 80% new oak.

Podere le Boncie

Strada delle Boncie, Loc. San Felice, 53019 Castelnuovo Berardenga	*+39 0577 359383*
info@leboncie.it	*Giovanna Morganti*
www.leboncie.it	*[map p. 45]*
	5 ha; 27,000 btl

Eric Morganti was a famed oenologist, who was in charge of San Felice (see profile), where he established an experimental vineyard that did much to preserve the indigenous varieties. He gave his daughter Giovanna a small farm with some olive groves in San Felice, and she planted a vineyard with vines from the experimental vineyard. Le Trame is a traditional blend of Sangiovese with the indigenous varieties, fermented in large open-topped wood tanks, and aged in wood. It started as a Chianti Classico, but has been IGT Toscana since 2011. A second wine, called Cinque ("5"), comes partly from declassified grapes and partly from younger vines, and is also IGT Toscana.

Castello di Bossi

Località Bossi in Chianti, 53019 Castelnuovo Berardenga	*+39 0577 359330*
agriturismo@castellodibossi.it	*Marco Bacci*
www.castellodibossi.it	*[map p. 45]*
	124 ha; 700,000 btl

Located in the mildest, southernmost part of the Chianti Classico area, the estate covers 510 ha, surrounding the castle, which dates back to 1099. The name comes from the Roman era. Wine production had all but ceased when Marco Bacci bought the estate in 1984. More recently, he also bought Renieri in Montalcino and Terre di Talamo in Morellino di Scansano. He son Jacopo joined him in 2004. The winery at Bossi is built into the hillside. All the cuvées of Chianti Classico are 100% Sangiovese. The Chianti Classico is the major production, with 600,000 bottles. There are 50,000 bottles of the Berardo Riserva, which like the Chianti Classico ages in a mix of barriques and 50 hl botti of French oak for 18 months or longer. The Gran Selezione, is a selection of the best lots from across the estate, with 20,000 bottles aged in 500-liter tonneaux for 24 months. In IGT Toscana there is a rosé and the red Corbaia, both from a blend of 70% Sangiovese and 30% Cabernet Sauvignon; the red ages in barriques for 9 months. Girolama comes from the oldest (more than 40-year) plots of Merlot, aged in barriques for two years.

Cantalici

Fraz. Castagnoli, Via Della Croce, 17-19, 53013 Gaiole In Chianti	*+39 0577 731038*
info@cantalici.it	*Daniele & Carlo Cantalici*
www.cantalici.it	*[map p. 45]*
	60 ha; 80,000 btl

The winery is on the site of an old kiln (L'Antica Fornace), which Loris Cantalici purchased in 1972. His sons Carlo and Daniele moved into viticulture, planting the first vineyards in 1999. (The official name of the estate is L'Antica Fornace di Ridolfo.) Vineyards extend across several villages. The Chianti Classico Cantalici is 85% Sangiovese, 10% Merlot, and 5% Cabernet Sauvignon, from albarese terroir at 400-560m; it ages for 12 months 70% in barriques with new half new oak, 30% in stainless steel. Chianti Classico Baruffo is 100% Sangiovese and has the same aging. The Riservas and Gran Selezione are 100% Sangiovese. The Riservas ages 70% in 20 hl French casks and 30% in stainless steel: Messer Ridolfo Riserva comes from vineyards at 350m, the Baruffo Riserva from 550m altitude. The Gran Selezione moves into French barriques for malolactic fermentation and aging for 18 months. Tangano is a super-Tuscan from a third each of Sangiovese, Merlot, and Cabernet Sauvignon, aged in barriques for 18 months.

Azienda Agricola Caparsa

Via Roma 17 (shop) *Via Case Sparse Caparsa 47, 53017 Radda in Chianti (winery)*	*+39 057 7738174*
caparsa@caparsa.it	*Paolo Cianferoni*
www.caparsa.it	*[map p. 44]*
	12 ha; 40,000 btl

Reginaldo Cianferoni purchased the property in 1965 and planted vineyards; his son Paolo took over in 1982. Vineyards are at 450m elevation, with soils of galestro and albarese. The cellars date from the seventeenth century. The estate bottles just under half of its production. The Chianti Classico is 100% Sangiovese and ages in concrete tanks. The Carpasino Riserva is also 100% Sangiovese, and ages in 18 hl botti for 1-2 years, while the Doccio a Matteo Riserva is a selection of the best grapes, including 2-5% Colorino, and ages in 10 hl oak casks for 1-2 years. The entry-level wines are IGT Toscana in all three colors, aged in concrete or steel. There is also a Vin Santo.

Tenuta di Carleone

Loc. Castiglioni, 53017 Radda in Chianti (winery) *VIA Guido Rossa 10b, Loc. La Villa, Radda In Chianti (tastings)*	*+39 0577 735613*
office@carleone.it	*Sean O'Callaghan*
www.carleone.it	*[map p. 44]*
	20 ha; 65,000 btl

Austrian industrialist Karl Egger (he makes cooling systems) and his sister Kristina bought this hamlet at Castiglioni in 2012 and began to restore it. Sean O'Callaghan left Somerset in England, qualified in winemaking in Germany, and came to Chianti thirty years ago, where he became chief winemaker at Riecine (see profile). He's known as Il Guercio as he was born blind in one eye. After 26 years, he left Riecine when it changed hands, started a brand called Il Guercio, and then started a collaboration at Tenuta di Carleone. In addition to the original 5 ha of vines at Castiglioni, more plots have been bought or leased in neighboring villages. Vineyards alternate between albarese and galestro. Sean describes his approach as, "I am convinced that Sangiovese should be elegant, light with a strong tannic backbone." So the Chianti Classico is handled simply, in stainless steel and concrete. Uno is a selection of the best Sangiovese, aged 90% in vat and 10% in new tonneaux. Il Guercio is 100% Sangiovese from the Mello vineyard in Gaiole in Chianti, picked late, fermented with 20% whole bunches, and aged in concrete. Due is 95% Sangiovese and 5% Merlot, aged in a mix of wood and vat.

Fattoria Carpineta Fontalpino

Loc. Carpineta, Montaperti, 53019 Castelnuovo Berardenga	*+39 0577 369219*
office@carpinetafontalpino.it	*Gioia & Filippo Cresti*
www.carpinetafontalpino.it	*[map p. 45]*
	31 ha; 100,000 btl

At the border between Chianti Classico and Chianti Colli Senesi, close to Siena, the name reflects history: Carpineta is a place where Carpini (silver birch) trees grow, and Fontalpino is a water source by the pines. Italo Cresti bought the 80 ha estate in 1967, and his children run it today. Gioia is the winemaker (trained in France) and Filippo manages the estate. Chianti Classico Fontalpino and Chianti Colli Senesi are 100% Sangiovese. Two single-vineyard cuvées in Chianti Classico were added with the 2015 vintage: Montaperto and Dofana (previously an IGT Toscana). Rather than using descriptions such as Riserva, they simply call the them the 'Crus.' Chianti Colli Senesi ages in cuve, and Chianti Classicos age in tonneaux for 15 months. In IGT Toscana, Montaperto is a blend of Sangiovese, Alicante, and Gamay, and Do Ut Des is a blend of Sangiovese, Merlot, and Cabernet Sauvignon.

Fattoria Casaloste

Via Montagliari 32, 50022 Panzano In Chianti	*+39 0558 52725*
infocasaloste@casaloste.com	*Giovanni Battista & Emilia d'Orsi*
www.casaloste.com	*[map p. 43]*
	10 ha; 60,000 btl

In the hills around Panzano, this small estate is the home of oenologist Giovanni d'Orsi and his wife Emilia. The 18 ha estate includes 2 ha of olive trees as well as the vines. The approach is modernist. The first vintage of Chianti Classico was 1993; it has 90% Sangiovese and 10% Merlot, and ages in barriques and larger casks of French oak. The Riserva is a selection of the best lots, with 95% Sangiovese and 5% of other varieties, and ages in barriques for 14 months. Gran Selezione is 100% Sangiovese, and has 30% new oak among the barriques. Don Vincenzo is a monovarietal single-parcel Sangiovese. It ages for 18 months in barriques including 12% new oak, followed by 18 months in 35 hl casks, and is produced only in top vintages, with under 300 cases. It is labeled as IGT Toscana. Reversing the proportions of the Chianti Classico, another IGT, Inversus, is 90% Merlot and 10% Sangiovese, aged in new and 1-year barriques.

Casavecchia Alla Piazza

Località La Piazza 37, 53011 Castellina In Chianti	*+39 0577 749754*
buondonno@chianticlassico.com	*Gabriele Buondonno & Valeria Sodana*
www.buondonno.com	*[map p. 43]*
	11 ha; 40,000 btl

Gabriele Buondonno and his wife Valeria Sodano, both agronomists, bought this property in 1988. Its history goes back to 1549, when it belonged to Michelangelo's nephew, and had a good reputation for its wine The IGT Toscana is the entry-level wine, mostly Sangiovese. Chianti Classico is the main product and includes small amounts of Merlot and Syrah. It ages in a mix of larger casks and barriques for a year, The Riserva comes from the best lots in the vineyards at the southern end of the property. There are also varietal wines from Merlot, Syrah, and Cabernet Franc. Lemme is unusual, a field blend from old vines of Sangiovese with some Canaiolo, Malvasia Nera, and Colorino (they call it an 'old Chianti'), trained on maple trees; it ages in ceramic vats and is only 1,000 bottles.

Tenuta Casenuove

Panzano In Chianti, 50020	*+39 0558 52009*
info@tenutacasenuove.it	*Philippe Austruy*
www.tenuta-casenuove.com	*[map p. 43]*
	28 ha

The estate was owned by the Gandolfini family for a long time until Philippe Austruy bought it in 2014. He already owned Commanderie de Peyrassol and Château Malescasse in Bordeaux and Quinta da Côrte in the Douro, and set about reviving Casenuove, renovating the cellars and installing new equipment. Stéphane Derenoncourt from Bordeaux was brought in to consult. The estate covers 105 ha (more than half is forest) and about half the vineyards were productive. The first vintage to show the effects of the new regime was 2018. Chianti Classico is a blend of 80% Sangiovese, 15% Merlot, and 5% Cabernet Sauvignon, aged mostly in concrete with some lots in wood. The Riserva has a similar blend and ages mostly in 500-liter barrels and 25 hl casks. There is an IGT Toscana blend of 60% Sangiovese with 40% Merlot, and a sparkling rosé, ZIIK, from Sangiovese.

Castell'in Villa

Loc. Castell'in Villa, 53019 Castelnuovo Berardenga	*+39 0577 359074*
info@castellinvilla.com	*Coralia Pignatelli*
www.castellinvilla.com	*[map p. 45]*
	50 ha; 120,000 btl

This is a historic estate, run down with only a hectare of vineyards when Coralia Pignatelli purchased it in 1967. Planting began in 1968, and the first Chianti Classico was released in 1971. The Riserva was an immediate success. The vineyard Poggio delle Rose was planted in 1990 and became the basis of a single-vineyard Riserva from 1996. Both Chianti Classico and Riserva are 100% Sangiovese. Santa Croce started in 1983 as a pure Sangiovese aged in barriques, but Cabernet Sauvignon was included from 1988. (The Cabernet was grafted over the old Canaiola vines in 1983). There is also a Vin Santo. Today the estate of 300 ha includes 32 ha of olive groves as well as the vineyards.

Castellare Di Castellina

Loc. Castellare, 53011 Castellina in Chianti	*+39 0577 742903*
info@castellare.it	*Paolo Panerai*
www.castellare.it	*[map p. 43]*
	33 ha; 250,000 btl

The estate of 80 ha is an example of polyculture, with 12 ha of olive groves and 15 ha of other agriculture, as well as the vineyards. It originated in 1968 when five farms were consolidated, and produced its first wine in 1971. It has been owned since the 1980s by Paolo Panerai. About half of production is Chianti Classico (including Riserva in the best vintages). There are about 35,000 bottles of I Sodi di San Niccolò, a super-Tuscan from Sangiovese and Malvasia that ages in 50% new barriques, and much smaller amounts of Coniale (100% Cabernet Sauvignon aged in 50% new barriques), Poggio ai Merli (100% Merlot aged in 100% new barriques), and some white wines based on Chardonnay and/or Sauvignon Blanc. The estate is best known for the I Sodi cuvée, which is distinctly modern in style. (I Sodi means hard soil.) It also owns Rocca di Frassinello (see profile) in Maremma.

La Castellina di Tommaso Bojola

Viale Rimembranza 28, 53011 Castellina in Chianti	*+39 0577 740454*
info@lacastellina.it	*Tommaso Bojola*
www.lacastellina.it	*[map p. 43]*
	42 ha; 200,000 btl

The 140 ha estate originally belonged to the aristocratic Squarcialupi family. La Castellina as such was founded in 1980 and is owned by the Bojola-Targioni family; Tommaso Bojola started producing wine in 1989. His son Cosimo, an oenologist, works with him. Production is 60% Chianti Classico and 40% of other wines, including production from Maremma. Vineyards in Castellina are at 400-500m altitude. Squarcialupi is the traditional range of Chianti Classico. The Classico is half Chianti production, from 95% Sangiovese with 5% Colorino, aged in 24-47 hl botti of Slavonian oak. The Riserva is 90% Sangiovese with 5% each of Merlot and Cabernet Sauvignon, aged for two years in botti followed by another 6 months in barriques and 500-liter barrels. The Gran Selezione is 100% Sangiovese and ages in 500-liter barrels and some barriques. The Tommaso Bojola Riserva is more international in style, with late harvest of 80% Sangiovese, 15% Cabernet Sauvignon, and 5% Merlot, fermented and then aged in barriques and tonneaux. Cosimo Bojola is 100% Sangiovese aged in amphorae. The Riccuda Chianti Classico and Riserva are organic. IGT Toscana include Reale (100% Merlot) and Rubisco (equal Sangiovese and Syrah). In addition to the Chianti Classico Vin Santo (from Trebbiano and Malvasia), Occhio di Pernice is a vin santo from 100% Sangiovese. The domain is into oenotourism and offers several tours and tastings for a fee, including a visit to the fifteenth century cellars of the Palazzo Squarcialupi.

Castello Della Paneretta

Strada della Paneretta 35, 50028 Barberino Tavarnelle (FI).	*+39 0558 059003*
paneretta@paneretta.it	*Alberto Albisetti*
www.castellodellapaneretta.com	*[map p. 43]*
	23 ha; 100,000 btl

With 309 ha of woods surrounding the vineyards, the estate is one of the largest in the area. At its center is a real castle, dating from a restoration in 1577. Wine has been made here at least since 1596. The Albisetti family bought the property in 1984. As they describe their philosophy, "We strongly believe that using exclusively Sangiovese and Canaiolo Nero is not only our tradition but also the only answer to the increasing popularity of the New World wines. Making good Merlot or Cabernet wines is possible wherever you are in the world, however, only the Chianti Classico region has the potentiality to produce outstanding Sangiovese and Canaiolo." There are no international varieties here, but the traditional varieties are married with French oak. The Chianti

Classico is 85% Sangiovese, 10% Canaiolo, and 5% Colorino. The Riserva is 90% Sangiovese and 10% Canaiolo. They age in 30 hl and 50 hl French casks for 12 months. Torre a Destra is pure Sangiovese from a single vineyard, and ages in French barriques for 24 months. Terrine is an IGT with half each of Sangiovese and Canaiolo, aged in barriques with 50% new oak. There is also an unusual 100% Canaiolo, aged in new barriques for 24 months. Quatrocentenario is an IGT from 100% Sangiovese aged in new barriques for 24 months.

Fattoria Castelvecchio

Loc. San Pancrazio, via Certaldese 30, 50026 San Casciano In Val di Pesa	*+39 0558 248032*
info@castelvecchio.it	*Filippo Rocchi*
www.castelvecchio.it	*[map p. 42]*
	27 ha; 120,000 btl

On the border between Chianti Classico and Chianti Colli Fiorentini, the property dates from the medieval period, and has belonged to the Rocchi family since 1962. The 70 ha estate includes 15 ha of olive groves. Renzo Rocchi built up the estate in the mid nineties, and today it is run by his children Filippo and Stefania. Just to the west of Chianti Classico, the DOCG wines are Chianti Colli Fiorentini. There are IGTs from international varieties, Il Brecciolino (70% Merlot, 20% Petit Verdot, and 10% Sangiovese), aged in tonneaux and barriques for 12 months. Solo Uno follows its name: it is a monovarietal, but the variety is whichever performs best each year. In 2009 it was Cabernet Sauvignon, but since then it has been Sangiovese. Irrespective of variety, it ages in new barriques.

Famiglia Cecchi

Località Casina Dei Ponti, 53011 Castellina in Chianti	*+39 0577 54311*
cecchi@cecchi.net	*Andrea & Cesare Cecchi*
www.cecchi.net	*[map p. 43]*
	385 ha; 8,500,000 btl

This the flagship winery in the Cecchi group. The first winery was Villa Cerna, established at the southern boundary of Chianti Classico in the 1960s, Castello Montauto in San Gimignano came in 1988, Val Delle Rose in Maremma was purchased in 1996, and Tenuta Alzatura in Umbria was added last. But Cecchi is somewhat of a catch-all name for activities of the group: wines include Brunello di Montalcino, Vino Nobile di Montepulciano and a long list from all around the area. In Chianti Classico, there are wines under the Villa Cerna label and also under Famiglia Cecchi, but no single cuvée stands out as epitomizing the house.

Fattoria di Cinciano

Località Cinciano 2, 53036 Poggibonsi	*+39 0577 936588*
info@cinciano.it	*Ferdinando & Ottavia Garrè*
www.cinciano.it	*[map p. 43]*
	24 ha; 140,000 btl

This property near Poggibonsi is a small hamlet of its own, with buildings and terraced gardens in an estate of 150 ha that includes 40 ha of olive trees as well as vineyards. It was owned by the Church from 1126 to 1900, and bought by the Garré family in 1973. There are also some vineyards in Barberino Val d'Elsa. The focus is very much on Sangiovese, with the Chianti Classico, Riserva, and Gran Selezione all 100% varietal, aged in botti of Slavonian oak for 8, 12, or 18 months respectively. There is a Chianti Classico Vin Santo (half Trebbiano, half Malvasia). In IGT Toscana there are also red (Merlot, Cabernet Sauvignon, and Sangiovese), rosé (Sangiovese), and white (Viognier, Chardonnay, and Sauvignon Blanc).

Collazzi

Via Colleramole 101, Loc. Tavarnuzze, 50023 Impruneta	*+39 0552 374902*
info@collazzi.it	*Carlo & Bona Marchi*
www.collazzi.it	*[map p. 41]*
	25 ha; 80,000 btl

Villa Collazzi is just south of the ring road around Florence, on a hilltop with a commanding view over the hills. It was designed by Michelangelo in 1560. The 960 ha estate was purchased by the Marchi family in 1933. In the 1990s, Carlo and Bona Marchi revived the vineyards. Most of the wines are IGT Toscana, including Collazzi (a Bordeaux blend) and Ferro (Petit Verdot), both aged for 18 months in barriques, and Libertà (Merlot, Cabernet Franc and Syrah (aged in wood and tank). The white Otto Muri is from the variety Fiano. The Chianti Classico, I Bastioni, comes from 7 ha in San Casciano (80% Sangiovese, 18% Merlot, 2% Malvasia Nero, aged in barriques for 12 months).

Castello di Gabbiano

Mercatale Val di Pesa, via Gabbiano 22, 50020 San Casciano In Val di Pesa	*+39 0558 21053*
castellogabbiano@castellogabbiano.it	
www.castellogabbiano.it	*[map p. 42]*
	165 ha; 1,000,000 btl

The winery is located in a historic castle, and this is a very old estate, but as one of the largest producers in the region, is today very much in the modern idiom. There are 120 ha in Chianti Classico and another 45 ha in IGT. The focus is on ripeness, and wines are aged mostly in barriques. Chianti includes the whole range, Classico, Riserva, and Gran Selezione Bellezza, (formerly a Riserva). The Classico is ripe, round, and modern, the Riserva moves towards black fruits and has more sense of structure. and the Gran Selezione is very much in the same style, but a touch deeper and blacker. The Alleanza IGT is a blend of Merlot and Cabernet Sauvignon. Gabbiano is owned by Treasury Wine Estates, who have used it as the basis for launching other brands.

Gagliole

Via Case sparse 3/5, Panzano in Chianti	*+39 0577 740369*
info@gagliole.com	*Monika & Thomas Bär*
www.gagliole.com	*[map p. 43]*
	20 ha

Monika and Thomas Bär changed careers when they bought the property in 1990: Thomas was a Swiss banker and layer, Monika was a gallery owner. Now several generations of the family are involved in making wine. Vineyards are divided equally between Castellina in Chianti, planted on terraces of galestro soil with trees offering shade, and Panzano, in the Conco d'Oro amphitheater where the soil has more clay and gravel. All the Chianti Classicos are 100% Sangiovese. Rubiolo comes from galestro soils, aged in vat. The estate Riserva ages in small oak casks. The Gallule Riserva comes only from

Castellina and ages in used barriques. There is a break in style for the IGT wines. The top Sangiovese is Pecchia, sourced from Panzano, aged for 18 months in new French barriques. Other IGT wines are Gagliole (Sangiovese with just 2% Cabernet Sauvignon aged in barriques with 40% new oak) and Valletta (50% Sangiovese, 50% Merlot, aged in barriques with 50% new oak).White IGTs are unconventional blends: Biancola is 50% Chardonnay, 50% Trebbiano; Il Bianco is 60% Procanico, 30% Chardonnay, and 10% Malvasia, aged in new barriques.

I Fabbri di Susanna Grassi

Via Casole 18, Loc. Lamole, 50022 Greve in Chianti	*+39 0339 4122622*
info@ifabbrichianticlassico.it	*Susanna Grassi*
www.ifabbrichianticlassico.it	*[map p. 44]*
	7 ha; 35,000 btl

The estate has belonged to the Grassi family since the seventeenth century. Although they began to bottle wine in the 1920s, the next two generations lost interest, and the estate was rented out. Susanna Grassi changed careers from fashion to wine when she took back the estate in 2000 and created I Fabbri. Vineyards are at elevations of 550-650m. The focus is on a local cultivar of Sangiovese: the only other variety is some Canaiolo in the Riserva. Chianti ages partly in vat and partly in 500 liter barrels: Riserva and Gran Selezione age only in 500 liter barrels of French oak. There are two IGTs: Due Donne is a equal blend of Sangiovese and Schiopetto, and Il Doccio is a monovarietal Merlot.

Istine

Loc. Istine Cs, 53017 Radda in Chianti	*+39 3920 082243*
info@istine.it	*Angela Fronti*
www.istine.it	*[map p. 44]*
	25 ha; 95,000 btl

Bruno Fronti created Istine in 1959 after starting a vineyard management company. Working with his sons Fabio and Stefano, he started by selling grapes., The winery is basically a warehouse. Vineyards are in three areas, two in Radda in Chianti, and one in Gaiole in Chianti, all at altitudes around 500m. The first estate wine was produced in 2009, with only 250 cases. In addition to the estate blend, today there are separate bottlings from Istine (between Radda and Castellina), Casanova (near Radda), and Cavarchione (in Gaiole). The lots that are most typical of the area go into these cuvées, and the others are blended into the estate wine or the Riserva. Each single-vineyard wine is not necessarily made every year. The top wine is the Riserva, LeVigne, which ages in Austrian oak from Stockinger. It shows a light, fresh balance with a red fruit spectrum, and goes for elegance rather than power. The approach is traditional, with only Sangiovese, and all wines aged in botti.

La Sala

Via Sorripa 34, 50026 San Casciano Val di Pesa	*+39 0558 240013*
info@lasala.it	*Francesco Rossi Ferrini*
www.lasala.it	*[map p. 42]*
	32 ha; 50,000 btl

La Sala has a long history dating back to 1260. The modern era started with its purchase in 1981 by Laura Baronti. Located at the northern edge of Chianti Classico (just south of Florence), the property was bought in 2014 by Francesco Rossi Ferrini who already owned La Torriano, about five miles away. About half of the 70 ha La Sala estate is planted with vineyards, all but 5 ha classified for Chianti Classico. There is a range of DOCG wines: Chianti Classico is 95% Sangiovese and 5% Merlot, and the Riserva is 90% Sangiovese and 10% Cabernet Sauvignon; both age half in large French oak casks, half in stainless steel. Gran Selezione is 100% Sangiovese, aged in large (39 hl) French oak. The IGT Toscana, Campo All'Albero, is half Merlot and half Cabernet Sauvignon, aged in barriques.

Lamole di Lamole

Via di Lamole, 50022 Greve in Chianti	*+39 0559 331256*
info@lamole.com	*Andrea Daldin*
www.lamole.com	*[map p. 44]*
	77 ha; 300,000 btl

Best known for its Pinot Grigio, the Santa Margherita group owns wineries all over Italy. The home base is in Alto Adige. Purchased in 1993, Lamole di Lamole is one of three wineries in Tuscany; the others are Villa Vistarenni in Gaiole in Chianti, and Sassoregale in Maremma. The historic building of the Lamole winery is now used for aging; there is a modern fermentation center in Lamole, and a visitor center at Greti in Chianti. The approach is modern. Chianti Classico is light and fresh, Chianti Classico Blue Label has 20% Cabernet Sauvignon and Merlot and is rather stern, the Riserva has 5% Canaiolo and is deeper than Classico but not as structured as Blue Label, and the Gran Selezione has 5% Cabernet and is the deepest and most modern.

Azienda Agricola Lanciola

Via Imprunetana Per Pozzolatico 210, 50023 Impruneta	*+39 0552 08324*
info@lanciola.it	*Giancarlo Guarnieri*
www.lanciola.it	*[map p. 41]*
	40 ha

South of Florence, just inside the ring road, the estate is located on the hills of Impuneta in the DOC of Colli Fiorentini. The 80 hectares are divided half into vines and half into olive trees. Wine has been made here since the sixteenth century. The Guarnieri family have owned the property since the 1970s. In addition to Chianti Fiorentini from the estate, they produce Chianti Classico from 14 ha in Greve in Chianti. The Chianti Fiorentini is a blend of Sangiovese and Canaiola, aged in a mix of steel and small botti. The vineyard in Greve, Le Masse di Greve, produces Chianti Classico, Riserva, and Gran Selezione, with a similar blend, but aged in a mix of barriques and the botti.

Le Cinciole

Via Case Sparse 83, Panzano In Chianti, 50020	*+39 0558 52636*
info@lecinciole.it	*Luca & Valeria Orsini*
www.lecinciole.it	*[map p. 43]*
	10 ha; 50,000 btl

Located in the center of the Conca d'Oro (golden conch) of Panzano, with vineyards above 400m in elevation, Le Cinciole (an old name for the location that may be a contraction of 'Le Terre di Quintius'), has been in the hands of Luca and Valeria Orsini since the 1990s. Vineyards range from 430-450m. There are three cuvées that are exclusively Sangiovese. About half of all production, the Chianti Classico ages in 20 hl casks of French oak for 12 months followed by another 12 months in concrete. The Riserva,

Aluigi, comes from a single vineyard at 430-450m, and ages for 24 months in the large casks. The top Sangiovese is the IGT Toscana, Petresco, aged in barriques for 24 months. Camalaione is an IGT Toscana from international varieties (Cabernet Sauvignon, Syrah, and Merlot) aged in 500-liter barrels. The entry-level wine is the IGT Toscana Cinciorosso, a blend of Sangiovese with Syrah and Merlot. There is also a rosé from Sangiovese.

Villa Le Corti

Via San Piero Di Sotto 1, 50026 San Casciano In Val di Pesa	*+39 0558 29301*
shop@principecorsini.com	*Duccio Corsini*
www.principecorsini.com	*[map p. 42]*
	50 ha; 150,000 btl

One of the oldest estates in Chianti, the property is located in the northern part of San Casciano, which is to say about as far north as Chianti Classico goes. It has been in the hands of the Corsini family for generations. Duccio Corsini took over in 1992. The Principe Corsini family also owns Tenuta Masiliana in Maremma. The 240 ha estate near Florence produces Chianti Classico and IGT Toscana. The Chianti Classico Le Corte is 95% Sangiovese with 5% Colorino and ages in concrete vats. The Cortevecchia Riserva has the same blend but ages in 27 hl botti for 16-20 months. Don Tommaso Gran Selezione is 80% Sangiovese and 20% Merlot, aged in 500-700-liter tonneaux for 16 months. The top wine returns to IGT Toscana; Zac is 100% Sangiovese from a single vineyard, and ages in used barriques. There are also Vin Santo, rosé, and sparkling wine.

Tenuta di Lilliano

Loc. Lilliano, 8, 53011 Castellina In Chianti	*+39 0577 743070*
info@lilliano.it	*Giulio Ruspoli*
www.lilliano.it	*[map p. 43]*
	40 ha; 160,000 btl

The Ruspoli family have owned this property of 460 ha., including 160 ha of woods and 42 ha of olive trees, and other crops, as well as vines. Giulio Ruspoli has been in charge since 1989. The family lives in the Ruspoli Palace in Rome. The estate has been bottling its own wines since 1958. It has three vineyards: Le Piagge at 300m facing south is planted with Sangiovese; Casina Sopra Strada facing east-southeast at 300m is planted with Sangiovese and Colorino; and Vigna Catena facing south-southwest at 280m is planted with Merlot. The Chianti Classico is 90% Sangiovese and 5% each of Colorino and Merlot, and ages partly in concrete, partly in large casks of French oak. The Riserva is based on selection and has 95% Sangiovese with 5% Merlot, and ages for 15 months in 28 hl and 34 hl casks of French oak. The Gran Selezione ahs the same blend as the Classico, and ages partly in the large casks and partly in tonneaux of French oak. Anagallis is a Bordeaux blend IGT Toscana. There is a rosé from Sangiovese.

Livernano

Loc. Livernano, 53017 Radda in Chianti	*+39 0577 738353*
info@livernano.it	*Martino Scheggi*
www.livernano.it	*[map p. 44]*
	25 ha; 100,000 btl

Just outside Radda in Chianti, Livernano is a hamlet in a 200 ha estate that was restored starting in 1990. The owners are Americans, Robert and Gudrun Cuillo. The estate includes a boutique hotel and offers cooking classes, as well as cellar tours and tastings. There's a wide range of wines. From Chianti there's a Classico and Riserva, which contain 20% Merlot: the top Sangiovese is the IGT Purosangue. The style is modern, with wines aged in 350-liter barrels. The eponymous Livernano is a Cabernet-Merlot blend. There are also some whites, including a Chardonnay. Caselvento nearby is under the same ownership: here the Chianti Classico and Riserva include 20% Cabernet Sauvignon; IGT Janus is 100% Cabernet.

Le Miccine

Località Le Miccine 44, Sp2, 53013 Gaiole In Chianti	*+39 0577 749526*
mail@lemiccine.com	*Paula Papini Cook*
www.lemiccine.com	*[map p. 45]*
	7 ha; 25,000 btl

This small property in Gaiole in Chianti sold wine in bulk until Americans Clifford and Donna Weaver bought it in 1996 and started estate-bottling. They sold in 2010 to Canadian Paula Cook, originally from Quebec. The Chianti Classico and Riserva now have 95-100% Sangiovese with (sometimes) Colorino an Malvasia Nero. They used to include Merlot, but Paula uses the 0.5 ha to make a separate IGT Toscana, Carduus. The Gran Selezione is 100% Sangiovese from albarese terroir. Wines age in larger oak casks.

Castello Di Monsanto

Loc. Monsanto, 50028 Barberino Tavarnelle	*+39 0558 059000*
monsanto@castellodimonsanto.it	*Family Bianchi*
www.castellodimonsanto.it	*[map p. 43]*
	72 ha; 450,000 btl

Located in the northern part of Chianti, this is one of the most charming estates in the region, with a view over to the towers of San Gimignano. It was founded when Aldo Bianchi bought the property in 1960; today it is run by his son Fabrizio. The entry-level wine is a Chianti DOCG, Monrosso, which comes from the Colli Senesi area. The three Chianti Classicos are quite traditional, with a blend of 90% Sangiovese and small amounts of Canaiolo and Colorino. The Chianti Classico matures in 50 hl botti, the Riserva ages in small wooden barrels, and the Il Poggio Riserva, produced only in top vintages, matures in French barriques. The wines show a modern, crowd-pleasing style, faintly nutty for Classico, a touch more structure for Riserva, and livelier for Gran Selezione. The Toscana IGTs are labeled as Fabrizio Bianchi, and include the Rosato, which is a second wine from young vines, a Sangiovese, and a Chardonnay. Nemo is a monovarietal Cabernet Sauvignon.

Monte Bernardi

Via Chiantigiana, Panzano In Chianti, 50020	*+39 0558 52400*
mb@montebernardi.com	*Michael Schmelzer*
www.montebernardi.com	*[map p. 43]*
	25 ha; 150,000 btl

This old estate has grown grapes for a long time, but the grapes were sent to the cooperative until wine production started in 1992. American Michael Schmelzer moved to Italy and bought the 53 ha property in 2003. The estate includes 10 ha of vineyards, he leased another 5 ha in 2011. Soils are rocky, with galestro (shale), arenaria (sandstone), and albarese (limestone). The Chianti Classico, Retromarcia, has been 100% Sangiovese since 2010, and comes from recent plantings (2003-2010). It ages in a mix of botti and concrete. The Monte Bernardi Riserva has 5% Canaiola and comes from 40-year-old vines; it ages only in wood. In 2016, because of a disagreement with the Consorzio—it was judged too light in color and structure—it was labeled as IGT Toscana. The Sa'etta Riserva is 100% Sangiovese from a single parcel, and ages in German and Austrian oak for 24-30 months. Tzingarella is an IGT based on a Bordeaux blend with 5% Colorino; Tzingana is Bordeaux blend where all four varieties are cofermented. Both IGTs age in a mix of barriques and tonneaux.

Monteraponi

Loc. Monteraponi, 53017 Radda in Chianti	*+39 0577 738208*
mail@monteraponi.it	*Michele Braganti*
www.monteraponi.it	*[map p. 44]*
	13 ha; 60,000 btl

The vineyards are part of a 200 ha estate, purchased by Michele Braganti's father in 1974. Vineyards were rented out, and the grapes sold off, until Michele decided to take over: his first vintage was sold in 2003. The cellars are underneath the medieval tower of the Monteraponi hamlet. Winemaking is traditional, with aging in large, old botti. The Chianti Classico and Riserva Il Campitello (from the oldest vineyard) are both Sangiovese with small amounts of Canaiolo or Colorino. Baron Ugo (named for the eleventh century owner of the village), which comes from the highest vineyard, was a Riserva until 2012, but then became an IGT to give more flexibility in production (but it has the same blend of Sangiovese, Canaiolo, and Colorino).

Fattoria Poggerino

Loc. Poggerino, 53017 Radda In Chianti	*+39 0577 738958*
info@poggerino.com	*Piero Lanza*
www.poggerino.com	*[map p. 44]*
	13 ha; 65,000 btl

Floriana Lanza inherited the family estate in 1980 and began to produce wine. In 1988, her children Piero and Benedetta started to run the state, and in 1999 they took over completely. It's a complex with old houses, some of which are used to offer accommodation. Only a small part of the 43 ha are planted with vines (and olive trees). All the Chianti Classicos are 100% Sangiovese. Two cuvées have different aging regimes: Chianti Classico ages in a mix of Slavonian botti and French barriques, while the Chianti Classico N(Uovo) ages in a concrete egg. The Riserva Bugialla ages in botti of Slavonian oak. There are two IGT Toscana: Il Labirinto is the entry-level, 100% Sangiovese aged in concrete; Primametria is a Sangiovese-Merlot blend, aged in 400-liter tonneau.

Podere Poggio Scalette

Via Barbiano 7, Località Ruffoli, 50022 Greve in Chianti	*+39 0558 546108*
fiorewines@gmail.com	*Adriana Assje' Di Marcora'*
www.poggioscalette.it	*[map p. 44]*
	15 ha; 45,000 btl

This is essentially a new winery in an old vineyard. The 40 ha estate had been abandoned for years when Vittorio Fiore, who had been working previously as a flying winemaker, bought it together with his wife Adriana in 1991. Their son Jurij Fiore makes the wine together with Vittorio, and sons Roberto and Alessandro are in charge of marketing. The

5 ha Il Carbonaione vineyard has 90-year-old Sangiovese vines (an example of the Lamole subcultivar) and gives its name to the flagship wine, produced since 1992. It's aged in half new and half one-year barrels of 350 liters, and is labeled as IGT Alta Valle della Greve. Since 2009 there's also been a Chianti Classico, also Sangiovese di Lamole, aged simply in cement tanks. There's also a very small production of the Capogatto IGT, made from an equal blend of Cabernet Sauvignon, Cabernet Franc, Merlot, and Petit Verdot, and the single vineyard Phantonaia varietal Merlot.

Poggio Torselli

Via Scopeti 10, 50026, San Casciano In Val di Pesa	*+39 0558 290241*
info@poggiotorselli.it	*Eduardo Colapinto*
www.poggiotorselli.it	*[map p. 42]*
	26 ha; 126,000 btl

Villa Poggio Torselli is a famous historic property, dating from the fifteenth century, when it belonged to the Machiavelli family. An avenue of cypresses leads to the current villa dates from a reconstruction in 1702. An extensive terraced Italian garden dates from the seventieth century. Maurizio Zamparini, owner of the Palermo football team, bought in 1990, restored it from a dilapidated state, and built a new cellar in 2003. He sold it in 2021 (asking price: $60 million) to Laura Giordani; winemaker Eduardo Colapinto stayed on. All the Chianti Classicos are 100% Sangiovese. The Chianti Classico is more than half of production and ages in 15 hl barrels of Slavonian oak. The Riserva and Gran Selezione (which comes from the single vineyard Montecapri) age for 24 months in French oak, with a mix from barriques to 15 hl barrels. The IGT Toscana range, Bizzaria, comes in red (100% Sangiovese aged in stainless steel and used barriques), white (Chardonnay, Gewürztraminer, and Sauvignon Blanc, aged in stainless steel), and rosé (Pugnitello).

Castello di Radda

Località Il Becco, 101/a, 53017 Radda in Chianti	*+39 0577 738992*
info@castellodiradda.com	*Maurizio Castelli*
www.castellodiradda.com	*[map p. 44]*
	40 ha; 150,000 btl

Together with Lo Sparviere in Montalcino and ForteMasso in Barolo, this is owned by Gussalli Beretta, the viticultural holding company of the Beretta firearms company. The Chianti Classico is 90% Sangiovese and ages in a mix of 20 hl Slavonian botti and tonneaux, the Riserva is 100% Sangiovese and comes from vineyards at 400m elevation and ages in French tonneaux including new oak and Slavonian botti, and the Gran Selezione, also 100% Sangiovese, ages in new tonneaux. The Classico and Riserva are close in style, both somewhat modern, and the Gran Selezione is a little denser. Grapes from younger Sangiovese vines go into a blend with Merlot in the Granbruno IGT Toscana, and Guss is a varietal IGT form the best lots of Merlot.

Riecine

Località Riecine, 53013 Gaiole In Chianti	*+39 0577 749098*
info@riecine.it	*Lana Frank*
www.riecine.it	*[map p. 45]*
	30 ha; 90,000 btl

John Dunkley founded Riecine in 1973 and made the first wine with Carlo Ferrini as his chief winemaker. After John died in 1996, Ferrini became a consulting oenologist. The estate passed through several owners. Sean O'Callaghan became chief winemaker and stayed until Lana Frank bought the property, when he started his own brand and made wine at Tenuta di Carleone (see profile). Alessandro Campatelli came as winemaker in 2015, and Carlo Ferrini returned to consult. Vineyards are at 450-500m on calcareous terroir. In a series of 100% Sangiovese wines, the Chianti Classico plays second fiddle to the IGT Toscana. The Chianti Classico and the Riserva both age in a mix of tonneaux and large casks of French oak, for 14 and 24 months respectively. The Classico is light and the Riserva is a rounder and more inclined to black fruits. Riecine di Riecine is IGT Toscana, aged for 36 months in concrete eggs. La Gioia is a selection of the best Sangiovese, aged for 30 months in new and 1-2-year tonneaux of French oak. TreSette is a small production of IGT from 100% Merlot, aged in three 700-liter barrels. There is also a rosé from Sangiovese.

Borgo Salcetino

Loc. Lucarelli, 53017 Radda in Chianti	*+39 0577 733541*
info@livon.it	*Tonino Livon*
15 ha; 95,000 btl	*[map p. 44]*

The Livon family have been making wine in Friuli for fifty years, expanding from their original winery to purchase two more estates, and an estate in Umbria, and then in 1996 they expanded into Chianti Classico by purchasing Salcetino. Relatively small, the estate of 30 ha is half planted to vineyards. There are three wines. The Chianti Classico and the Riserva each have 5% Canaiolo; a bit nutty for Classico, more oaky impressions on the Riserva, and strong aromatics of oak with the Gran Selezione. Rossole is an IGT with 70% Sangiovese and 30% Merlot, aged in new barriques.

Tenuta di Perano

San Donato In Perano, 53013 Gaiole in Chianti	*+39 0577 749563*
info@frescobaldi.it	*Frescobaldi*
www.frescobaldi.com	*[map p. 45]*
	52 ha; 500,000 btl

This is Frescobaldi's seventh estate in Tuscany, a 250 ha with vineyards that were first rented and then purchased, on gravelly terroir surrounded by woods. They are at a significant elevation in Gaaiole in Chianti, at 500m. The first Frescobaldi vintage was 2015. Chianti Classico is 90% Sangiovese and 10% Canaiolo, aged partly in vat and partly in large oak casks. The Riserva is 95% Sangiovese and 5% Merlot, aged in Slavonian oak for 24 months. Gran Selezione comes from the highest vineyard, Rialzi, and is Sangiovese aged in new French barriques for 24 months.

Fattoria San Giusto a Rentennano

Località San Giusto a Rentennano, 20, 53013 Gaiole in Chianti	*+39 0577 747121*
info@fattoriasangiusto.it	*Elisabetta & Luca Martini di Cigala*
www.fattoriasangiusto.it	*[map p. 45]*
	30 ha; 95,000 btl

A couple of miles away from the Castello di Brolio, this estate was a Cistercian monastery that became a fort that was destroyed in the wars of the Middle Ages. It came into the Martini di Cigala family by marriage in 1914, and since 1992 has been run by Enrico Martini di Cigala and his family. The estate extends over 160 ha. Chianti Classico and the

Riserva Baròncole include a little Canaiolo; Chianti Classico is aged in barrels of mixed sizes, but the Riserva ages exclusively in barriques, including 20% new oak. The top Sangiovese is the IGT Percarlo, aged in barriques and some larger casks. La Ricolma is 100% Merlot, aged in barriques. With the extensive use of barriques, including new oak, the approach here is decidedly modernist.

Savignola Paolina

Via Petriolo 58, 50022 Greve in Chianti	*+39 0558 546036*
info@savignola.it	*Luzius & Manuela Caviezel*
www.savignola.it	*[map p. 44]*
	5 ha; 22,000 btl

Originally a religious complex built early in the seventeenth century, then called Savignola, the estate was purchased by the Fabbri family in 1780; in mid twentieth century the owner of the day added her name, Paolina. Vineyards and cellar have been renovated, and a partnership with the Caviezel family from 2014 has brought new investment. The focus here is on harvesting late to achieve ripeness. The Chianti Classicos have up 15% Colorino and Malvasia Nero. They are all aged in French barriques. The IGT Il Granaio is 50% Sangiovese and 30% Merlot.

Tolaini

Loc. Vallenuova, 9 di Pievasciata 28, 53019 Castelnuovo Berardenga	*+39 0577 356972*
info@tolaini.it	*Pierluigi Tolaini*
www.tolaini.it	*[map p. 45]*
	50 ha; 250,000 btl

After spending fifty years building TransX Transportation in Canada, Pierluigi Tolaini (known as Louie in Canada) returned to his native Tuscany in 1999 and purchased vineyards in two locations near Castelnuova Berardenga (with a view to Siena from the highest point), Montebello and San Giovanni. The approach is modern, extending from optical sorting to get grapes of uniform ripeness, fermentation in large wood vats, and aging in barriques with new oak. The Chianti Classico is 100% Sangiovese, and the Gran Selezione is a single-vineyard wine from Montebello. There is a range of different blends under IGT Toscana. Al Passo is 85% Sangiovese and 15% Merlot, and resembles the Chianti Classico Gran Selezione in style: both are smooth and ripe, with a fruit-driven flavor profile, and slightly nutty on the palate. Valdisanti has 75% Cabernet Sauvignon blended with 5% Cabernet Franc and 20% Sangiovese, from San Giovanni. Picconero is a blend of 65% Merlot with 35% Cabernet Franc from Montebello that is intended to compete with Bordeaux.

Val Delle Corti

Loc. La Croce 141, 53017 Radda in Chianti	*+39 0577 738215*
info@valdellecorti.it	*Roberto Bianchi*
www.valdellecorti.it	*[map p. 44]*
	7 ha; 35,000 btl

Giorgio Bianchi moved from Milan to start this winery in 1974; his son Roberto took over in 1999. This is a very small estate, with only 4 ha of vineyards, plus 2 ha that are rented. The vineyards face east, which was a problem in the early years, but has proved beneficial during climate warming. The approach is traditional, with wines aged in large old casks. The Chianti Classico includes 5% Canaiolo; the Riserva is made only in top years, from the oldest (40-year) vines and is 100% Sangiovese. A rosé is made by saignée, and IGT Il Campino is an entry-level wine made from young Sangiovese. Lo Straniero is a Sangiovese-Merlot bland.

Vallepicciola

Sp 9 di Pievasciata, 21, 53019 Pievasciata, Castelnuovo Berardenga	*+39 0577 1698718*
info@vallepicciola.com	*Bruno & Giuseppina Bolfo*
www.vallepicciola.com	*[map p. 45]*
	105 ha

Industrialist Bruno Bolfo converted a medieval monastery northeast of Siena into the 5-star hotel La Fontenelle in the 1980s. The first vineyards for the winery were around the hotel. Vineyards have expanded greatly since then and there is a new winery. Riccardo Cotarella is the consulting oenologist. All the Chianti Classico releases are 100% Sangiovese. The Classico ages in large oak casks, the Riserva and the Lapina Gran Selezione in a mix of various sizes from barriques to large casks. In IGT Toscana, Pievasciata is a blend of Cabernet Sauvignon with Cabernet Franc and Sangiovese, and there is a range of varietals with Pinot Noir, Cabernet Franc, and Merlot, all aged in barriques. The only white is the Lugherino Chardonnay, aged in stainless steel. There are also rosé and sparkling wines. A series of tours and tastings is available, with lunch at the cellar door.

Castello di Verrazzano

Loc. Verrazzano, 50022 Greve in Chianti	*+39 0558 54243*
info@verrazzano.com	*Luigi Cappellini*
www.verrazzano.com	*[map p. 44]*
	52 ha; 280,000 btl

"Visit one of the most ancient but still working cellars in the area," the estate says. The Verrazzano family bought the property in the seventh century, and explorer Giovanni Verrazzano was born here in 1485. The Verrazzano Narrows Bridge in New York is named after him. Before then, the castle was first an Etruscan and then a Roman settlement. There are references to the vineyards from the twelfth century. The cellars date from the sixteenth century. The estate fell into some disorder during the twentieth century, and was restored after Cavalier Cappellini purchased it in 1958. Basically the present vineyards date from then. Chianti Classico and the Riserva are 95% Sangiovese, aged in 30 hl botti of Slavonian oak, while the Gran Selezione is 100% Sangiovese from a single vineyard, aged in new French barriques, which are also used for the super-Tuscan Bottiglia Particolare, a blend of Sangiovese and Cabernet Sauvignon. There is also an entry-level line of IGT Toscana in all three colors, and Vin Santo. The Chianti shows a modern style, with only small differences between Classico, Riserva, and Gran Selezione. The estate is well into oenotourism, with a series of tastings, wine-food pairings, and various tours.

Villa Calcinaia

Via Citille 84, 50022 Greve In Chianti	*+39 0558 54008*
ufficio@villacalcinaia.it	*Sebastiano & Niccolò Capponi*
www.villacalcinaia.it	*[map p. 44]*
	32 ha; 100,000 btl

The 200 ha estate has been owned by the Capponi family since 1524. Sebastiano Capponi was the first member of the family to manage the estate in person when he took over in 1992. Vineyards are on the west side of the Greve river facing east-southeast, on galestro (clay-schist) soils. There are several cuvées from single parcels. The Chianti Classico is 90% Sangiovese with 10% Canaiolo and ages in a mix of 30 hl casks, and tonneaux and barriques of French oak. The Riservas and Gran Selezione are 100% Sangiovese. The estate Riserva comes from older vines with the sunniest exposition and ages in Slavonian casks and French tonneaux. The Piegaia Riserva comes from higher plots, aged in tonneaux. The Classico shows a modern style, and the Riserva has impressions of oak. There are three Gran Selezione. Vigna La Fornace comes from a hectare of Sangiovese planted in 1975 close to the Greve river where the soil has sand and clay (used to produce bricks, which gave rise to the name 'Fornace'). The terroir here is like the Lamole area of Greve. Vigna Contessa Luisa is a west-facing block of 2 ha, planted in 1959 (there are small amounts of other varieties as well as Sangiovese.) Vigna Bastignano comes from a hill of calcareous clay. There are also IGT wines from Merlot, Sanforte (at one time called Sangiovese Forte and thought to be a relative of Sangiovese), and the unusual indigenous variety Occhiorosso.

Vignamaggio

Via Petriolo 5, 50022 Greve In Chianti	*+39 0558 546653*
agriturismo@vignamaggio.com	*Patrice Paul Taravella*
www.vignamaggio.com	*[map p. 44]*
	70 ha; 250,000 btl

Villa Vignamaggio has an estate spreading over 400 ha with a working farm that includes 9 different vineyards, mostly in Greve in Chianti. The farm includes animals as well as crops, and there is accommodation in the farmhouse and villas, and a restaurant. The property was bought by a group of investors in 2014, and a major renovation project has been going on ever since. The Terre di Prenzano Chianti Classico is 100% Sangiovese, aged in botti, and is generally quite light and fresh. The Gherardino Riserva is 80-90% Sangiovese with 10-20% Merlot; aged in small oak including barriques, it presents a more modern style. The Monna Lisa Gran Selezione is a blend of 85% Sangiovese with 15% Merlot and Cabernet Sauvignon, aged first in barriques and then in botti; made only in the best vintages, it shows the extra weight of the international varieties. They are all rather modern in style, which is to say tending towards black fruits with nutty impressions from oak. I find it hard to identify Sangiovese. Under IGT Toscana there are varietal wines from Merlot and Cabernet Franc, produced in small amounts, and the entry-level Il Morino (a blend of Sangiovese and Merlot, aged in steel).

Fattoria di Viticcio

Via San Cresci 12/a, Greve in Chianti	*+39 0558 54210*
info@viticcio.com	*Beatrice Landini*
www.viticcio.com	*[map p. 44]*
50 ha; 250,000 btl	*Chianti Classico Riserva, Beatrice*

Viticcio has extended from its origins in Chianti in 1964 to vineyards in Bolgheri and Maremma. Viticcio at Greve in Chianti remains the main estate, devoted mostly to the production of Chianti Classico, although there are 10 ha of Cabernet Sauvignon for the Monile super-Tuscan blend with Merlot, introduced in 1998. At the other extreme, Bere is an IGT Toscana blend from all the young vines. The Chianti Classico is Sangiovese with 2% Merlot, the Riserva has 5% Merlot and 5% Syrah, and Beatrice Gran Selezione has 5% Cabernet Sauvignon. Prunaia is a 100% Sangiovese, originally an IGT Toscana, but now a Chianti Classico Gran Selezione. All are aged in a mixture of Slavonian oak casks and barriques. Under the name of Tenuta I Greppi, the 15 ha vineyard in Bolgheri produces the Greppicaia Bordeaux blend, and its second wine, Greppicante. The only white wine is the small production of Greppico from Vermentino at Maremma. The wines are quite modern in style, and perfectly well made, but for me do not really exhibit the typicity of Tuscany. Supposedly it's possible to make an appointment to see the winery, but you are more likely to get a brief tasting in the tasting room.

Montepulciano

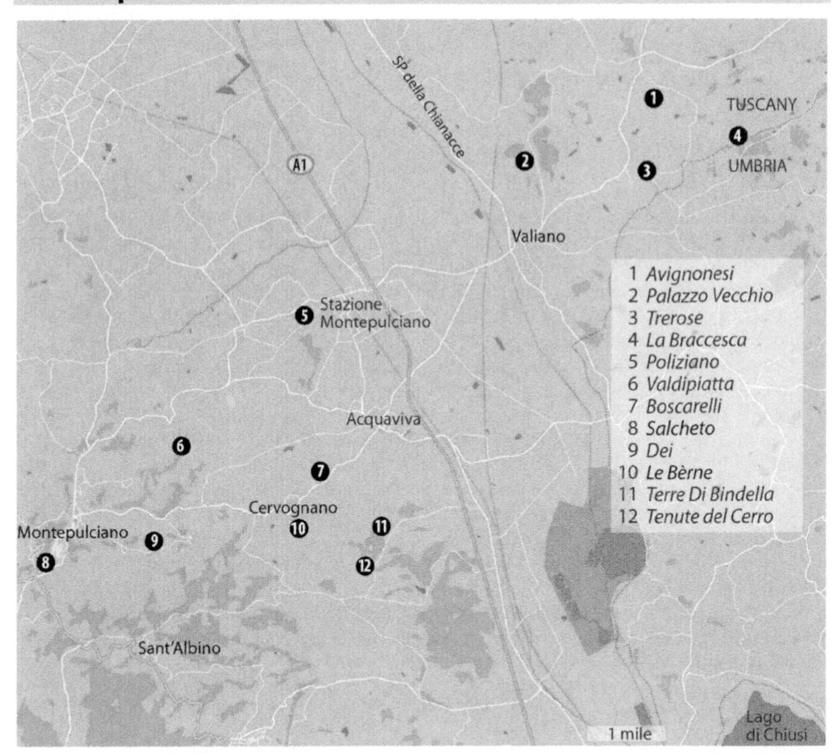

Profiles of Important Estates

Avignonesi

Via Colonica 1, 53045 Montepulciano	*+39 0578 75787234*
info@avignonesi.it	*Virginie Saverys*
www.avignonesi.it	*[map p. 93]*
	169 ha; 500,000 btl

Avignonesi is one of the oldest estates in Tuscany, founded by a family who followed the Pope from France to Italy in 1377. The Falvo brothers bought the property in 1974 and moved the focus towards indigenous varieties. Virginie Saverys, a lawyer in Belgium who was the heiress to a major shipping business, was a minority shareholder, and bought the company in 2009. The large estate includes seven properties, generally about 300m in altitude. Vine Nobile comes from the largest property, Le Capezzine. Other vineyards in the Cortona DOC, adjacent to the east, are planted with international varieties. Since the change of ownership, the focus on Sangiovese has increased. There's an ongoing project to map all the soils. There are several cuvees exclusively from Sangiovese. The Rosso di Montepulciano ages for 6 months in botti of Slavonian oak. The Vino Nobile ages mostly in botti with some barriques. Grandi Annate is based on selection of the best lots in the top years, and also ages in a mix of botti and barriques. Avignonesi is a member of the Alliance Vinum group of leading producers, and their cuvée is Poggetto di Sopra, which comes from a single plot of 40-year-old vines, and ages 75% in 2-year barriques and 25% in botti. Dai-Di is Sangiovese vinified entirely in terracotta amphorae made in Tuscany. Desiderio is a super-Tuscan from 100% Merlot, aged for 20 months in barriques with 15% new oak. 50:50 is an unusual cuvée, a blend of 50% Merlo from Avignonesi and 50% Sangiovese from Capannelle in Chianti Classico, aged in barriques. The domain is into oenotourism and offers a range of tours and tastings.

Podere Le Bèrne

Via di Poggio Golo, Loc. Cervognano, 53040 Montepulciano	*+39 0578 767328*
leberne@libero.it	*Andrea Natalini*
www.leberne.it	*[map p. 93]*
	12 ha; 50,000 btl

Egisto Natalini and his son Giuliano founded this estate in the top area of Cervagnano in the late 1960s. Half of the 21 hectares are planted with vines and another 3 ha are olive groves. Giuliano's son, Andrea, who now runs the estate, has been President of the Consorzio since 2012. All the DOCG wines are exclusively Sangiovese. The Rosso ages for 3 months in botti of Slavonian oak, the Vino Nobile for 24 months with 60% in 25 hl botti and 40% in French barriques, and the Riserva for 36 months with the proportions of cask sizes reversed. The IGT Toscana L'Affronto is an unusual blend of two indigenous varieties, Colorino and Mammolo, aged in stainless steel.

Bindella

Via Delle Tre Berte, 53100 Siena	*+39 0578 767777*
info@bindella.it	*Giovanni Capuano*
www.bindella.it	*[map p. 93]*
	54 ha; 190,000 btl

The Bindella family started with a wine shop in Zurich. The Italian connection was that Bindella was the first importer of Chianti into Switzerland. The company now owns forty restaurants in Switzerland. The winery was founded in 1983 when Rudi Bindella he bought the Tenute Vallocaia estate in rather dilapidated condition with a small area of vines. He bought more vineyards and built a winery in 1986. The winery was extended with contemporary buildings in 2020. The Rosso di Montepulciano, Rossulupaio, has a slightly unusual varietal mix, 85% Sangiovese with 15% Syrah; it ages in stainless steel. The Vino Nobile, Bindella, is 85% Sangiovese and 15% Colorino and Mammolo, and ages for 20 months in botti. The single vineyard I Quadri vineyard is more modern: 100% Sangiovese aged for 18 months in French oak. The Riserva, Vallocaia, is 90% Sangiovese and 10% Colorino, aged in mix of barrels and larger casks of French oak. "Many of our colleagues looked on doubtfully as we created the first Sauvignon Blanc," they say, but since 2004 this has been the basis for the IGT Toscana white, Gemella. Other IGT Toscana include varietal Syrah, Cabernet Sauvignon, and Merlot, aged in French oak

Boscarelli

Via Di Montenero 24/26, Loc. Cervognano, 53045 Montepulciano	*+39 0578 767277*
cantina@poderiboscarelli.com	*Luca & Nicolò De Ferrari*
www.poderiboscarelli.com	*[map p. 93]*
	22 ha; 100,000 btl

Egidio Corradi founded the estate in 1962 and his daughter Paolo ran it, at first with her husband, and then alone after he died in 1983. Today her sons are in charge, with Luca making the wine and Nicholò managing the vineyards. The winery and original vineyards are in the Cervagnano area, considered to be one of the best terroirs of Montepulciano. They are around 300m altitude, facing north and northeast. There is also a small holding in Cortona DOC. The entry-level wine is an IGT Toscana blend of 90% Sangiovese with 10% Merlot. Rosso di Montepulciano is a quarter of production, from 85% Sangiovese and 15% Mammolo, aged in concrete. Vino Nobile is half of production, from vines at least ten years old, also 85% Sangiovese, but with the rest a mix of Colorino, Canaiolo, and Mammolo. A Riserva was released until 1992 and then stopped as the vineyards were replanted with better clones: production resumed in 2010 when the vines were judged old enough. It is 88% Sangiovese and 12% Colorino, aged for more than 28 months as opposed to 18 months. The top Riserva comes from the small Sotto Casa vineyard, and is 80% Sangiovese, 15% Cabernet Sauvignon, and 5% Merlot, aged for 28 months. Boscarelli is a member of the Alliance Vinum group of leading producers, and produces a 100% Sangiovese from the 4 ha plot Il Nocio. Susino is a selection from the Vigna Grande vineyard that produces a wine in a more powerful style. The Vino Nobile cuvées age in French tonneaux and Slavonian botti. Boscarelli dei Boscarelli is a super-Tuscan of Sangiovese, Merlot, Cabernet Sauvignon, Syrah, and Petit Verdot, aged in barriques.

La Braccesca

Via Stella di Valiano, 10, 53045 Montepulciano	*+39 0578 724252*
visite@labraccesca.it	*Fabrizio Balzi*
www.antinori.it/tenuta/estates-italy/la-braccesca-estate	*[map p. 93]*
	340 ha; 550,000 btl

La Braccesca is Antinori's estate in Montepulciano, which was purchased in 1990. The 508 ha property is divided into two parts: the larger block has 237 ha of vineyards in Cortona DOC on the border with Montepulciano, mostly planted with Syrah and Merlot; the remaining 103 ha are spread among three areas in Montepulciano, mostly planted with Sangiovese. The Rosso di Montepulciano, Sabazio, is a blend of Sangiovese and Merlot, aged for 4 months in stainless steel. The estate Vino Nobile is the same blend, but ages in oak for 12 months. The Riserva is Sangiovese from the 15 ha vineyard of Santa Pia, located below the town of Montepulciano, with soils known locally as 'scheltro,' sandy loam with rocks,; it ages in tonneaux. La Braccesca is a member of the Alliance Vinum group of leading producers, and their single-vineyard Sangiovese cuvée comes from Podere Maggiarino, also aging in tonneaux. Achelo and Bramasole are cuvées of Syrah from Cortona; Achelo ages 30% in stainless steel and 70% in barriques, and Bramasole ages in barriques including new oak. The estate offers several activities in oenotourism, including a cooking school as well as tours and tastings.

Fattoria del Cerro

Via Grazianella, 5, Fraz. Acquaviva, 53045 Montepulciano	*+39 0578 767722*
fattoriadelcerro@tenutedelcerro.it	
www.tenutedelcerro.it	*[map p. 93]*
	181 ha; 1,300,000 btl

Fattoria del Cerro is one of five estates held by Tenute del Cerro, the viticultural holding company of Gruppo Unipol, one of Italy's largest insurance companies. The others are La Poderina in Montalcino, Monterufoli in Val di Cornia (Pisa), Colpetrone in Montefalco (in Umbria), and Montecorona (in Umbria).Fattoeria del Cerro covers 600 ha, and half (93 ha) of its vineyards are classified for Vino Nobile, making it the largest producer in the appellation. A Chianti Colli Senesi is 90% Sangiovese and 10% Canaiolo, aged in large wood casks. The Rosso di Montepulciano is 90% Sangiovese and 10% Mammolo, aged in barriques and tonneaux for 6 months. The first Vino Nobile, Silìneo, is Sangiovese and ages in botti for 18 months. Vigneto Antica Chuisina is 90% Sangiovese and 10% Colorino from a single parcel, aged for 12 months in barriques. The Riserva is 90% Sangiovese with 5% each of Colorino and Mammolo, aged for 18 months in barriques and tonneaux.

Cantine Dei

Via Di Martiena 35, Villa Martiena, 53045 Montepulciano	*+39 0578 716878*
info@cantinedei.com	*Caterina Dei*
www.cantinedei.com	*[map p. 93]*
	60 ha; 230,000 btl

Alibrando Dei founded the estate when he bought a vineyard in the Bossona cru in 1964. A few years later, he bought the Villa Martiena, a mile east of the town of Montepulciano, where the winery was built in 1989. His son, Glauco, had a business in marble, and the winery was constructed of travertine built into the hillside. Glauco's daughter Caterina took over in 1991. Vineyards are in several crus: the original holding in Bossona is calcareous, Martiena and Piaggia are mostly sandstone, Ciarlina is clay and limestone, and Cervognano is tufa and clay. The Rosso di Montepulciano is 90% Sangiovese with 5% each of Canaiolo and Merlot, aged for three month in botti of Slavonian oak. Vino Nobile is 90% Sangiovese and 10% Canaiolo, aged in botti for 18 months. The Riserva Bossona is 100% Sangiovese from the Cru, aged for 3 years on tonneaux. Dei is a member of the Alliance Vinum group of leading producers, and their 100% Sangiovese cuvée for the Alliance, Madonna della Querce, comes from a 1.5 ha plot facing south, aged in botti for 24 months. Sancta Catharina is a super-Tuscan blend with 30% each of Cabernet Sauvignon, Merlot, and Sangiovese, plus 10% Petit Verdot, aged in barriques with 50% new oak.

Palazzo Vecchio

Via Terra Rossa 5, Valiano, 53045 Montepulciano	+39 0578 724170
palazzovecchio@vinonobile.it	Marco and Luca Sbernadori
www.vinonobile.it	[map p. 93]
	7 ha; 45,000 btl

The Fattoria di Valiano was an important farm, dating from 1300, that was donated to a charity in 1552. It was sold in 1837 and became the basis for an agricultural research institute. Riccardo Zorzi purchased the central part of the land in 1970. He renovated the estate and began to focus on viticulture in the 1980s, producing his first Vine Nobile in 1990. He changed the name to Palazzo Vecchio, and handed the estate on to his daughter Alessandra, whose husband Marco Sbernadori and son Luca now run the winery. The Rosso di Montepulciano, the Vino Nobile Maestro, and the Riserva, are blends of 85% Sangiovese with 10% Canaiolo and 5% Mammolo, with Rosso aged for 4 months, Maestro for 24 months, and the Riserva for 36 months, in French oak. Vino Nobile Terrarossa is a selection of Sangiovese planted in the 1950s in the vineyard Vigna des Bosco, also aged for 24 months in French oak, only made in the best years from the part of the vineyards in Cortona DOC, there is an approachable blend of 85% Sangiovese with 15% Syrah, aged for 12 months in barriques.

Poliziano

Via Fontago 1, Fraz. Montepulciano Stazione, 53045 Montepulciano	+39 0578 738171
info@carlettipoliziano.com	Federico Carletti
carlettipoliziano.com	[map p. 93]
	170 ha; 650,000 btl

One of the leading producers in Montepulciano, Poliziano was founded when Dino Carletti bought 22 ha on 1961. The name refers to a humanist poet of the fifteenth century. Dino's son Federico took over in 1980. Vineyards are distributed all over the area, from around the town of Montepulciano in the west to beyond Valiano in the eastern sector. Overall 47 ha are used for Vino Nobile, 58 ha for Rosso di Montepulciano, 11 ha for Chianti Colli Senesi, 7 ha in Cortona DOC, and 20 ha for IGT Toscana. There are another 18 ha in Maremma for Morellino di Scansano. Wines ferment in tronconique stainless steel vats, followed by aging in oak barrels and casks of various sizes, in an aging cellar built in 2005. The Rosso di Montepulciano is the largest production, with around 250,000 bottles, and is 80% Sangiovese and 20% Merlot, aged partly in stainless steel and partly (20-40%) in oak. Vino Nobile increases Sangiovese to 85%, with Colorino, Canaiolo, and Merlot, aged two thirds in barriques and tonneau of French oak, and a third in vat. There are two single-vineyard wines from Montepulciano. The 12 ha Asinone is 100% Sangiovese in the best vintages, but other vintages may include 10% of Colorino and Canaiolo. It ages in French tonneaux. Poliziano is a member of the Alliance Vinum group of leading producers, and their top DOCG wine is the 100% Sangiovese cuvée from the single-vineyard Le Caggiole, aged in tonneaux for 16-18 months. Le Stanze is an IGT Toscana blend of Cabernet and Merlot aged in new barriques. The white is Ambrae, a blend of 80% Chardonnay with 20% Sauvignon Blanc, aged in stainless steel.

Salcheto

Via di Villa Bianca 15, 53045 Montepulciano	+39 0578 799031
enoteca@salcheto.it	Michele Manelli
www.salcheto.it	[map p. 93]
	58 ha; 390,000 btl

Michele Manelli took over the estate in 1997 and turned it into a showcase for a sustainable winery. The property was acquired by the Lavinia group (owners of the former famous wine shop in Paris) in 2003, but Michele continued to run the winery. The winery was gutted and rebuilt in 2011. Located just outside the town of Montepulciano, vineyards are at one of the highest points in the appellation, around 450m altitude. The Rosso di Montepulciano is 85% Sangiovese, 8% Canaiolo, and 7% Merlot, from the youngest vines and ages in stainless steel. Vino Nobile is 100% Sangiovese and ages in a mix of barrels and large casks for 18 months. This is the major wine, almost half of all production. The Riserva is 95% Sangiovese and 5% Colorino, and is unusual in using the old Governo method, where grapes are dried before fermentation; it ages in a mix of small and large oak. The top wines come from the Salco vineyard and are 100% Sangiovese. Salco ages for 24 months, 30% in botti and 70% in tonneaux, and Vecchie Viti del Salco comes from 2 ha of the oldest vines in the vineyard, aged half in botti and half in tonneaux. Salcheto is a member of the Alliance Vinum group of leading producers. There's an entry-level range in all three colors in IGT Toscana called Obvius.

Tenuta Valdipiatta

Via Della Ciarliana, 25/a, 53040 Gracciano Di Montepulciano	*+39 0578 757930*
info@valdipiatta.it	*Miriam Caporali*
www.valdipiatta.it	
	23 ha; 80,000 btl

Valdipiatta was founded in 1973 and acquired its present reputation after Giulio Caporali bought the estate in 1990. Giulio replanted the vineyards with more Sangiovese and expanded before excavating an underground cellar from the rock. Giulio's daughter Miriam took over in 2002. The approach is modernist, with wines aged in barriques from Alliers in France. The Rosso di Montepulciano is a blend of Sangiovese with Canaiola and Mammolo, aged in barriques; Vino Nobile is Sangiovese and Canaiolo, aged for 15-18 months in a mix of barriques and 30 hl and 50 hl botti of Slavonian oak; the Riserva is made only in top years from the same blend, and ages in a mix of French tonneaux and 30 hl botti; for 15-18 months; Vigna d'Alfiero is 100% Sangiovese from a single parcel, with the same aging. There is also a an entry-level Chianti Colli Senesi, Sangiovese and Canaiolo, briefly aged, sometimes in oak. The IGT Toscana range includes a Bordeaux blend, a blend of Sangiovese and Cabernet Sauvignon, and a Pinot Noir. The only white wine is the IGT Toscana Nibbiano, unusual in that half comes from immediate pressing of Sangiovese (effectively a Blanc de Noirs treatment), the other half from white varieties. The winery offers a range of tours and tastings.

Tenuta Trerose

Via Della Stella, 3, 53040 Montepulciano	*+39 0578 724018*
g.capitani@bertani.net	*Bertani Domains*
www.tenutatrerose.it	*[map p. 93]*
	101 ha; 600,000 btl

Pharmaceutical company Angelini moved into viticulture in 1994 by purchasing three domains in Tuscany: Tenuta San Leonino in Castellina in Chianti Classico, Val di Suga in Montalcino, and Tenuta Trerose in Montepulciano. They already owned Fazi Battaglia in the Marche, and subsequently purchased Tenuta Puaitti in Collio, and Bertani in Valpolicella. In 2014 they moved all the producers into a holding group called Bertani Domains. Trerose is in the eastern sector of the appellation, extending for 200 ha over five hills. The Rosso di Montepulciano, Salterio, is 90% Sangiovese with 10% of Merlot and Cabernet Sauvignon, aged in 55 hl casks of French oak and chestnut. Vino Nobile,

Villa Romizi (named after the Renaissance villa at the center of the estate) is 90% Sangiovese with 10% of Cabernet Sauvignon and Petit Verdot, aged for 6 months barriques followed by 18 months in 50 hl botti of Slavonian oak. Santa Catarina is a single-vineyard Vino Nobile, coming from the Santa Catarina hill, and is 100% Sangiovese, aged in a mix of 10, 30, and 40 hl casks. The Simposia Riserva is a selection from the best lots, aged in barriques for 12 months and 50 hl botti for 6 months. Borgo Tre Rose, a medieval hamlet that has been restored to become a hotel, is within the estate.

Brunello di Montalcino

1 *Silvio Nardi*
2 *Castiglion del Bosco*
3 *Donatella Colombini*
4 *Pertimali*
5 *Romitorio*
6 *Luce Della Vite*
7 *Villa Poggio Salvi*
8 *Sanlorenzo*
9 *Le Potazzine*
10 *Pian delle Vigne*
11 *Camigliano*
12 *Mocali*
13 *Centolani*
14 *Caprili*
15 *Case Basse*
16 *Gaja*
17 *Poggio Antico*
18 *Fattoi*
19 *Collemattoni*
20 *Argiano*
21 *Talenti*
22 *Il Poggione*
23 *Lisini*
24 *Podere Giodo*
25 *Banfi*
26 *Col d'Orcia*
27 *Piancornello*

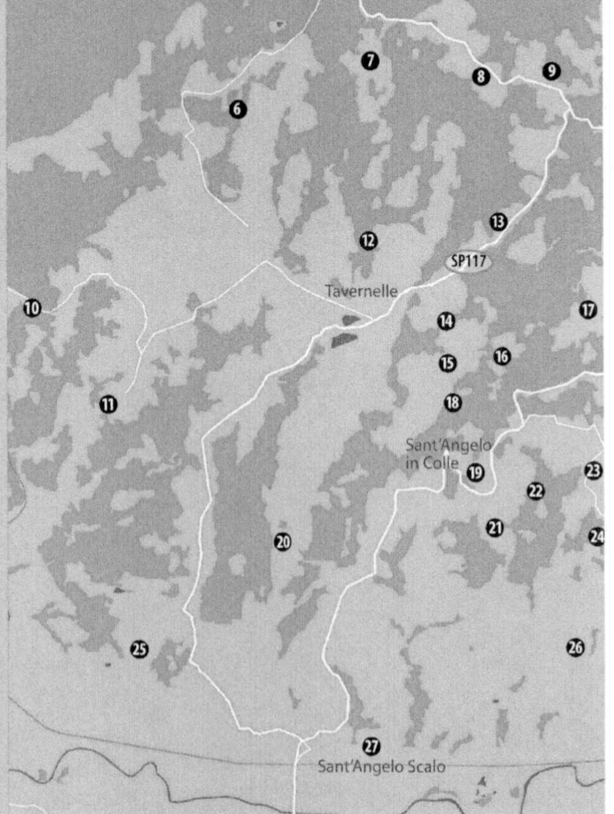

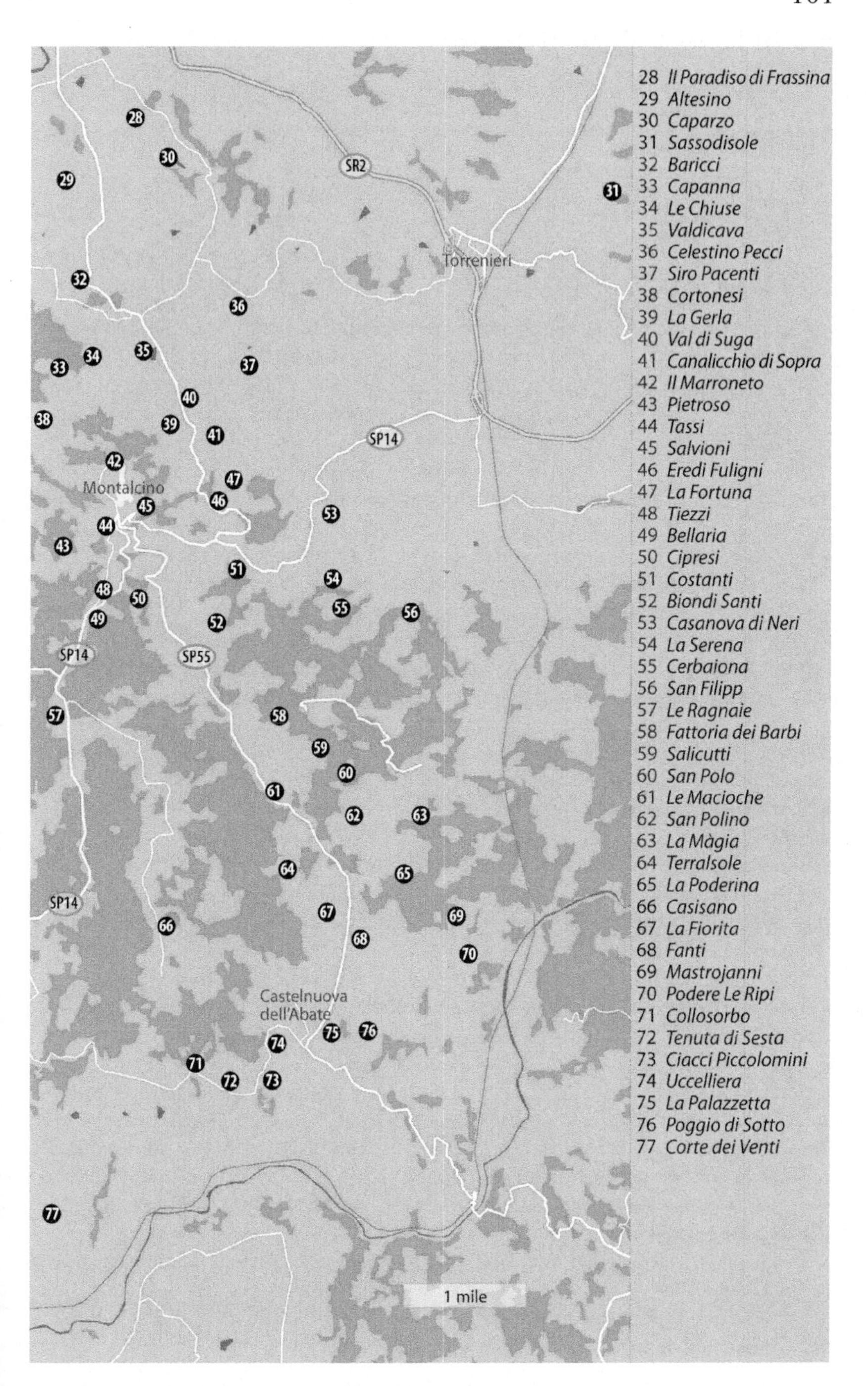
SR2
Torrenieri
SP14
Montalcino
SP55
Castelnuova dell'Abate
1 mile
28 Il Paradiso di Frassina
29 Altesino
30 Caparzo
31 Sassodisole
32 Baricci
33 Capanna
34 Le Chiuse
35 Valdicava
36 Celestino Pecci
37 Siro Pacenti
38 Cortonesi
39 La Gerla
40 Val di Suga
41 Canalicchio di Sopra
42 Il Marroneto
43 Pietroso
44 Tassi
45 Salvioni
46 Eredi Fuligni
47 La Fortuna
48 Tiezzi
49 Bellaria
50 Cipresi
51 Costanti
52 Biondi Santi
53 Casanova di Neri
54 La Serena
55 Cerbaiona
56 San Filipp
57 Le Ragnaie
58 Fattoria dei Barbi
59 Salicutti
60 San Polo
61 Le Macioche
62 San Polino
63 La Màgia
64 Terralsole
65 La Poderina
66 Casisano
67 La Fiorita
68 Fanti
69 Mastrojanni
70 Podere Le Ripi
71 Collosorbo
72 Tenuta di Sesta
73 Ciacci Piccolomini
74 Uccelliera
75 La Palazzetta
76 Poggio di Sotto
77 Corte dei Venti

Altesino **

Località Altesino 54, 53024 Montalcino	*+39 0577 806208*
info@altesino.it	*Simone Giunti*
www.altesino.it	*[map p. 101]*
47 ha; 220,000 btl	*Brunello Di Montalcino*

The northernmost producer in Montalcino, Altesino was owned by the Consonno family before being sold in 2002 to Elisabetta Angelini, owner of the adjacent Caparzo property. Altesino and Caparzo had been one property before 1970, but remain separate today. "Altesino is more masculine, it's on the north side of the hill, the weather is colder," Elisabetta says. About 18 ha of vineyards surround the winery, the 7 ha vineyard on the Montosoli hill is a couple of miles from the winery, and the remaining vineyards are in the south of Montalcino.

"It's important to have vineyards in both places because there are a lot of differences between north and south, and in some vintages the quality is different," says production manager Simone Giunti, expressing the traditional view that the best wines come from blends between the firmer south and more elegant north. Montosoli is the exception that makes a single-vineyard wine. Montosoli has long been regarded as special for the power of its wines, and Altesino were among the first to introduce the Cru concept into Montalcino when they started to make a separate cuvée in 1975. The vineyards are maintained using their own cultivars. "When we replant the vineyards we see a big difference between using our cultivars (which come from selection massale) and commercial clones," Simone says.

Vinification is traditional for the DOC wines. An entry-level IGT is 80% Sangiovese with Cabernet Sauvignon and Merlot. The grapes come from Montalcino, and can include some declassified from the DOC. It ages for 6 months in steel. Rosso di Montalcino is based on selection, but usually comes from more or less the same vineyards each year. It ages for a year in 100 hl botti. The Brunello ages in 50 hl botti and favors elegance rather than power. Riserva is only made some years. "During the harvest the best grapes are separated to see if they will make a Riserva, but the final decision isn't taken until the end of aging," Simone says.

Going from IGT to Rosso there is a big step-up in smoothness. The Rosso previews the Brunello, which is smoother, rounder, and more intense, but favors elegance over power. The Riserva has more evident structure behind its chocolaty tannins. Montosoli has an extra dimension, with greater density and structure. If you are looking for a wine to drink five years after the vintage, the Brunello is ready, but Montosoli needs more time, and will have the greatest longevity.

At one point, Altesino had more IGTs, but the number has been reduced to focus on the appellation. Barriques are used for the two super-Tuscans. Palazzo Altesi is 100% Sangiovese, but is labeled as IGT to distinguish it from the DOC wines. Alte d'Altesi is a blend of Sangiovese with Cabernet Sauvignon and Merlot.

Argiano **

Sant'Angelo In Colle, 53024 Montalcino	*+39 0577 844037*
argiano@argiano.net	*Bernardino Sani*
www.argiano.net	*[map p. 100]*
58 ha; 350,000 btl	*Brunello Di Montalcino*

One of the founding members of the Consorzio, Argiano is an old estate, but now undergoing a transition resulting from changes in ownership. Dating from the sixteenth century—the original villa from 1598 is still standing—it was owned by the Cinzano spirits company before it passed to Noemi Cinzano in 1992 after Cinzano was sold to a drinks conglomerate. Introducing French oak, she followed a generally modernist style, with the famous oenologist Giacomo Tachis as her consultant. About half of the vineyards are classified for Brunello, and another 7 ha of the youngest vines are dedicated to Rosso. It's located in the southwest, and Argiano sees itself as representing the warmer part of Montalcino.

Argiano was sold in 2013 to a group of Brazilian investors, who have put resources into replanting the vineyards and renovating the winery. Following a soil survey, vineyards are being changed, a new aging cellar was built in 2015, and a new vinification cellar is planned. "They are returning to tradition, using concrete vats for fermentation and MLF, and as of the 2015 vintage there won't be any use of French oak (in Brunello)," says Claudia Cherubini at Argiano. (Previously vinification in stainless steel was followed by aging in one year barriques and Slavonian botti for the Rosso, and in a mixture of barriques and tonneaux for the Brunello.)

The IGT Suolo, a monovarietal Sangiovese from the oldest vineyards, aged exclusively in new French barriques, has been discontinued. "The focus is on Brunello, they don't want to make an IGT from Sangiovese any more." A more conventional super-Tuscan, Solengo, with half Cabernet Sauvignon, and equal proportions of Petit Verdot, Merlot and Syrah, continues to be aged in new barriques of French oak. Introduced by Tachis, the intention was to show how powerful and long lived it could be. The most recent cuvée was the IGT NC (Non Confunditur), a blend of Cabernet Sauvignon, Merlot, Syrah, and Sangiovese, intended to be easy to drink and directed at the market in the United States; it is now almost half of all production. Argiano is definitely moving from the camp of the modernists towards tradition for its Brunello, with the IGTs remaining more international in style.

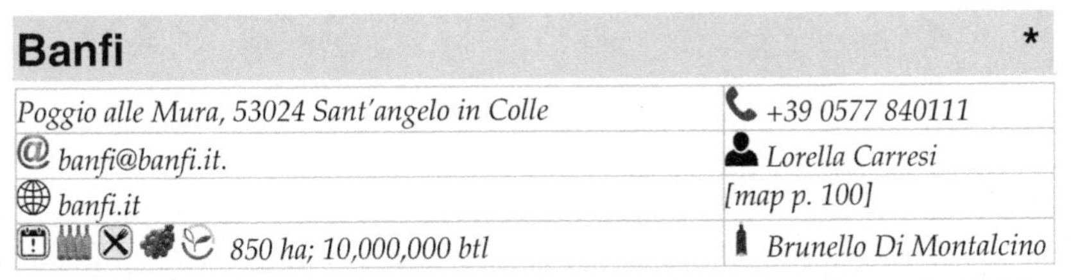

Banfi *

Poggio alle Mura, 53024 Sant'angelo in Colle	*+39 0577 840111*
banfi@banfi.it.	*Lorella Carresi*
banfi.it	*[map p. 100]*
850 ha; 10,000,000 btl	*Brunello Di Montalcino*

Banfi Wines was founded as an American importer of wines from Europe in 1919 by John Mariani and is run today by his grandchildren. Castello Banfi in Montalcino was

founded in 1978 with the purchase of vineyards in Chianti Classico, Bolgheri, and Maremma. It includes a complex of old buildings at the southern border of Montalcino, in the former hamlet of Poggio alle Mura, which also includes a hotel and restaurant. A purpose-built modern winery is nearby.

Vineyards were planted through a land-clearing program that involved removing several hills. Around the complex, six lakes have been constructed for irrigation (of IGT wines). Banfi is the largest producer in Montalcino, although somewhat controversial locally because a major part of its plantings started with international varieties. The winery is full of modern equipment, including tanks specially designed for Banfi which are stainless steel at top and bottom, but wood in between, designed to give the advantages of wood without hygiene problems. Winemaker Lorella Caresi says the tanks "give wine with better aromatics and color, although science does not explain the difference between wood and steel."

Banfi started by producing wines under all the DOCs of the region (Brunello and Rosso di Montalcino and Sant'Animo), but then moved away from Sant'Animo to the IGT Toscana—"no one knows Sant'Animo." So Summus (a blend of Sangiovese, Cabernet Sauvignon, and Syrah), Excelsus (a Merlot-Cabernet Sauvignon blend) are now super-Tuscans. These and the newer super-Tuscan cuvées are aged in barrels. The Rosso and Brunello di Montalcino age in a mixture of different wood sizes; the smallest barrels are usually 350 liters.

With about 30% new oak on average, there tends to be a noticeable oak in the super-Tuscans, and the Brunellos are quite powerful, often needing time for tannins to resolve. The single-vineyard wines, identified as Poggio alle Mura, come from the oldest vineyards, immediately by the castle (planted in 1984) and age mostly in barrels. There are both Rosso and Brunello from the Poggia alle Muro vineyard, and the structure is more evident than in the communal wines. The Poggio all'Oro super-cuvée, made only in top years, ages in only barrels. Banfi also produces Chianti Classico, and here you can see an influence from making Brunello: the Classico has a touch of obvious structure from some Cabernet Sauvignon, the Riserva has more fruits and better balance, and the Gran Selezione is quite dense and stern. There is an impression locally that the wines are intended to appeal to the American palate.

Fattoria Dei Barbi **

Loc. Pordernovi 170, Strada Consorziale dei Barbi, 53024 Montalcino	*+39 0577 841111*
info@fattoriadeibarbi.it	*Laura Cerundolo*
www.fattoriadeibarbi.it	*[map p. 101]*
66 ha; 600,000 btl	*Brunello di Montalcino*

"We have more or less lived the history of Montalcino," says Stefano Colombini, whose family came to the area in 1352. Initially they built a castle at Poggia alle Mura (now part of the Banfi estate), and they acquired the Barbi estate by marriage in 1790. The family also own estates in Chianti, and they purchased an estate in Maremma in 1997. The vine-

yards of the estate in Montalcino are mostly near the winery, but there are also rented vineyards elsewhere.

Barbi is firmly in the camp of traditional producers. "I believe in tradition, I believe we have to work in the spirit of tradition, but we need to use modern methods. So we have been pioneers for using dry ice for fermentation, we use the most modern stainless steel fermenters. We follow a mixture of the best traditions and the best techniques to produce Brunello that must be as similar to tradition as possible." Aging is mostly in large botti, but this is not rigid, with smaller casks used for smaller plots. And there's a distinction based on conditions. "We use smaller vats for wines that have more tannins. For lighter vintages we use larger vats."

Five wines come from the estate in Montalcino. Brusco dei Barbi, labeled as IGT Toscana, is a second wine from Sangiovese plus small amounts of indigenous varieties. Rosso di Montalcino comes from younger vines, and the Brunello is the major wine, about 40% of production; its blue label is one of the best known in Montalcino. The top two wines are made only in the best vintages: the Riserva is made by selection from the estate, and Vigna del Fiore is a selection from a single (5.7 ha) vineyard in the southern part of the appellation. Compared with the 200,000 bottles of Brunello, there are only 10,000 bottles of Riserva and 4,000 bottles of Vigna del Fiore.

The Rosso and Brunello show the same smooth style, with finely textured tannins, but the Brunello has more depth and flavor variety. The Riserva is more complex and structured. Vigna del Fiore shows greater silkiness on the palate, with more refinement rather than power. Stefano's objective is to make wines that can be drunk on release but that age well, and accordingly the Brunello 2011 was already ready to drink in 2016, but the Vigna Del Fiore needed another couple of years. The wines age for decades: a tasting at the winery showed the 2007 just beginning to develop, the 1986 still going strong, and the 1982 fully developed—after 35 years! Barbi is unusual in keeping back enough wines from each vintage that they can still offer quite old vintages for sale.

Biond-Santi Tenuta Greppo ***

Villa Greppo 183, 53024 Montalcino	*+39 0577 848023*
biondisanti@biondisanti.it	*Christopher Descours*
www.biondisanti.it	*[map p. 101]*
32 ha; 60,000 btl	*Brunello Di Montalcino*

This is really the grandfather estate for all Brunello since the appellation was more or less created by Biondi Santi in the nineteenth century. Ferruccio Biondi-Santi was instrumental in planting a strain of Sangiovese which he called Brunello (little brown one) at a time when most plantings were white. From phylloxera through the first part of the twentieth century, his son Tancredi Biondi-Santi was one of the few to continue producing Brunello. The estate was managed by Tancredi's son Franco from 1970, and by Franco's son Jacopo since 2013.

The tradition of selecting cultivars has continued with a project started in 1970 which culminated in development of clone BBS/11 (Brunello Biondi Santi), which is now used for replanting. The heart of the estate is the Greppo vineyard and winery just south of Montalcino (but sometimes a little difficult to find; people with morning appointments have been known to turn up in the afternoon...) Vineyards face east, with elevations up to 500m. There are also vineyards at Pieri (close to Il Greppo), and north of Montalcino, allowing Biondi-Santi to follow the traditional model of blending wines from the south and north. In fact, this is probably the most traditional producer in Montalcino; accordingly, the wines can be unbending when young, and require years to age. Cuvées are distinguished by age of vines.

The White Label Rosso di Montalcino comes from vines less than ten years old, the Fascia Rosso comes from older vines from lots that are declassified in the lesser vintages (the entire crop was declassified in 2002), the Annata Brunello comes from vines of 10-25 years age, and the Riserva comes from vines over 25 years only in top vintages. Needless to say, vinification is entirely traditional: after fermentation in cement tanks, the wine is transferred to Slavonian botti for aging. The wines tend to elegance rather than power, with that faintly savage quality of Sangiovese in the background, and the Brunello beginning to come around after a decade, the Riserva just a little longer. They remain the archetypal Sangiovese. Biondi-Santi is committed to Sangiovese even to the extent of making a 100% Sangiovese from a separate estate, the Castello di Montepo, in Maremma, but this is a quite different expression of the variety, softer and denser, and more southern.

Given the history in Montalcino, It was a shock when it was announced at the end of 2016 that a majority stake had been sold to the owners of Charles Heidsieck and Piper Heidsieck Champagne, although Jacopo continues to make the wine. Biondi Santi seems to have become more bureaucratic, and it's more difficult to make an appointment now.

Castello di Camigliano *

Via d'ingresso 2, 53024 Montalcino	*+39 0577 844068*
info@camigliano.it	*Sergio Cantini*
www.camigliano.it	*[map p. 100]*
92 ha; 350,000 btl	*Brunello di Montalcino*

When you arrive in the hamlet of Camigliano, the only sign of the winery is a shop and tasting room just below the village. The offices for the winery are in one of the houses just off the little square that is the center of the village. The old winery, and a new extension, are built unobtrusively into the hillside just beside the village (total population: 25). The estate of 500 ha is all around the village, at an elevation about 300m. It was acquired in 1957 by entrepreneur Walter Ghezzi, and today is run by his son Gualtiero.

Camigliano is a traditional producer. "We use large wood casks, I prefer big barrels, especially when the grapes are perfect, and I don't like to smell vanilla or wood in the wine. I don't like too much extract, which makes the first glass taste good, but not the second," says winemaker Sergio Cantini. Brunello is about half of total production, and the Rosso is about a quarter.

Camigliano is in the south of Montalcino, but the wine style is fresh. A white comes from a 2 ha plot of Vermentino and is quite lively. The entry-level red is an IGT Toscana, Poderuccia, a Merlot-Cabernet blend, with a little Sangiovese, intended for immediate consumption. A Chianti Colli Senesi comes from a negociant activity. The Rosso di Montalcino is distinct from the Brunello. "For us it is important the Rosso should be fresh and drinkable."

The Brunello makes a savory impression, quite fresh and crisp; the Gualto Riserva is more structured. A single-vineyard wine, Paessagia Inatteso (which means unexpected landscape) was introduced with the 2012 vintage (the next was 2015). It is matured in 25 hl barrels (compared with 60 hl for Brunello), and moves more towards black fruits. Whereas the Brunello is ready five years after the vintage, Paessagia Inatteso is more structured and requires longer. The wines are a solid representation of the traditional style.

Canalicchio di Sopra ***

Loc. Casaccia, 53024 Montalcino	*+39 0577 848316*
info@canalicchiodisopra.com	*Francesco Ripaccioli*
www.canalicchiodisopra.com	*[map p. 101]*
20 ha; 70,000 btl	*Brunello di Montalcino*

"Our wines are an expression of the blend between Canalicchio and Montosoli," says winemaker Francesco Ripaccioli, who runs this estate with his brother Marco (who manages the vineyards) and sister Simonetta. The estate was founded by Primo Pacenti in 1962, Primo's son-in-law, Pier Luigi Ripaccioli joined in 1987, and now it is in the hands of the third generation. The property is just off the main road going north from Montalcino, and although it looks entirely modern, there's a huge excavation for building a new underground cellar. It is focused entirely on Brunello.

The original vineyards are in Canalicchio—just on the other side of the road from the winery is the original house together with a hotel—and the vineyards on Montosoli came into the family in 1985. An extra 2 ha were planted in 2014 and another 2 ha were purchased in 2015; "it wasn't the right moment, " says Francesco, "because we are building a new cellar and this is a very big investment, but the plot was in the middle of our vineyards so we decided to buy." Presently 70% of the vineyards are in Canalicchio and 30% on Montosoli hill. "We are one of the few producers to have vineyards only in the north. The two zones of production are very close but very different. Our wine represents the north side of Montalcino but it also represents our style; the minerality comes from Montosoli and the richness comes from Canalicchio."

The major distinction between cuvées is age of the vines, with vines of 3-10 years age used for Rosso, 10-25 years for Brunello, and the oldest vines for the Riserva (in the best vintages only). The Rosso ages in an equal mix of French tonneaux and Slavonian botti, the Brunello only in Slavonian botti, and the Riserva uses tonneaux followed by botti. The Rosso shows a fine balance between red fruits and minerality, the Brunello is more powerful and complex, more black fruits than red, but retains that characteristic balance with minerality although showing more vintage variation—"we like to make different wines depending on the vintage," says Francesco—and the Riserva (made only 15 times since 1970) shows the rich side of Brunello, but matures in the elegant house style. For me, the Brunello is the perfect compromise.

Although the Ripacciolis believe in blending, the current project is to introduce a single-vineyard wine with the 2015 vintage. This is Vigna Casaccia—"this is the most elegant vineyard we have, not the best, but the most elegant." Barrel samples promise a wine with the richness of the vintage but the elegance of the house style. I believe that right across the range, these were the most elegant wines I tasted on my most recent visit to Montalcino.

Caparzo **

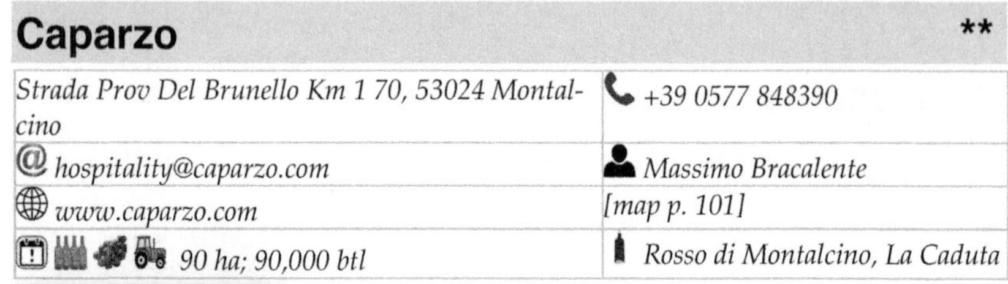

Strada Prov Del Brunello Km 1 70, 53024 Montalcino	*+39 0577 848390*
hospitality@caparzo.com	*Massimo Bracalente*
www.caparzo.com	*[map p. 101]*
90 ha; 90,000 btl	*Rosso di Montalcino, La Caduta*

Caparzo was founded in 1970, just after the establishment of the Consorzio in Brunello. By the nineties, after several changes of ownership, it was somewhat in decline, until it was purchased by Elisabetta Gnudi Angelini in 1998, when vineyards were replanted and the winery was modernized. Elisabetta also owns Borgo Scopeto in Chianti Classico, and DOGA delle Clavule in Maremma. After Caparzo, she subsequently bought the adjacent Altesino property, but "Caparzo is on the south side of the hill, it's more feminine, but very strong," she says.

The estate covers 200 hectares, with nine separated vineyards in several different areas of the appellation devoted to Brunello. The most famous is La Casa, a 5 ha vineyard on the hill of Montosoli with galestro terroir, which has been the basis of a single-vineyard wine since 1977. Production is poised between modernism and tradition. The "classic" Rosso, Brunello, and Riserva are blends from vineyards in both the north and south, and are aged only in large casks, but the two single-vineyard wines, Brunello La Casa and Rosso La Caduta use tonneaux of French oak. The Riserva comes from La Casa, La Caduta, and Il Cassero. Rosso La Caduta is an unusual Rosso, coming from a single vineyard, a plot of 7.5 ha in the south of the appellation; the explanation is that "the winemaker really wanted to do it." The super-Tuscan, Cà del Pazzo is a blend of Sangiovese and Cabernet Sauvignon, aged only in tonneaux, and there is also a dry white wine, Le Grance, that ages in small barrels.

The style is rich and firm, more modern than traditional, and going from the Rosso La Caduta or Brunello to the Riserva and La Casa, the wines become denser and more chocolaty; overall the style is more modern than traditional.

Caprili **

F.lli Bortolommei, 53024 Montalcino	*+39 0577 848566*
info@caprili.it	*Giacomo Bartolommei*
www.caprili.it	*[map p. 100]*
21 ha; 110,000 btl	*Brunello di Montalcino*

The Bartolommei family were tenants on the Villa Santa Restituta estate in the southwest quadrant of Montalcino, until they purchased the Caprili property in 1965. "They were making wine, but it was just table wine," says Giacomo Bartolommei. The estate has 60 ha, including 18 ha of Sangiovese, 3 ha of white grape varieties, and 4 ha of olive trees. Vineyards are maintained by an equal mix of selection massale from the original vineyard, and a clone Giacomo found in Chianti. "We want a clone where the berries are not too large and the bunches are not too compact," Giacomo explains. The new winery, completed in 2015, and built on two levels into the hillside, sits in the middle of what feels like a broad plateau extending to mountains in the distance.

The first Brunello dates from the 1978 vintage, and since 1983 the Riserva has been made from the oldest vines (dating from 1955) in the best vintages, thirteen times to date. It essentially comes from one 3,000 liter cask. The Rosso comes from the youngest vines. "We consider ourselves a traditionalist in using large casks for aging. Just in the past few years we've started to use some smaller sizes (700 liter)," says Giacomo. Wood is mostly Slavonian oak, with a little French. The style shows a classic progression from the light, attractive palate of the Rosso to the refined palate of the Brunello, where fruits make a precise impression on the palate. Purity of the fruits of Sangiovese drives the palate, which is traditional in prizing elegance over power. The IGTs include a red from Sangiovese and a white from Vermentino; there's also a Sant'Antimo white as a "hobby wine," which is aged in barrique, and a sweet Moscadello.

Casanova di Neri *

Podere Fiesole, 53024 Montalcino	*+39 0577 834455*
info@casanovadineri.com	*Giacomo Neri*
www.casanovadineri.com	*[map p. 101]*
65 ha; 220,000 btl	*Brunello di Montalcino, Cerretalto*

"We believe our vineyards give us the possibility to produce three different expressions of Montalcino," says Giacomo Neri. Giacomo's father bought the estate in 1971, and it has remained a family property. A modern winery operating by gravity feed on three levels was built into the hillside in 2005, just beside the house where the tasting room and offices are located. The vineyards are located in several areas, some around the winery in the northeast, some farther east, and some to the south at Sant'Angelo.

The entry-level wines are IGT Toscana, one white and one red. The Rosso comes from dedicated vineyards. "To us it's the first wine of our hierarchy, not a second wine," says Giacomo, who regards the IGT as the second label (the red is a blend of Sangiovese with Colorino). I find the Rosso easy going. The Brunello, known as the white label, comes from three vineyards in the northeast; aged in botti, it gives more structured impression, but remains generally soft in its approach. Then there are three single-vineyard wines, or perhaps more accurately, three single terroir wines.

Coming from the most recently acquired vineyards, Figurante represents two vineyards, one the highest of the estate in the northeast, the other on a plateau in the east. Tenuta Nuova comes from two very similar vineyards at high elevation in the south, where conditions are dry, and represents the more opulent side of Montalcino. Cerretalto comes from the oldest vineyard, close to the winery, at one of the coolest locations in Montalcino (it ripens three weeks after Nuova): it has by far the most structured impression. Made only in the best vintages, and aged in small barrels for an extra year, it could be a Riserva, but "Cerretalto is Cerretalto," Giacomo says.

Made since 2000, the super-Tuscan monovarietal Cabernet Sauvignon, Pietradonice, comes from a vineyard in the south, and even after a decade's aging conveys a powerful impression of warm climates; "this is a Montalcino version of Cabernet," according to Giacomo. The style here ranges from the quaffable IGT or Rosso, to more solid Brunello, and expressions of terroirs ranging from mineral to opulent.

Case Basse Di Soldera ***

Loc. Case Basse, 53204 Montalcino	*+39 0577 848567*
soldera@casebasse.it	*Monica Soldera*
www.soldera.it	*[map p. 100]*
10 ha; 15,000 btl	*IGT Toscana Soldera Casse Basse*

"My wine, like all the finest wine in the world, is simply not for everyone," said Gianfranco Soldera, which gives a pretty good impression of the prickly personality behind what were formerly some of the best wines of Brunello di Montalcino. "Formerly," because after a disagreement with the Consorzio in 2013, Gianfranco resigned, and then was expelled just to make sure; since then the wines have been labeled as IGT Toscana.

It can be difficult to track the identity of the individual cuvées. When Gianfranco, then an insurance broker, bought the estate in 1972, the land had been more or less abandoned, and he planted two vineyards, Case Basse and Intistieti, about 400m apart, more or less at the same elevation of 320m. The Brunello used to come sometimes from Case Basse, sometimes from a blend of the two vineyards. Riservas might come from either or both. At one period there was a Vino da Tavola labeled Intistieti, but actually coming from both vineyards; this was effectively a second wine. The current IGT Toscana is a blend from both vineyards.

Gianfranco is one of the most vociferous advocates for keeping Brunello as 100% Sangiovese, so it is not surprising that winemaking is traditional: the underground cellar was constructed using only natural materials (stone and iron), grapes are destemmed and go into vats of Slavonian oak, and the temperature of fermentation (by indigenous yeast only, of course) is not controlled; malolactic fermentation usually starts immediately the alcoholic fermentation has finished, and then the wine ages for four or five years in Slavonian botti. Gianfranco had strong views on barriques: "they are for deficient wines that don't get enough tannins and flavor from the grapes."

The wine is held in the cellar before release; the 2013 was the most recent vintage on the market in 2019. Intended to be the definitive description of Sangiovese, the wines are certainly the most expensive coming from Montalcino. Gianfranco died early in 2019; the domain continues under his wife Monica.

Castiglion del Bosco *

Località Castiglion del Bosco, 53024 Montalcino	*+39 0577 1913750*
wine@castigliondelbosco.com	*Filippo Lazzerini*
wine.castigliondelbosco.com	*[map p. 100]*
62 ha; 250,000 btl	*Brunello di Montalcino, Campo del Drago*

The hamlet of Castiglion del Bosco used to be a commune focused on producing honey and wine. Today the hamlet has been turned into a hotel; the spa is where the communal winery used to be. After Massimo Ferragamo purchased Castiglion del Bosco in 2003, a new gravity-feed winery was built just along the road. Ferragamo's ownership shows in the professional arrangements for hospitality: most visitors come from the hotel. There is a wine club (with its own room in the winery), and there are events and dinners.

There are two separate vineyards. Just to the south, the main vineyard of 42 ha, south-facing at 420m elevation with classic galestro soils, produces Brunello. Just east of the hotel, on slightly lower ground with more clay, a 20 ha vineyard produces Rosso di Montalcino. A single-vineyard wine, Campo del Drago, comes from a 1 ha plot at the northeast corner of the main vineyard: this is the highest elevation, with the best exposure. The Riserva comes from 8 ha close by.

The style has been changing towards a more traditional approach, but is still more modernist than traditionalist. "The market makes it sensible for us to produce wine that people can drink immediately," says Communication Manager Anna Malvezzi. Aging regimes differ with the cuvée. "Before Ferragamo came in 2003, there was a very French style here, with lots of barriques. Now we are trying to go back to tradition and we are buying larger casks for aging." The Brunello ages for one year in small casks and one year in large casks. Campo del Drago spends two years in barriques. The Riserva spends three years in large casks.

Intended for immediate consumption, the Rosso is fresh and lively. The Brunello adds some weight, but the overall impression remains fresh. Campo del Drago shows greater refinement, with a smooth roundness reflecting its time in barriques. The Riserva shows a greater sense of power and an increased sense of concentration. The overall impression remains relatively modern.

Massimo also has a winery on the Tuscan coast, Prima Pietra, north of Bolgheri, making a Bordeaux blend. There are plans to introduce a limited edition all-Cabernet blend of 85% Cabernet Sauvignon with 15% Cabernet Franc. The wines were made at Castiglion del Bosco until 2017, when a new cellar was built at Prima Pietra.

Cerbaiona ***

Località Cerbaiona, 53024 Montalcino	*+39 0342 9057826*
fioretti@cerbaiona.com	*Matthew Fioretti*
www.cerbaiona.com	*[map p. 101]*
4 ha; 20,000 btl	*Brunello di Montalcino*

"This destination is not on the digital map," the GPS announced, when I entered the coordinates for Cerbaiona, but we knew the destination was in sight when we saw the huge crane looming over the construction. The buildings were in full flight of reconstruction with a two year project to renovate and extend the cellars, improve the vineyards, and plant a new vineyard. Cerbaiona is one of the mythic producers of Brunello, created when Diego Molinari left Alitalia in 1977, and instead of flying planes, began making wine. Winemaking might have been called idiosyncratic rather than traditional, with vinification in cement tanks with fiber glass lining, and aging in very old botti. But the wines won worldwide acclaim.

Cerbaiona was a manor house, and the east-facing vineyards just below the house are adjacent to the La Cerbaiola estate. Cerbaiona was purchased in 2015 by a group of investors led by Matthew Fioretti, a Californian who spent some of his education in Italy, and started in wine by importing Italian wines into the United States. Now he is living at Cerbaiona and managing the massive reconstruction. "I thought we could do it one step at time, but I realized we would have to do everything at once," Matthew explains. Just below the house a 1 ha olive grove has been replanted with vines, and an additional vineyard may be added at slightly higher elevation (the estate is at 450 m).

"The Molinaris were the ultimate garagistes, making some wine in the basement," is how Matthew describes the previous situation. Working around the construction, the current vintage is being made in new equipment, with wood fermenters and new botti. So there may be a bit more wood showing for the next year or so. Tastings of the Rosso and Brunello presently maturing in botti show the characteristic combination of density with elegance. Will there be any permanent change in style? "Well, it's the vineyards that count," Matthew says, but there will be better handling of the fruit, so look for increased purity in the wine. Estate grapes provide 75% of production, the rest are purchased.

Ciacci Piccolomini d'Aragona *

Località Molinello, Castelnuovo Dell'abate, 53024 Montalcino	*+39 0577 835616*
marketing@ciaccipiccolomini.com	*Alessandra Avanzati*
www.ciaccipiccolomini.com	*[map p. 101]*
	Brunello di Montalcino, Pianrosso
56 ha; 300,000 btl	*Sant'Antimo, Fabius*

The winery name reflects the conjunction of two families, Ciacci and Picolimini d'Aragona, in an arranged marriage in 1921. In 1985, the Countess died without progeny and left the estate to the winemaker, Giuseppe Bianchini. He designed and built the new facility in 2003. His children Paulo and Lucia took over in 2004.

The estate of 220 ha is on the unpaved road between Saint Angelo and Castelnuova dell'Abate. In addition to vines, it has 40 ha of olive trees. A new winery was built into the hillside in 2003; previously the wine was made in the Palazzo (acquired from the Church in the nineteenth century) in the village of Castelnuova dell'Abate. A wine shop and tasting room were built on the other side of the road in 2013.

"We are absolutely a traditional producer," says Alessandra Avanzati. "Everything is aged in 60-75 hl botti of Slavonian oak. We think the Slavonian oak is less aggressive, softer, than French or American oak. We are looking for the elegance of Sangiovese rather than the power of oak." The Rosso ages for a few months, a second Rosso, called Rossofonte, for a year, Brunello for 36 months, and Riserva for 42 months.

The estate produces two Rosso di Montalcino, and three Brunellos in top vintages. The classic Rosso is soft and approachable and comes from dedicated vineyards. Produced in smaller amounts, Rossofonte is declassified from Brunello, and is more restrained, intense, and structured, but still shows the juiciness of Rosso. It bears much the same relationship to the classic Rosso as the Riserva does to the regular Brunello. Most of the vineyards are at 250-350m, but the Riserva and single-vineyard wine, Pianrosso, come from 7 plots at 180m, totaling 12 ha, just above the river Orcia, in a warm area that has the oldest vines. Pianrosso is the most sophisticated of the Brunello cuvées, smooth and silky, with precise mineral impressions. The Brunellos make a more modern impression than might be expected from the traditional production methods.

The estate produces two wines under Sant'Antimo DOC from international varieties, aged in barriques. Ateo's name is a joke, meaning atheist (as opposed to Sangiovese's meaning of God). It started in 1989 as a blend of Cabernet Sauvignon, Merlot, and Sangiovese, but it has been a Bordeaux blend since the Sangiovese was removed in 2007. It shows more the plushness of Merlot than austerity of Cabernet, although it has 50% of each. Fabius is a monovarietal Syrah made from a 2 ha plot since 1996: its style follows the Northern Rhône, and it has the lowest alcohol of any of the Ciacci wines. There is also an entry-level IGT Toscana based on Sangiovese plus some international varieties. In addition, Ciacci owns Santo Stefano in Grosseto, which produces a Montecucco Sangiovese.

Col d'Orcia **

Col d'Orcia, Via Giuncheti, 53024 Montalcino	*+39 0577 80891*
info@coldorcia.it	*Count Francesco Marone Cinzano*
www.coldorcia.it	*[map p. 100]*
149 ha; 800,000 btl	*Rosso di Montalcino, Banditella*

Located on the Sant'Angelo hill, this is a beautiful property with vineyards all around the complex of stone buildings at the end of a long unpaved road. In the thirteenth century, Fattoria di Sant'Angelo included 32 farms; it remained as a single estate until 1956 when

it was split between two brothers. One half of the original estate, Col d'Orcia was purchased by Alberto Cinzano in 1973, and Francesco took over in 1992. The winery is at 100m elevation, and vineyards extend to 350m.

Col d'Orcia is one of the larger producers in Montalcino (with 108 ha registered for Brunello), but still retains the feel of a small family winery. Vineyards are planted with 18 clones that were developed on the property. The approach to viticulture and winemaking is traditional, looking for subtlety rather than extraction. "We pick each vineyard three to four times," says Francesco Cinzano, "not necessarily waiting for the highest ripeness at each picking; some are picked to preserve acidity, some are picked to get high sugar levels. Our intention is to get a good blend of acidity, sugar, and phenolics in the wine."

"This is the largest traditional cellar in Montalcino, we follow the old style," Francesco says, as we go into a huge cellar filled with 150 hl botti to sample current vintages. The Rosso ages for a year, Brunello ages for 36 months as in the old protocol, and the Riserva age for 48 months. However, there was a change of style in 2009. "In the last century, people were proud of how long they kept wines on the skins and extracted, but now e are using a lighter hand," Francesco explains. "We have reduced maceration before fermentation by more than half." This shows itself by greater generosity in the modern wines.

The Rosso makes a smooth, elegant, almost perfumed red fruit impression. The Brunello moves towards black fruits and a more mineral impression with a great sense of precision. Based on selection, the Riserva is deeper yet and ages for a very long time: the 1978 was still vibrant and lively in 2018. The top wine is the single vineyard Poggio al Vento Riserva, which comes from a single plot in the center of the estate, and is made about one year in two. The current release, the 2010, is still undeveloped: the 1995 has come into its own and is now at its peak, although it will easily last another decade or so.

Francesco believes you get the best results for Sangiovese by reducing oxidative exposure, so the traditional DOC wines age in botti, but there are also some cuvées that age in smaller casks. The Rosso comes from selection at harvest with young vines as a major source, but has now been divided into a simple Rosso and the Banditella Rosso. "We felt there was a big gap between Rosso with one year aging and Brunello with 5 years aging," Francesco explains, so the Banditella Rosso is a selection that is aged mostly in tonneaux. It retains the elegance of the house, but with a more modern aspect due to faint impressions of oak. As the result of experiments with alternative aging methods, there is also now a Nastagio cuvée of Brunello which is aged in tonneaux and barriques for a year, followed by 2-3 years in botti. It's richer and more aromatic than the regular Brunello.

International varieties are labeled under the Sant'Animo DOC: Olmaia is a monovarietal Cabernet Sauvignon, and Nearco is a blend of Cabernet, Merlot, and Syrah. The elegance of the house style comes through even here.

Donatella Cinelli Colombini *

Casato Prime Donne, Loc Casato, 53024 Montalcino	*+39 0577 849421*
casato@cinellicolombini.it	*Antonella Marconi*
www.cinellicolombini.it	*[map p. 100]*
17 ha; 90,000 btl	*Brunello di Montalcino Riserva*

This is a relatively new estate as an independent venture, but a very old one in terms of the history of the family and the region. The Colombini family owned Barbi (in southeast Montalcino), Casato Prime Donne (in northwest Montalcino), and Fattoria del Colle (in the Orcia region to the northeast). "The estate was inherited from my grandmother to my mother, who divided it in 1998," explains Donatella, who now runs both Casato Prime Donne and Fattoria del Colle. At Casato Prime Donne she produces Rosso and Brunello di Montalcino [before 1998 the grapes went into Barbi (see profile), which is now a separate estate]; at Fattoria del Colle she produces IGT Toscana and Orcia Sangiovese-based blends. Casato Prime Donne and Fattoria del Colle each has roughly the same area of vineyards. The same team, consisting exclusively of women, makes the wine at both.

The estate is in a single parcel, located on a very long unpaved road, but can be quite busy when coach parties arrive at the tasting room. The winery is behind the old buildings. "This was all in disrepair, I had to rebuild it," Donatella says. There are four wines: Rosso and Brunello each account for about 45% of production; Selection Prime Donna and Riserva are about 5% each. Lots are assigned to Rosso on the basis of ripeness—"when you taste, it is obvious which should be Rosso and which should be Brunello," Donatella says. "Prime Donna is a selection from a plot where the quality is better every vintage, but no one has explained why."

"We are a traditionalist: wines are aged in botti. The innovation here is a return to the past; in the Middle Ages, vats were small and open, so that's what we use here," she says. "The open tops mean the wine gets oxygenation during fermentation, and we get a better balance." Quantities for Selection Prime Donna and the Riserva are small, so the wines are fermented in concrete eggs rather than vats. The Brunello ages in tonneaux for a year and then for another year in Slavonian foudres. Selection and the Riserva age for longer in botti, and go back in the concrete eggs for six months before bottling.

The Rosso is immediately approachable with a hint of structure at the end. The Brunello is a little deeper, and a classic representation of Sangiovese, tending towards a savory flavor spectrum, the Riserva is riper and if anything more approachable, and Prime Donna moves in a more chocolaty direction. Going from Brunello to Riserva to Prime Donne, the wines become more finely textured and silkier, more elegant rather than more powerful. I would be inclined to describe the style as moving from more traditional towards more modern along the series.

Conti Costanti *

Loc. Colle Al Matrichese, Via San Saloni 33, 53024 Montalcino	*+39 0577 848195*
info@costanti.it	*Andrea Costanti*
www.costanti.it	*[map p. 101]*
10 ha; 50,000 btl	*Brunello di Montalcino*

The Costanti family moved to Montalcino after being on the losing side in the battle for Siena in the sixteenth century. This is one of the oldest wineries in Montalcino, claiming to be second only to Biondi Santi. Costanti started growing Sangiovese in the nineteenth century, producing a red wine that they called Brunello in 1865. Just outside the town of

Montalcino, the winery consists of a group of long, low buildings, with vineyards were planted on 10 ha of galestro soils in the 25 ha estate in the 1970s. Andrea Costanti, a geologist by training, took over in 1983 from his uncle Emilion.

Production is split between 15,000 bottles of Rosso and 35,000 of Brunello (including about 7,000 Riserva when one is made). The Rosso is based on selection. The view here is that Rosso is a completely different wine from Brunello—"it is meant for enjoying young, whereas Brunello is a wine for aging"—and it ages for one year in tonneaux, whereas the Brunello and Riserva both age for one year in tonneaux followed by two years in botti of Slavonian oak. However, in the difficult vintage of 2014, the Brunello was declassified to a special cuvée, the Vermiglio Rosso, which aged for a year in a mixture of tonneaux and botti, and this is being continued as a second Rosso, intermediate in style between the original Rosso and the Brunello.

The house style is firm. The Rosso is relatively powerful, the Vermiglio Rosso is quite weighty, and the Brunello is firmly structured, although the tannins tend to be hidden behind the black fruits. The impression overall is quite traditional. The only wine that is not DOC is Ardingo, a Merlot IGT Toscana coming from a 2 ha plot in the north.

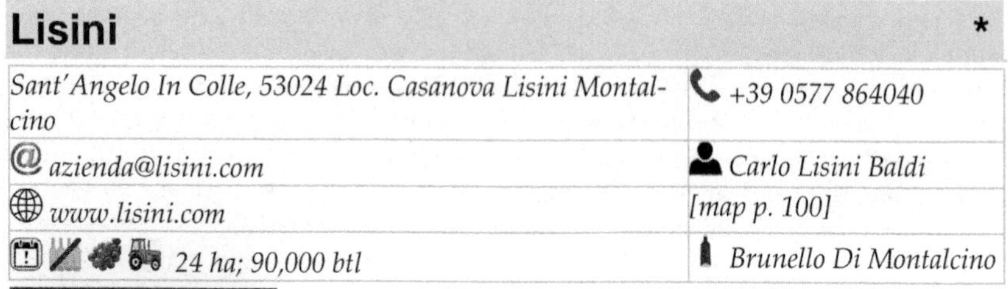

Lisini *

Sant'Angelo In Colle, 53024 Loc. Casanova Lisini Montalcino	*+39 0577 864040*
azienda@lisini.com	*Carlo Lisini Baldi*
www.lisini.com	*[map p. 100]*
24 ha; 90,000 btl	*Brunello Di Montalcino*

One of the oldest estates in Montalcino, the property has been in the family since the mid nineteenth century, and was one of the founding members of the Brunello Consorzio in 1967. Today it's run by third generation cousins Lorenzo, Carlo, and Ludovica. The estate covers 154 ha, of which only a small part is planted to vineyards. The oldest plantings of the modern era date from the 1930s, although within the estate there's an isolated half hectare vineyard with pre-phylloxera vines dating from the mid-nineteenth century, and for more than twenty years from 1985 this was bottled as the separate prefillossero cuvée, until production from the vineyard became too low.

The vineyards are exclusively devoted to Sangiovese, planted with clones that were developed on the estate. Vinification is traditional, with fermentation in glass-lined or stainless steel tanks followed by maturation in Slavonian botti, briefly for the Rosso, longer for Brunello and the Riserva, which comes from a selection of the best lots. There is also a single-vineyard wine, Ugolaia, from a 1.5 ha vineyard high up in the estate. The IGT San Biagio is effectively a second wine that is aged only in stainless steel. The style is pure Sangiovese, with a savory palate showing some savage hints, a classic representation of the unsullied variety.

Tenuta Luce **

Loc. Castelgiocondo, 53024 Montalcino	*+39 0577 841311*
info@lucewines.it	*Lamberto Frescobaldi*
www.lucedellavite.com	*[map p. 100]*
88 ha; 400,000 btl	*IGT Toscana, Luce*

Adjacent to Castelgiocondo, which is Frescobaldi's estate in Montalcino, Luce della Vite started in 1995 as a joint project between Frescobaldi and Robert Mondavi of Napa Valley. It became Frescobaldi's alone in 2006 after Mondavi was sold to Constellation. In 2016, they purchased the 55 ha neighboring estate (formerly Logonovo), including 11 ha of vineyards and a new underground winery, which is now used to produce Luce.

The focus is really on a super-Tuscan blend of Sangiovese and Merlot, not on Brunello. The first two vintages of Luce, 1993 and 1994, the super-Tuscan, were released together in 1997. It's 55% Sangiovese and 45% Merlot, and aged in French barriques with 85% new oak. The style is powerful, dense, and international.

Lucente is a second wine, from the same vineyards, and has been made since the 1995 vintage. It's 70% Merlot and 30% Sangiovese, and ages in a mix of new and used barriques. It follows the same international style as Luce, but is not so intense. There are generally up to 100,000 bottles of Luce and 300,000 of Lucente.

The Brunello was introduced in 2013, and comes from a specific part of the estate, where 12 ha are registered for Brunello. Its production is small compared with the super-Tuscans, only about 20,000 bottles. It also ages in barriques, but they come from Slavonian oak instead of French, and there is only 10% new wood. The style seems more like a Sangiovese-based super-Tuscan than Brunello, very dark and very modern, with high alcohol (up to 15.5%).

Lux Vitis is the newest wine, a cuvée of Cabernet Sauvignon with a little Sangiovese, first released in 2015.

Mastrojanni *

Poderi Loreto San Pio, Castelnuovo dell'Abate, 53024 Montalcino	*+39 0577 835681*
info@mastrojanni.com	
www.mastrojanni.com	*[map p. 101]*
39 ha; 140,000 btl	*Brunello di Montalcino*

The estate was created in 1975 by Gabriele Mastrojanni, a lawyer who lived in Rome. By the 1990s it was managed by his son, Antonio, but after Gabriele died in 2008, it was sold to the Illy family (of coffee fame). In 1997, Francesco Illy had purchased the neighboring property, Podere Le Ripi, so when Mastrojanni became available, he was instrumental in the Illy group's decision to purchase it. Andrea Machetti arrived as winemaker in 1992, and still is involved today. The new winery, a practical modern building on the track from Castelnuova dell'Abate to Sant'Antimo, was constructed in 2011. The vineyards are all around, at an elevation of 420m. There's also a guest house, the Mastrojanni Relais, with accommodation.

"We consider ourselves a traditional producer," they say. Fermentation takes place in concrete vats because "we believe that stainless steel damages the wine." The wines age in relatively small botti (16-40 hl) of Allier oak. There are no barriques: "we don't want toast and oak in our wines." There are four wines from Montalcino. The Rosso di Montalcino is declassified from Brunello, there is just a little less of the regular Brunello than Rosso, and there are two single-vineyard wines, Vigna Schiena d'Asino and Vigna Loreto, produced in only 300-400 cases each. There is no Riserva—"we prefer to focus on the single vineyards"—so all the Brunellos spend the same 36 months in wood. In addition, San Pio is a blend of 20% Sangiovese with 80% Cabernet Sauvignon, which spends 18 months in tonneaux, and is now labeled as IGT Toscana instead of Sant'Antimo as previously.

The style is quite sleek and elegant. The Rosso gives a good preview of the style of the Brunello, which is rounder and deeper. The Sant'Antimo follows the same general style, but has less persistence. Notwithstanding the exclusive focus on botti, the elegant style seems poised somewhere between full fledged tradition and modernist.

Siro Pacenti ***

Podere Pelagrilli, 53024 Montalcino	*+39 0577 848662*
info@siropacenti.it	*Giancarlo Pacenti*
www.siropacenti.it	*[map p. 101]*
	Brunello di Montalcino
25 ha; 60,000 btl	*Brunello di Montalcino*

This estate is generally considered an arch modernist, but it has always been one of my favorites because the style is never overdone and the purity of fruits shines out. Before 1970 the Pacentis were farmers rather than wine producers; they owned the property, but it was given over to polyculture. Siro started producing wine in 1970, but the current style and reputation date from his son Giancarlo's return from Bordeaux, where he studied oenology.

When Giancarlo came back he wanted to follow the French philosophy, but with traditional grapes. He received a lot of criticism at the beginning, when he introduced selection in the field, a sorting table, and French oak. Rosso and Brunello are aged only in barriques; the Riserva ages in tonneaux. All cuvées receive the same mix of new and old oak, with about one third new. A new cellar was built in 2008; Giancarlo wanted to represent his style—he likes modernity—and it's very stylish in an ultramodern fashion.

The estate is focused entirely on Brunello. There are vineyards around the cellar in the northern part of the appellation, and some more about 25 km away in the southern area. There are no dedicated vineyards for Rosso; the Rosso is about half of production, but comes entirely from declassification. "Our Rosso has the same character as Brunello, sometimes people call it a baby Brunello. But there was no choice between Rosso and Brunello, we wanted to have something more approachable, but with the character of Brunello." This led to the introduction of Pellagrilli in 2006.

The main distinction between the three cuvées is the age of the vines: less than 15 years for Rosso, 15-25 years for Pellagrilli, more than 30 years for Brunello. The Riserva (produced in small amounts, around 400 cases), only in top vintages, comes from a specific 2 ha vineyard, half of which has vines planted by Siro in 1967. With the exception of the Riserva, all cuvées are blends in the traditional way from vineyards in both north and south. The style is consistent across the range: the Rosso is a baby Brunello with some wild edges, Pellagrilli is smoother but lighter than the Brunello, which is rich and chocolaty, and displays the full style of the house. Sweetness and concentration of fruits increase going up the scale. However, it seems to me that the style has moved in a more aromatic, more overtly modern direction in recent years.

La Palazzetta *

Podere La Palazzetta, 53024 Castelnuovo Dell'Abate Montalcino	*+39 0577 835631*
palazzettafanti@gmail.com	*Luca Fanti*
www.palazzettafanti.it	*[map p. 101]*
20 ha; 70,000 btl	*Brunello di Montalcino*

This is very much a family business, now making its transition to the next generation, Luca Fanti and his sister Tea. "My parents (Flavio and Carla) started in 1980 with animals and cereals," Tea says, "with only 1 ha." The first Brunello was produced in 1988: now there is also a Rosso and a Riserva. A Sant'Antimo Rosso has been made since 1999.

The winery is on a high point overlooking the village of Castelnuova dell'Abate, off the track that leads to Sant'Antimo. A small cluster of buildings house a fermentation cellar with stainless steel vats, an aging cellar crammed with botti, and a small bottling line. It's very hands on: Flavio established the style of a firmly traditionalist producer, his wife Carla designed the labels, Luca is now the winemaker, and Tea is in charge of marketing.

"We only have indigenous grapes, you won't find any international varieties here," Tea explains. In fact, the only variety aside from Sangiovese is Colorino. "Grandfather had some Colorino, which he used for governo (using partially dried grapes to help with fermentation), but now it's blended with Sangiovese in the Sant'Antimo." Brunello ages in old 40 hl botti of oak from Allier, now circular rather than the original ovals, "to preserve the fruit better." The Rosso and Sant'Antimo age in 500 liter casks, because the wine is not intended for long aging; a little new oak is used for the first three months.

The style is firmly traditional, but is moving towards greater approachability. When I arrived, Luca was engaged in a blending session with consulting oenologist Maurizio Saettini. "The wine should be ready to drink almost as soon as it goes on the market," Maurizio says "The wines have been very good, but used to need a lot of time. We are working to make them rounder, but they should also last."

There are five separate vineyards. The oldest vineyards tend to be used for Brunello, vineyards of 10-20 years age for Rosso di Montalcino, and the youngest vineyards for Sant'Antimo, but all are treated the same. "Everything is picked as though for Brunello," says Tea, "the lots that are more fruity and fresh are used for the Rosso to give a more forward style." The Riserva comes from a specific plot of calcareous terroir in the best years. They may be committed to a traditional style, but there is some innovation. In 2016, Luca produced a rosé as an experiment, and the Sant'Antimo is bottled using a new type of cork produced from sugar cane.

The same style runs through the range, but shows greater depth and refinement moving along the hierarchy. The rosé, all Sangiovese, is quite full. Sant'Antimo actually contains several indigenous varieties, "planted all together in the ancient style." It's forward and fruity, and attractive for enjoying immediately. The Rosso di Montalcino is a little darker, with more of a sheen. The Brunello is a smoother version of the Rosso, more restrained and less obvious, with a very fine structure. Rosso and Brunello both show a touch of salinity at the end—"this is something you find in all our wines," Luca says.

Il Paradiso di Frassina *

Loc. Frassina 14, 53024 Montalcino	*+39 5778 39031*
info@alparadisodifrassina.it	*Federico Ricci*
www.alparadisodifrassina.it	*[map p. 101]*
10 ha; 35,000 btl	*Brunello di Montalcino*

Located just below the Montosoli hill, the vineyard resonates with the music of Mozart. "This musical vineyard is not some silly romantic dream, but part of a long-term scientific research to see how sound waves can beneficially affect the vineyard and its vines," explains the domain. They have patented the system. Giancarlo Cignozzi, who founded the domain, cites regions of the Orient where it's common to play music to plants, and has had researchers from local universities measure the effects. "The music must not be too sharp or modern," he says, "Wagner doesn't work." He has settled on Mozart.

The estate was founded in 2000 after the sale of Caparzo, where Carlo, a lawyer from Milan has been a founding partner in 1970. Carlo has a fervent dislike of large wineries. "I hate large wineries, to make good wine you have to go to a small winery. Big wineries make the same wine every year, our wine is different every year," he says. So he decided to start a small winery. Il Paradiso had been abandoned after the second world war, and it took two years to renovate the buildings and replant the vineyards with Sangiovese.

The Rosso di Montalcino ages in 2- and 3-year 300- and 500-liter barriques, the Brunello has 30% new oak, and the Riserva in 70% 1- and 2-year oak; the oak is a mix of barrels from 300 to 700 liters, and Slavonian botti. It's actually only the 1.5 ha Mozart Vineyard used to make the Riserva (named Fluto Magico, only 1,500 bottles) that has music played to it, 24/7, from 50 Bose loudspeakers. There are also loudspeakers in the cellars. I cannot say that I see an effect on the wine.

The house style is quite delicate: the Rosso shows light red fruits, the Brunello is a little richer and more structured, and Fluto Magico is a little rounder and riper, but along the same lines. The estate offers tours with an explanation of the Music and Vines project, and also has accommodation. There is also a similar sized estate in Maremma, which makes an IGT called 12 Uve. "We call this the crazy blend," says Carlo's son, Ulisse, as it has 6 Bordeaux and 6 Italian varieties. It's more powerful than the Brunello, but not overwhelming.

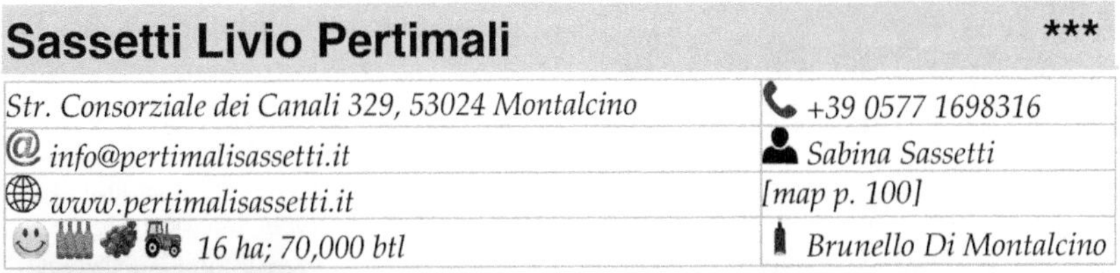

Sassetti Livio Pertimali ***

Str. Consorziale dei Canali 329, 53024 Montalcino	+39 0577 1698316
info@pertimalisassetti.it	Sabina Sassetti
www.pertimalisassetti.it	[map p. 100]
16 ha; 70,000 btl	Brunello Di Montalcino

The Sassettis have been making wine in Sant'Angelo for three generations, but Pertimali is a relatively recent creation, dating from the 1970s when Livio Sassetti sold the property in Sant'Angelo and bought the Pertimali property on a hill in the northwest part of Montalcino. About 10 ha surround the vineyard, with another 2 ha in the south. "Blending between the vineyards from north and south is important for producing high quality wine," Livio says. There are no vineyards dedicated to Rosso, which is produced exclusively from declassified Brunello, and is vinified exclusively in steel. The amount of Rosso varies widely, depending on the vintage; in 2002 it was the whole crop.

The Brunello and Riserva (made only in top vintages) are produced traditionally, with aging in Slavonian botti. The super-Tuscan Fili di Seta is a blend of 60% Sangiovese to 40% Cabernet Sauvignon; originally it was equal proportions of each variety, "but the Cabernet overwhelmed the Sauvignon," Livio explains. The Sassettis bought an estate in Maremma in 2000 and make wine under the Montecucco DOC. "The attraction is that you can buy land and convert it to vineyards; it is not affordable to buy more vineyards in Montalcino," Livio says. The wines have a classic flavor profile, showing the savory side of Sangiovese; and Fil di Seta shows Sangiovese more clearly than Cabernet. The style conveys an impression of refinement.

Pian Delle Vigne **

Località Pian delle Vigne, 53024 Montalcino	+39 0577 816066
antinori@antinori.it	Dora Pacciani & Fabio Ratto
www.antinori.it	[map p. 100]
65 ha; 156,000 btl	Brunello Di Montalcino

Just to the south of Montalcino, Pian delle Vigne takes its name from an old railroad station located on the property. Antinori bought the property in 1995. The estate is about 185 ha, with about a third planted as vineyards. The vineyards run from 130 to 200m elevation (relatively low for the region); about half are used for producing Brunello. There are a couple of hectares of olive trees, and the rest of the estate consists of woods.

Brunello has always been produced, but the Rosso di Montalcino was introduced with the 2012 vintage. The Rosso is smooth and elegant, but perhaps more in line with the top Chianti Classicos than the Brunello, which can be rich (reflecting the southern location of the vineyards in Montalcino) or more restrained, depending on the year. Although the

style seems modern, they are both aged in large (80 hl) casks of Slavonian oak. The Rosso ages for 7 months, compared with 24 months for the Brunello.

The Riserva, Vigna Ferrovia, taking its name from the railway station, comes from a 4 ha plot adjacent to the old station. The soil is calcareous clay and rather stony. The Riserva is made only in the best vintages, ages first in tonneaux and then is transferred to 30 hl casks. It's not really more concentrated or intense than the Brunello, but shows a wider flavor spectrum of spicy and savory notes, with a tannic presence indicating greater longevity. These are very reliable wines.

Gaja **

Loc. Chiesa Santa Restituta, 53024 Montalcino	*+39 0577 848610*
info@pievesantarestituta.com	*Gaia Gaja*
	[map p. 100]
35 ha; 100,000 btl	*Brunello di Montalcino, Rennina*

Pieva Santa Restituta is one of those estates where the quality of the terroir shines out from the wines. The property belonged to the local diocese until 1972 until it was sold (including the church) The wines were good, but improved after Gaja bought the property in 1994. At first they continued to be labeled under the Pieve Santa Restituta name, but in due course this was replaced by Gaja's striking black and white labels.

There was a large-scale restructuring of the vineyards between 2005 and 2010, but the same two cuvées continue to be made: Rennina, which is a blend of three parcels with sandy soils; and Sugarille, which comes from a single parcel with more calcareous soils. Rennina tends to be more savory, Sugarille is denser and more structured and chocolaty. In addition, there is a Brunello *tout court* , which comes from a 9 ha vineyard Gaja purchased in 2007 in the north of Montalcino. A new underground winery was constructed in 2005.

Vinification isn't determinedly either modern or traditional as the Brunellos are all fermented in stainless steel and then have same aging regime of a year in barriques (first to third year) followed by a year in botti. The style of the wines seems to have become more obviously modern in the past decade, but remains in the direction of elegance rather than power, showcasing purity of fresh black fruits. The wines age unusually well for Brunello: the 1997 and 1999 were showing well in 2020, with Rennina still showing overt fruits, and Sugarille more restrained and textured.

Poggio Antico **

Loc. Poggio Antico, 53024 Montalcino	*+39 0577 848044*
mail@poggioantico.com	*Federico Trost*
www.poggioantico.com	*[map p. 100]*
33 ha; 90,000 btl	*Brunello di Montalcino*

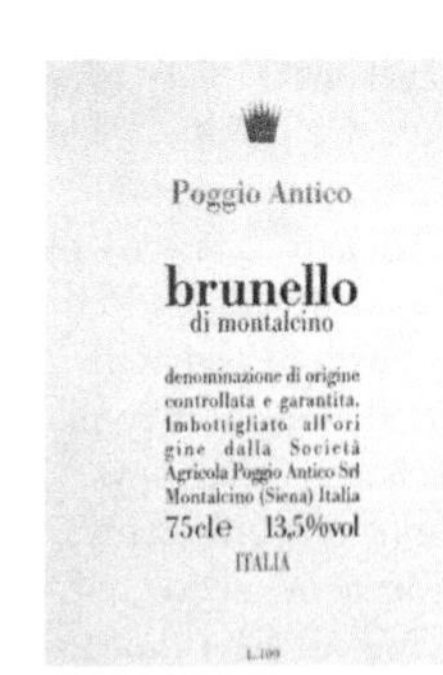

"I would say we are a modernist producer, but we want to accommodate all tastes, this is why we produce two different styles of Brunello," said Paola Gloder. Located just to the south of Montalcino within an estate of 200 ha, mostly forested, Poggio Antico is one of the highest wineries in the appellation, sitting on top of a hill at 450m. The estate was created in 1984 when Giancarlo and Nuccia Gloder came to Montalcino from Milan; then it was managed by their daughter Paola until it was sold to Dutch businessman Marcel van Poecke in 2017.

The buildings were renovated in 2002, and the winery is underground. Vineyards are all around the winery—"all are within five minutes of the sorting table," they like to say. All 30 ha of Sangiovese are declared for Brunello (although some goes into the super-Tuscans), and there are also 2 ha of Cabernet Sauvignon and 1 ha of Petit Verdot. The Rosso is exclusively declassified from Brunello; it ages in French tonneaux, but achieves a light style.

It is impossible to define a style for the Brunellos, because there are two extremes. The traditional Brunello ages in Slavonian botti and conveys a savory impression with mineral notes. Altero comes from the same vineyard, but is aged for two years in new French tonneaux, and makes a much riper, richer impression. (When it was introduced in 1983 it was an IGT, because the rules then required more than two years' aging for Brunello; now it is a Brunello) The Riserva comes from the oldest vines and spends a year in new tonneau followed by two years in Slavonian oak, but the overall impression is much closer to Altero than to the traditional Brunello. I find the traditional Brunello to be the most elegant, and it ages beautifully, reaching a peak of delicacy after more than a decade. The two super-Tuscans, Madre (equal proportion of Sangiovese and Cabernet Sauvignon), and Lemartine (half Sangiovese and quarter each of Cabernet Sauvignon and Petit Verdot) are powerful wines in the international style.

I would say that all the wines except the Rosso and the "traditional" Brunello are well into modernism, and I'd give Poggio Antico one star as a modernist but two stars as a traditionalist. There is an excellent restaurant at the winery, where it's possible to have dinner after a tour and tasting.

Villa Poggio Salvi *

Loc. Poggio Salvi, 53024 Montalcino	*+39 0577 847121*
vps@villapoggiosalvi.it	*Luca Belingardi*
www.villapoggiosalvi.it	*[map p. 100]*
42 ha; 200,000 btl	*Brunello di Montalcino*

"The estate was created in 1979 by my grandfather, who came from Milan and bought a country house with a couple of hectares of vineyards. There wasn't any intention to make wine, but little by little the estate enlarged and now there are 20 ha in a single block around the winery. They are on galestro soils at 350-500m elevation. In 1998, he bought another 20 ha in Chianti Colli Senesi," says Luca Belingardi, who has been at the winery since 2008, and took charge in 2012.

Driving into the estate, you pass a group of imposing buildings that include the residence, and then you come to the purpose-built concrete winery, buried in the hillside. Grapes from all the vineyards are vinified here.

Two wines come from the vineyards in Chianti. Just over half the vineyards are classified for Chianti Colli Senesi; the minor part is used for IGT Toscana. The grape mix is similar, Sangiovese with 10-15% Merlot, but the Chianti ages only in steel and is more overtly fruity and fresh, while the IGT Toscana has six months in oak, and is a little smoother. "Considering that we have Rosso di Montalcino, we like the Chianti Colli Senesi to be easy and approachable," Luca says.

On the local estate, the Rosso comes mostly from younger vines, but may include some declassified Brunello, and continues theme of showing direct fruits. Moving to the Brunello, there is a jump in intensity and more of a savory edge. In addition to the general Brunello, there are two special cuvées; both Pomona and the Riserva come from specific 1 ha plots. All the wines are aged in botti. "We don't use barriques, only big botti of Slavonian oak, 60-110 hl. We think Sangiovese ages better in the botti," Luca says. Rosso ages for 12 months, Brunello and Pomona for 30 months, and the Riserva for 36 months. Moving from the general Brunello to the special cuvées, there is more flavor variety and extraction; Pomona is much in the same style as the Brunello, but fruits are more obvious and it's a little more structured, while the Riserva shows more power and a sense of minerality in the classic traditional style.

Il Poggione *

Loc. Monteano, 53024 Sant'angelo in Colle	*+39 0577 844029*
info@ilpoggione.it	*Fabrizio Bindocci*
www.tenutailpoggione.it	*[map p. 100]*
140 ha; 600,000 btl	*Brunello di Montalcino*

Il Poggione has been in the Franceschi family since the nineteenth century. Originally Fattorio St. Angelo, the name changed in 1956 when the brothers who were the current owners split their estate into Il Poggione and Col d'Orcia. (Col d'Orcia was subsequently sold to the Cinzano family). The winery buildings form a complex about 2 km below St. Angelo, down a steep unpaved road. The winery was built in 2004, and is much larger than it appears, with a vast fermentation hall behind the offices, and separate halls with botti and tonneaux underground. In the center of the vineyards, it's partly built into the hillside. Before it was built, wine was made in a series of buildings in the village.

The vineyards form something of an amphitheater, part of a 600 ha estate which also includes 12,000 olive trees, and are ringed by mountains to the west. "We are aware that to make great wines you need old vines and we have some of the oldest vineyards in the region. We never uproot old vineyards, but we replace individual vines. One of the things we are proud of is that Il Poggione ages well, for up to twenty years," says winemaker Fabrizio Bindocci. "We consider ourselves a traditional producer, but open to technology."

Rosso and Brunello are each about a third of production. The Brunello and Riserva age only in 52 hl botti of French oak. "The botti are not toasted," Fabrizio explains. "Brunello spends 3 years in botti, Riserva spends 4 years, so we don't want oak influence to be strong. New barrels would be too strong. Barriques tends to homogenize wine; we don't want to adapt our wine to consumers, we want consumers to appreciate our wine. We want to maintain typicity, we want to make wine that you can see comes from this region. The botti allow Sangiovese to evolve over years of aging."

The regular Rosso, intended for consumption sooner, is aged mostly in botti, with 20-30% in tonneaux, and makes a nicely restrained impression. It comes partly from specific vineyards and partly from young vines in Brunello vineyards. A second Rosso, Leopoldo Franceschi, is a barrel selection, aged mostly in tonneaux, and is more of a young Brunello. "We've always taken the view that we should make a serious Rosso," Fabrizio says. The Brunello gives a mineral impression of black fruits and usually needs some time. "When our Brunello is released, it may not be as pleasant as wines aged in barriques, but it will age longer," Fabrizio says. The Riserva, Vigna Paganelli, comes from the oldest vines, a 12 ha vineyard planted in 1964, and shows the concentration of old vines with a smooth palate of black fruits, moving in a more chocolaty direction than the Brunello; it is not so much more powerful as smoother and deeper. These are very fine wines, but patience is required.

Castello Romitorio *

Loc. Romitorio, 53024 Montalcino	*+39 0577 847212*
info@castelloromitorio.com	*Filippo,Chia*
www.castelloromitorio.com	*[map p. 100]*
15 ha; 150,000 btl	*Brunello di Montalcino*

Castello Romitorio takes its name from a twelfth century fortress in the northwest quadrant of Montalcino. Two thirds of the vineyards are in the vicinity of the winery, and the other third are at Poggio di Sopra, near Castelnuovo dell'Abate in the southeast. The striking paintings on the labels reflect ownership by artist Sandro Chia, who purchased the estate in 1984 and planted vineyards largely with Sangiovese. The additional vineyards at Poggio di Sopra were added in 1990. Famed oenologist Carlo Ferrini is a consultant.

The hierarchy of Sangiovese varietal wines ascends from Chianti Colle Senesi (which spends six months in Slavonian oak), to Rosso di Montalcino (12 months in French barriques), and Brunello di Montalcino (12 months in French barriques and 12 months in Slavonian oak). The Riserva comes from a single vineyard, and spends 36 months in a mixture of French and Slavonian oak, and the top Brunello is the Filo di Seta, which is based on selection of the best lots, and spends 30 months in French barriques.

The house is a modernist and the style is refined: the Brunello is relatively light, but Filo di Seta moves up a notch with more structure evident in the background and an increased sense of precision. The Riserva is deeper and rounder, but still in the elegant style of the house. There's also a Sant'Antimo blend of Sangiovese, Cabernet Sauvignon, and

Canaiolo, and an IGT Toscana Bordeaux blend, as well as a white blend of Vermentino and Chardonnay. Another estate in Maremma was purchased in the mid nineties.

Salvioni ***

Piazza Cavour 19, 53024 Montalcino	*+39 0577 848499*
info@aziendasalvioni.com	*Alessia Salvioni*
www.aziendasalvioni.com	*[map p. 101]*
4 ha; 14,000 btl	*Brunello di Montalcino*

The tiny scale of production at La Cerbaiola is indicated by its aging cellar, underneath the family house in Piazza Cavour in the town of Montalcino: it has 6 botti of 20 hl. That's the total production for one of the mythic producers of Montalcino. The property at La Cerbaiola, three vineyards totaling 4 ha in a 20 ha estate immediately adjacent to Cerbaiona, has been in the Salvioni family for three generations, but winemaking is relatively recent.

"Our story started in 1985 when my father decided to make wine," says Alessia Salvioni. Giulio Salvioni's first vintage in 1985 was an immediate success: the traditional approach, using indigenous yeast, botti (albeit of medium size), and lack of filtration, marked the wines firmly in the artisanal camp. The entire vineyard is declared for Brunello, but some is declassified to Rosso when the crop is unusually large or there is a poor vintage. There are certainly ups and downs in production. In 2012 there were 12,000 bottles of Brunello, in 2013 there were only four botti (about 10,000 bottles), in 2014 the entire crop was declassified to Rosso, and in 2015 there will probably be 15,000 bottles, all Brunello. The wines have that combination of full flavor and density, yet elegant expression, that marks the vineyards of Cerbaiola and Cerbaiona.

San Filippo *

Loc. San Filippo 134, 53024 Montalcino	*+39 0577 847176*
info@sanfilippomontalcino.com	*Roberto Giannelli*
www.sanfilippomontalcino.com	*[map p. 101]*
10 ha; 65,000 btl	*Brunello di Montalcino, Le Lucère*

"I was in real estate and fifteen years ago I was asked to help sell the winery. I ended up buying it myself," says Roberto Giannelli. "I changed everything, the first five years were difficult." The winery occupies a group of buildings at the end of a track that winds down from the main road to San Filippo, where there are half a dozen producers. Dating from 1977, this is one of the older established wineries in Montalcino. The vineyards, all in San Filippo, were planted in the seventies, so the oldest vines are now almost fifty years old.

All wines are DOC, ranging from the Rosso di Montalcino (coming from dedicated vineyards) to the Brunello and the Le Lucère single vineyard of the oldest vines (also produced as a Riserva in top vintages). Are you a traditionalist or a modernist, I asked Roberto? "Oh, for me it's the grapes that matter. We have both large oak and small oak. Brunello ages in large oak, the single vineyard ages 14 months in each small and large oak, Riserva has an extra six months all in barriques. Maybe we are more traditionalist than new. We look for good fruits, fermentation that isn't too long or aggressive, maximum of 20 days on the skin. We want a clean style with good aromas, not too aggressive. In general we have soft wine, not too powerful."

The Rosso is quite light and fresh, the Brunello is more serious but remains relatively soft, and the single vineyard Lucère shows the style to best effect, a deeper, richer version of the Brunello, but elegant rather than powerful, poised between savory and chocolaty. The style to me seems to veer increasingly in a modernist direction along the range.

Sassodisole *

Pod. Sasso di Sole 85, 53024 Montalcino	*+39 0577 834303*
info@sassodisole.it	*Roberto Terzuoli*
www.sassodisole.it	*[map p. 101]*
10 ha; 50,000 btl	*Brunello di Montalcino*

Sassodisole is a new name for an old estate. Originally it was owned by two brothers, who split their holdings 25 years ago. The Terzuoli family has been involved in agriculture since the seventeenth century; Bruno and Graziella Terzuoli moved into winemaking during the 1970s, and Sassodisole is run today by their grandson Roberto, who worked at Biondi-Santi before taking over the estate. (The neighboring estate, Santa Giulia, is the other half of the original property.)

Vineyards are on slopes all around the cellar, facing south or southwest, at 350m. The small winery is stuffed with modern equipment. There is a stylish tasting room, where you may be greeted by manager Lorenzo Moscatelli, who is Roberto's sole assistant in the winery. "We are a traditional producer," Lorenzo explains, "we use only 35 hl or 50 hl botti of Slavonian oak for aging."

Located in the northeast corner of Montalcino, the estate overlaps with the Orcia DOC. The focus is exclusively on Sangiovese. The entry-level wine is Orcia Rosso, which comes from the youngest vines; the size of the estate was more or less doubled when 4 ha were planted to make the Orcia. A sparkling rosé was introduced in 2016, also from this vineyard. The Rosso di Montalcino and Brunello come from the original vineyards. The Riserva is based on selection. "Usually the best grapes come from the top of the hill. We harvest first for the Brunello and then go back three or four days later to harvest the smallest berries and bunches. This means we have to decide at harvest whether to select for the Riserva," Lorenzo says.

The Orcia Rosso spend 4-5 months in oak, the Rosso di Montalcino spends 8-9 months, but Brunellos have extended aging. "Brunello ages for 3 years, Riserva for 4 years, so we need very light wood," says Lorenzo. The Orcia is a nice summer wine showing light red fruits, the Rosso is slightly deeper and has more fruit complexity and a little restraint, the Brunello adds a sense of structure to the smooth sheen of the fruits, and there is a sense of minerality to the Riserva. Overall the style is elegant rather than powerful. "We follow the same style for all the wines, I think we can see the same hand, the same philosophy, in all our wines," Lorenzo says.

Tenuta Silvio Nardi *

Loc. Casale Del Bosco, 53204 Montalcino	*+39 0577 808332*
italia@tenutenardi.com	*Emilia Nardi*
www.tenutenardi.com	*[map p. 100]*
80 ha; 250,000 btl	*Brunello Di Montalcino*

Silvio Nardi purchased the Casale del Bosco estate in 1950, and then in 1962 purchased the Manachiara estate. Silvio's daughter, Emilia, has been in charge of the estate since 1990; the consulting oenologist is Eric Boissenot from Bordeaux. Casale del Bosco is to the west, and Manachiara is to the east of Montalcino. The fruit from Casale del Bosco tends to elegance, whereas Manachiara is riper. The combination anticipated the later trend of blending between north and south. About half the vineyards are in each of the estates, with a total of 36 different plots.

The Rosso comes from the Casale del Bosco estate, the Brunello is a blend from Casale del Bosco and Manachiara, while Manachiara is a single-vineyard wine from old vines, and Poggio Doria comes from a vineyard in the northwest corner of Casale del Bosco. Other wines include Sant'Antimo (Sangiovese plus international varieties), Chianti Colli Senesi (85% Sangiovese with 10% Merlot and 5% Colorino), Moscadello, and also Grappa.

The overall impression is modern but not ultra modern. The Brunellos age for 12 months in French barriques, followed by 12 months in Slavonian botti (Poggio Dora includes some new oak). The Brunello blend is smooth with just a hint of structure, while Manachiara shows the same modernist style but with greater structure, and can even be a little stern when young, needing some time to come around.

Talenti *

Podere Pian Di Conte, 53024 Sant'Angelo in Colle	*+39 0577 844064*
info@talentimontalcino.it	*Riccardo Talenti*
www.talentimontalcino.it	*[map p. 100]*
22 ha; 100,000 btl	*Brunello Di Montalcino*

Pierluigi Talenti founded this estate in the 1950s, and today it is run by his grandson Riccardo. There were 6 ha when Ricardo took over. The property is just off the main road opposite the village of Sant'Angelo in Colle. There are 4 ha immediately around the winery, and other vineyards along the road to Montalcino, with some additional plots near Castelnuovo dell'Abate. Everything is in the southeast quadrant. New cellars were built for the 2010 vintage, partly underground.

Vinification is similar for the Rosso, Brunello, and Riserva: fermentation in stainless steel is followed by aging in a mix of French tonneaux (500 liter barrels) and Slavonian botti, the basic difference being the length of aging. New oak is a maximum of 20%. "Wines are tasted in January, and I decide which lots go in tonneaux or botti," Riccardo says, "with the richer lots going into tonneaux. During aging, tasting is used to decide which lots go into the Rosso, by selecting those that are sweeter and more ready." The Rosso is bottled after eight months, and the remaining lots continue aging for the Brunello. The Riserva from the 2 ha Paretaio vineyard at the winery.

The approach is fresh but shows some structure to the black fruits, with the savory tang of Sangiovese. The Rosso previews the Brunello, which is a little smoother and more structured; the Riserva shows greater refinement rather than more power. There are also two IGTs: Trefolo, a blend of Sangiovese, Syrah, and Canaiolo, and Rispolla, a blend of 40% Cabernet Sauvignon, 30% Merlot, and 30% Petit Verdot. "This is a different philosophy and style," Riccardo says, with Rispolla intended for everyday drinking.

Uccelliera **

Loc Castelnuovo Dell'Abate, 53024 Montalcino	*+39 0577 835729*
anco@uccelliera-montalcino.it	*Andrea Cortonesi*
www.uccelliera-montalcino.it	*[map p. 101]*
6 ha; 60,000 btl	*Rosso di Montalcino*

Andrea Cortonesi was at Ciacci Piccolomini when he purchased his first four hectares from Ciacci in 1986. They included an old farmhouse and half a hectare of old vines at 250m elevation. Andrea renovated the house and extended the old underground cellar. His first vintage was 1991. He subsequently acquired two more plots, Pianrosso lower down at 150m, and Quercione higher up on the other side of Castelnuovo dell'Abate.

There is cold soak with dry ice before fermentation. Aging is in a mix of 40 hl botti and 2- and 3-year barriques. Andre decides after MLF which lots go into botti and which into barriques. The proportion of botti to barriques changes with the vintage. A strong vintage will have more new French oak. Production is divided roughly equally between Rosso and Brunello, and there is also an IGT Toscana. Sometimes a Riserva is made from an 0.35 ha plot of the oldest vines. In addition there's a special cuvee, Costabate, aged in untoasted barrels coming from a single 300 year old oak tree. It's an IGT, but is aged like a Brunello.

The style is modernist, deepening from the fresh impression of Rosso to the more mineral impression of Brunello, and becoming smoother, riper, and more obviously structured with Riserva. Smoky oak is evident on the Riserva, enhancing the modernist impression. Costabate is quite different from the Brunello, moving from modernist to arch-modernist, and really needing time to come out. There is also an IGT, Rapace, which is a blend of Sangiovese with Merlot, and Cabernet Sauvignon; very rich and powerful, this is certainly a super-Tuscan. High alcohol goes along with the modernist approach. The olive oil is powerful like the wines.

Andrea also makes small amounts of Rosso and Brunello from high altitude vineyards under the separate label of Voliero (sources have varied, but are 200m higher than Uccelliera). Like Uccelliera, the wines are vinified in traditional style in large casks of Slavonian and French oak. While Uccelliera is intended to showcase the local terroir of Castelnuovo dell'Abata, Voliero is intended to demonstrate the effect of blending different high altitude vineyards.

Val di Suga

Loc. Val Di Suga, 53024 Montalcino	*+39 0577 804101*
wineshop@angelini.it	
valdisuga.it	*[map p. 101]*
55 ha; 250,000 btl	*Brunello di Montalcino Riserva*

Val de Suga was founded in the 1970s, and its ownership has changed as it has passed through various conglomerate mergers. It became part of Tenimenti Angelini in 1994 when privately-owned pharmaceutical company Angelini simultaneously bought Val di Suga in Montalcino, Tre Rose in Montepulciano, and San Leonino in Chianti Classico. Then in 2011 Angelini bought Bertani, the well known producer in Valpolicella. In 2014 all of the estates were united under the banner of Bertani domains. It's probably fair to say that all of these domains are mid-range: they achieve a certain reliability in quality, but rarely scale the heights.

Since Angelini bought Val di Suga, however, there has been investment in vineyards and cellar. The focus is exclusively in Brunello, with the range ascending from the Rosso, to the Brunello, to the Riserva, and three single-vineyard wines, Poggio al Granchio, Vigna Spuntali, and Vigna del Lago, which represent distinct areas (southeast, southwest, and north, near the winery). The Brunello is aged mostly in botti, but the single-vineyard wines see new barriques, and age as long as Riserva although not labeled as such. From Rosso to Brunello to single vineyard, the style is light and quite attractive, with intensity increasing along the series, but not offering the prospect of increasing complexity with age. The single-vineyard wines are definitely in the modern idiom, but are over-oaked for my palate, and I worry about their aging capacity. Vigna Spuntali is closest in style to the Riserva, then the sense of oak builds with Poggio al Granchio and finally Vigna del Largo.

Valdicava ***

Loc. Valdicava, 53024 Montalcino	*+39 0577 848261*
+39 5778 48008	*Vincenzo Abbruzzese*
www.valdicava.it	*[map p. 101]*
27 ha; 70,000 btl	*Brunello di Montalcino*

When I visited Valdicava, we had to go a long way round to the back entrance, because the front was blocked by massive reconstruction works. Driving through the extensive estate on the way to the winery, we passed the Madonna del Piano, a small building that used to be a church, and which is just above the famous 8 ha vineyard of its name. The work is to build a new winery, a stable for the racing horses (another interest), and a tasting room. The present winery is small facility, packed with equipment and botti.

One of the older established producers in Montalcino, Valdicava was turned into something of a cult wine after Vincenzo Abbruzzese took over in 1987. The estate was founded by his grandfather, Bramante Abbruzzese, in 1953. Valdicava was a founding member of the Consorzio, and has been bottling wine under the Valdicava label since 1977 (previously they carried a generic description from the Consorzio with the winery's name). The vineyards occupy only a small part of the 135 ha estate, located in the northeast quadrant (and extending into Montosoli), where the most powerful wines of Montalcino are produced.

Valdicava produces three wines: Rosso (from the youngest vines), Brunello, and the single vineyard Madonna del Piano Riserva, produced only in the best vintages in small amounts (around 800 cases). Wines are aged only in botti, which are natural wood with no toast. The style is forceful, and at all levels the wines give an impression of the density that comes from low yields (in fact some of the lowest in the region), and the wines correspondingly need time to come around. Although forceful, Valdicava does not lose elegance and purity of fruits. Madonna is not so much more intense than Valdicava as different in its profile, with an intriguing blend of minerality on the bouquet and chocolate on the finish. "It's different but it's just between the other vineyards, there must be something in the soil." Its character comes right through vintage variation, but it needs a long time to come around, perhaps twenty years. How long will these wines age? Vincenzo has been quoted as saying, "I guarantee the Riserva for the lifetime of the buyer."

Profiles of Important Estates

Baricci

Loc. Colombaio di Montosoli 13, 53024 Montalcino	*+39 0577 848109*
baricci1955@libero.it	*Pietro Buffi*
www.baricci.it	*[map p. 101]*
	5 ha; 30,000 btl

Nello Baricci purchased this estate in 1955, and was one of the founders of the Consorzio in 1967. Now run by his grandsons, Federico (winemaker) and Francesco Buffi, the estate has stayed true to its roots, with wines aged only in old botti of Slavonian oak. "We want to resist the trend (to new oak)," Nello said. Vineyards are in a top location, in 6 plots on the Montosoli hill. Until recently, the only Baricci wines were Rosso and Brunello di Montalcino, but a Riserva was introduced with the 2010 vintage. The estate also produces grappa and olive oil.

Bellaria

Loc. Bellaria, 53024 Montalcino	*+39 5778 48574*
info@aziendabellaria.it	*Gianni Bernazzi*
www.aziendabellaria.it	*[map p. 101]*
	3 ha; 15,000 btl

Assunto Pieri and Bruna Tempori created the domain when they bought the farmhouse and land in 1963. Their nephew Gianni Bernazzi took over in 2000. The property covers 40 ha, but only 3.5 ha is planted with vines, and another 1 ha with olive trees. The regular range includes Rosso and Brunello. In 2004, Gianni added the Assunto range, which is a selection from older (40-year) vines, and also includes a Riserva and a Vin Santo. The wines ferment in stainless steel and age in barriques of French and Slavonian oak.

Capanna

Loc. Capanna, 53024 Montalcino	*+39 0577 848298*
info@capannamontalcino.com	*Patrizio Cencioni & Amedeo Cencioni*
www.capannamontalcino.com	*[map p. 101]*
	23 ha; 75,000 btl

In the northeast quadrant of Montalcino, the Capanna estate looks out over the nearby Montosoli hill. Purchased by the Cencioni family in 1957—subsequently they were among the founders of the Consorzio—it is now run by Patrizio, grandson of the founders, and the next generation, Amedeo. Vineyards are all in the local area, at elevations of 250-350m, planted with 80% Sangiovese, and some Moscato and a couple of other varieties. Wines are aged traditionally in large (10 or 30 hl) casks of Slavonian oak. "Capanna today represents one of the most traditional styles of Brunello in the area," manager Daniele says. The Rosso offers a preview of the Brunello, which follows the smooth, chocolaty style, brought to its peak in the Riserva. At a lower level, there's a Merlot Sangiovese blend, which is very Merlot-ish, under the Sant'Antimo label, and also a Pinot Grigio. Visitors can stay at the Capanna Wine Relais.

Casisano

Loc. Casisano 52, 53024 Montalcino	*+39 5778 35540*
wine@tomassi.com	*TommasiFamily Estates*
www.casisano.it	*[map p. 101]*
	22 ha; 100,000 btl

Tommasi Family Estates was founded in 1902 when Giacomo Tommasi bought a small plot in Valpolicella. Today it owns 600 ha, including estates in Valpolicella (still the home base where there is also a hotel), Poggio al Tufo in Maremma, Masseria Surani in Puglia, Caseo in Oltrepò Pavese, and Pater Noster in Basilicata. Casisano was a recent purchase, in 2015. The estate was founded in 1990, and Tommasi have renovated and expanded the vineyards. Winemaking is traditional, with aging in large botti of Slavonian oak. There are three cuvées, the Rosso di Montalcino, the Brunello from 9 ha specifically dedicated to the DOCG, and the Colombaiolo Riserva, from a single vineyard. Tommasi offers a series of tours and has a shop at its main winery in Valpolicella.

Agricola Centolani

Tenuta Friggiali, 53028 Montalcino	*+39 0577 849314*
info@tenutafriggialiepietranera.it	*Peluso Centolani*
www.tenutafriggialiepietranera.it	*[map p. 100]*
	70 ha; 260,000 btl

This is really two estates. Tenuta Friggiali is the original holding, in the southwest quadrant, with Sangiovese planted on slopes of mostly galestro terroir at 200-450m. (The name might be derived from 'frigid,' indicating exposure to the wind.) The Peloso Centolani family also bought Pietranera, farther south, near the abbey of Sant'Animo, in 1979 as a hunting preserve of only 10 ha. A single vineyard on the southeast side of the hill faces Mont Amiata; volcanic soil is darker and richer here. The winery is at Tenuta Friggiali. The Brunello cuvées from the two locations are labeled Tenuta Friggiali and Pietranera. There is also a Rosso di Montalcino from each location. A separate Brunello is made from the Poggiotondo cru at the southernmost end of the Friggiali vineyards. The wines ferment in stainless steel and age traditionally in large botti.

Le Chiuse

Loc.Valdicava, 53024 Montalcino	*+39 0338 1300380*
info@lechiuse.com	*Lorenzo Magnelli*
www.lechiuse.com	*[map p. 101]*
	8 ha; 30,000 btl

The estate belongs to a branch of the Biondi Santi family—Simonetta Valiani is Ferruccio Biondi Santi's great granddaughter, and the vineyards were rented to Biondi Santi for their Riserva until Simonetta decided to make wine in 1993. Aging is traditional, in botti of 20-40 hl. The house style is quite light; the Rosso di Montalcino shows fresh red fruits and is a little reminiscent of Chianti; the Brunello moves towards black fruits, but still in a lighter style. Wines are ready to enjoy soon after release.

Collemattoni

Località Collemattoni 100 53024 Montalcino	*+39 5778 44127*
collemattoni@collemattoni.it	*Marcello Bucci*
www.collemattoni.it	*[map p. 100]*
	11 ha; 50,000 btl

The presence of the Bucci family at the Collemattoni farmhouse close to Sant'Angelo in Colle can be traced back to 1798. The cellar was renovated in 2012. There are three vineyards close to the winery in the southwest, and another two in the southeast quadrant at Castelnuovo dell'Abata. The Rosso di Montalcino and the Brunello are blends from the various vineyards and age in 32 hl botti of Slavonian oak. The Riserva comes from the 0.5 ha Fontelontano vineyard at 380m altitude close to Collemattoni, and ages in tonneau of French oak. Other wines include the Adone IGT Toscana (a blend of Sangiovese and Merlot) and a rosé from Sangiovese.

Tenuta Di Collosorbo

Loc. Villa A Sesta, 53020 Castelnuovo Dell'Abate	*+39 0577 835534*
info@collosorbo.com	*Giovanna Ciacci*
www.collosorbo.com	*[map p. 101]*
	30 ha; 160,000 btl

Located in the south on the road from Sant'Angelo in Colle to Castelnuovo dell'Abate, this was originally part of the Tenuta de Sesta estate, which was divided in 1995, into two parts, each run by a different branch of the Ciacci family. The Rosso and Brunello age in Slavonian botti with a small proportion in French barriques; the Riserva comes from a selection of the best lots, and ages only in French oak. The interest here is really in the Brunellos, but under the Sant'Antimo label, Le Due Gemme is a blend of Sangiovese with international varieties, and the Rosso is a blend of Bordeaux varieties with Syrah. Lula is an IGT Toscana blend of Sangiovese with Cabernet Sauvignon.

Corte dei Venti

Loc Piancornello 35, 53020 Castelnuovo Dell'Abate	*+39 0577 844035*
info@cortedeiventi.com	*Clara Monaci*
www.lacortedeiventi.it	*[map p. 101]*
	5 ha; 20,000 btl

The name, which means confluence of winds, gives a clue as to style, surprisingly fresh for the south of Montalcino, due to the microclimate which maintains a constant wind. In fact, the estate was originally called Quattroventi, but the name had to be changed because it clashed with another estate. Originally this was part of the Piancornello estate, which the Pieri family bought in 1943, and divided among three daughters in 1990. In addition to vines, the estate includes 3 ha of olive trees, 4 ha of other arable land, and 3 ha of forest. Within the vineyards, 2.8 ha are classified for Brunello. The range starts with IGT Toscana (Sangiovese, Syrah, and Merlot, aged in stainless steel) and Sant'Antimo (Sangiovese, Merlot, Cabernet, and Syrah, aged in barriques and tonneaux. The Rosso di Montalcino ages in a mix of small and large barrels, and the Brunello and Riserva age in 20-25 hl of botti of Slavonian oak.

Cortonesi

Loc. La Mannella 322, 53024 Montalcino	*+39 0577 847126*
info@cortonesimontalcino.it	*Tommaso Cortonesi*
www.cortonesimontalcino.it	*[map p. 101]*
	8 ha; 45,000 btl

The estate established its reputation under the name La Mannella, from its location north of Montalcino, near Montosoli. It started growing grapes in 1970 when Leonardo Cortonesi replaced some of his olive trees with Sangiovese grapevines. The terroir at La Mannella is mostly clay and limestone, at 280-350m altitude. There is also another vineyard, Poggiarelli, in the south near Castelnuovo dell'Abate, rocky and very sunny, at 420m altitude. Leonardo's son Marco moved into producing wine after 1985 (the first vintage was bottled in 1990), and worked with his son Tommaso, who changed the name of the estate to Cortonesi in 2018. (Tommaso also became Vice President of the Consorzio in 2017.) The Rosso comes from the youngest vines. The Rosso, Brunello La Mannella, and Riserva, all age in 30 hl Slavonian botti, Rosso for 6 months, Brunello for 40 months, and Riserva (about 2000 bottles made only in top years from the oldest vines) for up to 60 months. A separate cuvée is made from the Poggiarelli vineyard and ages in French tonneaux for 24 months. The only wine that is not labeled under the DOCG is the entry-level Leonus, a 100% Sangiovese IGT Toscana, aged in wood for 6 months.

Tenuta Fanti

Località Podere Palazzo 14, 53024 Castelnuovo dell'Abate	*+39 0577 835795*
info@tenutafanti.it	*Elisa Fanti*
www.tenutafanti.it	*[map p. 101]*
	50 ha; 200,000 btl

With the vineyards lying within a 300 ha estate, close to the village of Castelnuovo dell'Abata, this is one of the larger properties in Montalcino, and a major producer of wine and olive oil. A very old family estate, it has been run by Filippo Fanti since the early seventies, joined by his daughter Elisa in 2007. The general approach is to age the wines in a mix of French tonneaux and larger casks, but the style is certainly modern across the range: The Rosso and Brunello are soft and approachable, there's a little more weight to the Vallochio Brunello (which comes from the Vallochio area), but even the Macchiarelle Riserva, which comes from the oldest vines, has that some approachability. There are also red, white, and rosé under the Sant'Antimo label.

Fattoi Ofelio e figli

Loc. Santa Restituta, 53024 Montalcino	*+39 0577 848613*
info@fattoi.it	*Leonardo Fattoi*
www.fattoi.it	*[map p. 100]*
	10 ha; 60,000 btl

Ofelio Fattoi bought this property in the area of Santa Restituta in 1965, and began to produce Brunello in 1979. Today it is run by his sons Leonardo and Lamberto. In addition to vineyards, the 70 ha estate includes 3 ha of olive trees. A new winery was built in 2012. Production is confined to DOCG wine, grappa, and olive oil. Rosso is about 16,000 bottles, Brunello 34,000, and Riserva 5,000 bottles in top years only. The Rosso ages in large casks, while the Brunello and Riserva age in a mix of large casks and tonneaux.

La Fiorita

Loc. Podere Ballavista, 53020 Castelnuovo Dell'Abate Montalcino	*+39 5778 35657*
info@lafiorita.com	*Natalie Oliveros*
www.lafiorita.com	*[map p. 101]*
	9 ha; 45,000 btl

La Fiorita was created by Roberto Cipresso, consultant oenologist at Casse Basse, Poggio Antico, and Ciacci Piccolomini, as well as being involved with Archaval Ferrer in Argentina. Initially in 1992 there were just 0.5 ha of vines and wine was made in an old building in Castelnuovo dell'Abate. Further plots were added later. In 2011 Roberto partnered with Natalie Oliveros, originally an actress from New York, and in 2014 she purchased full ownership. Natalie expanded the vineyards further and built a new two storey winery in 2019 operating on gravity feed. The Rosso comes from two thirds estate grapes and one third purchased grapes and ages in botti of French oak for 12 months. The Brunello is a blend from three estate vineyards located to the south, west, and east, and ages for 24 months in botti of Slavonian oak. The Riserva comes from the Pian Bossolino vineyard at Castelnuovo dell'Abate, and ages in 26 hl botti of French oak. Fiore Di No is a new cuvée that Natalie introduced in 2020, made only in top vintages from a selection of grapes, aged in botti. She also added a rosé, Ninfalia.

La Fortuna

53024 Montalcino	*+39 0577 848308*
info@tenutalafortuna.it	*Angelo & Romina Zannoni*
www.tenutalafortuna.it	*[map p. 101]*
	11 ha; 60,000 btl

The Zannoni family have been at La Fortuna since 1907, and purchased the estate in 1965. The winery and original vineyards are in the northeast sector of the area, and some parcels were added later at Castelnuovo dell'Abate in the southeast. The 33 ha estate is divided into vineyards, olive groves, and other arable land. Both the traditional Slavonian botti and French barriques are used in aging. The entry-level IGT Toscana, Fortunello, is 100% Sangiovese, aged in barriques for 6 months. The Rosso ages for 6 months in 25 hl botti and for another 6 months in barriques. The Brunello is close to half of all production and ages only in botti. The Riserva ages for 12 months in barriques and for 24 months in botti. Under the Sant'Antimo DOC there are both red (Sangiovese, Cabernet Sauvignon, and Petit Verdot) and white (Viognier).

Eredi Fuligni

Loc. Matrichese Via San Saloni 33, 53024 Montalcino	*+39 0577 848710*
info@fuligni.it	*Roberto Fulgini*
www.fuligni.it	*[map p. 101]*
	10 ha; 55,000 btl

The Fulignis were originally a Venetian family; they moved to Maremma in 1770, and then came to Montalcino in 1900. The domain dates from 1923. Maria Flora Fuligni is the present owner, helped by her nephew Roberto Guerrini Fulgini. Vineyards, on east-facing slopes at 380-450m elevation, are about 10% of the 100 ha estate. Plantings are Sangiovese plus some Merlot. Winemaking is a mix of modern and traditional; the Rosso and Brunello age first in stainless steel and then in a mix of French barriques and Slavonian botti; the Riserva ages in the botti. The style is elegant rather than powerful, relatively light for Brunello, more sense of structure for the Riserva. The S.J. super-Tuscan is a blend of 60% Sangiovese with 40% Merlot, aged in tonneaux of French oak.

La Gerla

Rossi Sergio, 53024 Montalcino	*+39 5778 48599*
lagerla@tin.it	*Alberto Passeri*
www.lagerla.it	*[map p. 101]*
	12 ha; 80,000 btl

Sergio Rossi was in advertising when he bought the estate in 1975 from Tedina Biondi-Santi, who had inherited it from her father, It included an old farmhouse and 6.5 ha of vines, just north of Montalcino; Sergio added another 5 ha at Castelnuovo dell'Abate in the south. After his death, the winery continued to be run by manager Alberto Passeri and oenologist Vittorio Fiore. The IGT Toscana, Poggio Degli Angeli, is the entry level wine, 100% Sangiovese, aged for 4 months in botti. Another IGT, Birba, also 100% Sangiovese, is the only wine to age in French oak, for 10 months in tonneaux. The Rosso (declassified from Brunello) and Brunello age in 50 hl and 100 hl botti of Slavonian oak, the Rosso for 10 months and Brunello for 24 months. The Riserva Degli Angeli comes from the Vigna gli Angeli vineyard at the winery, planted in 1976, and ages for four years in botti.

Podere Giodo

Loc. Poderino, 53024 Montalcino	
info@giodo.it	*Bianca and Carlo Ferrini*
www.giodo.it	*[map p. 100]*
	6 ha; 22,000 btl

Carlo Ferrini is probably Italy's most famous oenologist. He started his own personal project on a small scale in the southeast quadrant of Montalcino with his first vintage in 2009. He planted 15 different clones of Sangiovese that he had selected from his experience as a consulting winemaker. There are 2.5 ha classified for Brunello and 3.5 ha classified for IGT Toscana (also 100% Sangiovese). Both Brunello and the IGT age in casks ranging from 700 liter to 25 hl, the IGT, La Quinta, for 12 months, and the Brunello for 30 months. Carlo also has another small winery on Etna, Alberelli di Giodo.

Le Macioche

S.p. 55 di Sant'Antimo km 4,85, 53024 Montalcino	*+39 0577 849168*
info@famigliacotarella.it	*Famiglia Cotarella*
www.famigliacotarella.it	*[map p. 101]*
	3 ha; 18,000 btl

The Cotarellas are one of Italy's most famous winemaking families. Renzo is the chief winemaker at Antinori. His brother Riccardo founded the Falesco winery in Umbria. In 2017, Riccardo's daughters, Dominga, Marta, and Enrica, took over Le Macioche, which had been founded in 1985 and changed hands in 2014. Dominga's husband, Pier Paolo Chiasso, is the winemaker. Located just southeast of the town of Montalcino, this is one of the smallest estates in Montalcino, with just half of its 6 ha planted to vines. The vineyard faces southwest, at around 450m elevation. Winemaking is traditional, with wines aged in 30 hl botti of Slavonian oak. Brunello is about two thirds of production, with the rest divided between Rosso and Riserva. The winery has been known for its elegant, leaner style, and the Cotarellas have made only minor changes, such as introducing a cold soak before fermentation, but otherwise staying with the traditional approach.

La Màgia

Podere La Magia 53, 53024 Montalcino	*+39 5778 35667*
info@fattorialamagia.it	*Fabian Schwarz*
www.fattorialamagia.it	*[map p. 101]*
	15 ha; 60,000 btl

The estate was planted in 1974, and the founders sold it in 1979 to the Schwartz family, from Alto Adige. Harald and Gabriella Schwartz built the cellar in 1979 and renovated it in 1998. Their son, Fabian, took over in 2011. The estate covers 52 ha, with the vineyards occupying a single, contiguous plot, overlooking the abbey of Sant'Antimo. The Brunello is the major part of production, and there are also a Riserva (made only in top years) and the single vineyard Cilegio (made in very small quantities, just a couple of tonneaux). The Brunellos mature in 500 liter tonneaux of French oak. The Rosso di Montalcino ages half in tonneaux and half in stainless steel. Under IGT Toscana, there are entry-level red and rosé, coming from Sangiovese.

Il Marroneto

Loc. Madonna Delle Grazie 307, 53024 Montalcino	*+39 0577 849382*
info@ilmarroneto.it	*Alessandro Mori*
www.ilmarroneto.it	*[map p. 101]*
	6 ha; 30,000 btl

The name of the property reflects its origins in a chestnut drying room near the Montosoli hillside. Giuseppe Mori, a lawyer at the time, purchased the land, planted vineyards, and converted the building into a winery. The estate has been run by his son Alessandro since 1993. The vineyards are relatively old, planted in stages between 1975 and 1984. Only Rosso and Brunello di Montalcino are produced. The style of the wine is fairly tight. All wines are aged in large oak casks. The domain is best known for its single vineyard bottling, the Madonna delle Grazie, made only in top years, which takes its name from the church by the vineyard.

Mocali di Ciacci Tiziano

Loc. Mocali, 53024 Montalcino	*+39 0577 849485*
mocali1956@gmail.com	*Tiziano & Pamela Ciacci & Alessandra Mililotti*
www.mocali.eu	*[map p. 100]*
	14 ha; 180,000 btl

Dina Ciacci created the Mocali estate, and was one of the founders of the Brunello Consorzio in 1967, but the property was in polyculture, and sold its grapes, until his grandson Tiziano took advantage of the freeze that killed the olive trees in 1985: he planted vineyards and started bottling wine with the 1990 vintage. Production at Mocali is a mix of traditional and modern: Rosso di Montalcino, Brunello, and Riserva, are all aged in large casks. Vigna delle Raunate comes from the oldest vines and ages in 350 liter barriques. The Vigna delle Raunate Riserva is produced only in top vintages and ages in 400 liter barrels. In 1996, Tiziano and his wife Alessandra revived the neighboring Poggio Nardone property, and this separately produces Rosso, Brunello, and Riserva in a more modern style, with aging including a proportion of new oak. There are also several IGT Toscanas from Mocali, consisting of blends of Sangiovese with other varieties. Production was also expanded by purchasing the Suberli estate in Maremma in 2001.

Padelletti

Via Giuseppe Mazzini 36, 53024 Montalcino	*+39 5778 48314*
padelletti_claudia@yahoo.it	*Claudia Susanna Padelletti*
www.padelletti.it	
	6 ha; 8,000 btl

This is one of the oldest wineries in Montalcino, and the only one in town center. The family has owned vineyards since 1571. Carlo Padelletti was one of the founders of the first cooperative in Montalcino after the first world war. Guido Padelletti was one of the founders of the Consorzio when the DOC was created in 1967. Claudia Susanna Padelletti was a banker before she took over the estate, at first working there part-time only at weekends, before taking over full-time in 1990. She made the transition from selling grapes to estate-bottling. The cellars are below the family's sixteenth-century home. Vineyards are on slopes to the north of the town, with 2 ha for producing Rosso and 4 ha for producing Brunello. The wines ferment in concrete with maceration for 20-30 days. The Rosso ages for 6-12 months in large barrels of French oak, and the Brunello ages for 2-3 years in a mix of French and Slavonian oak. A Riserva is made in top years.

Celestino Pecci

Loc. Viti-San Carlo, 53024 Montalcino	*+39 5778 47046*
info@aziendapeccicelestino.com	*Tiziana Pecci*
www.aziendapeccicelestino.com	*[map p. 101]*
	40 ha

The domain was created when Celestino Pecci bought 40 ha of land and two old farmhouses in 1968. One of the farmhouses remains the family home. His only daughter Tiziana joined the estate in 2003 and is now in charge. All grapes come from the estate, where the vineyards face south-southwest at about 350m elevation. The Rosso di Toscana is 100% Sangiovese and ages in a mix of barriques and tonneaux. The Rosso and

Brunello di Montalcino age in 10hl and 35hl botti of Slavonian oak. The top wine is the Poggio al Carro Brunello, which ages in 35hl botti. The two Rossos age for 12 months, the Brunellos age for 36-40 months.

Piancornello

Loc. Piancornello, 53020 Castelnuovo Dell'Abate Montalcino	*+39 3495 997260*
info@piancornello.it	*Claudio Monaci*
www.piancornello.it	*[map p. 100]*
	10 ha; 50,000 btl

The Peri family purchased the Piancornello vineyard in 1950, and sold the fruit until they started bottling their own Brunello in 1991. The winemaker today is Claudio Monaci, grandson of the founders. In addition to the main estate in the southeast quadrant, there are 2 ha in the Valdicava area to the north. The Brunello is a blend from both. Use of about a third new oak gives a modern impression to the wine. The Rosso is a little lighter, and the Riserva is a fraction deeper, but I find the style generally to be on the light side and a little obvious. In 2015, they bought the estate of Podere del Visciolo in Montecucco, just to the west of Montalcino. The IGT Campo della Macchia combines grapes from both estates; otherwise the wines are separate.

Pietroso

Podere Pietroso 257, 53024 Montalcino	*+39 5778 48573*
info@pietroso.it	*Gianni Pignattai*
www.pietroso.it	*[map p. 101]*
	5 ha; 30,000 btl

Domenico Berni started to make wine in the 1970s from less than a hectare just outside the Montalcino town walls. Three generations later, his nephew Gianni Pignatti runs this small estate with vineyards around the winery (just west of Montalcino), near Sant'Antimo abbey in the south, and at Montosoli in the north. The Rosso and Brunello ferment in stainless steel and age in 30 hl botti of Slavonian oak. Villa Montosoli comes from a single vineyard on top of the Montosoli hill, and is an IGT Toscana, mostly Sangiovese, but also including small amounts of other Tuscan varieties including Colorino, Ciliegiolo, and Canaiolo; it ages for 24 months in tonneaux of French oak.

Podere Le Ripi

Loc. Le Ripi, 53021 Montalcino	*+39 0577 835641*
info@podereleripi.it	*Nasello Sebastian*
www.podereleripi.it	*[map p. 101]*
	33 ha; 90,000 btl

Podere Le Ripi was Francesco Illy's first project in Montalcino, before he purchased adjacent Mastrojanni (see profile), which is now somewhat better known. Podere Le Ripi was virgin land when the first vineyard was planted in 1998. It made a stir for its "bonsai vineyard," just a tenth of a hectare, planted with vines at the extraordinary density of 62,500/ha. This was the basis for the Rosso di Montalcino in 2007. There are several Brunellos: Lupi e Sirene, and its Riserva, come from "regular" dense plantings, at 11,000 vines/hectare. Cielo d'Ulisse and Zapuntel (from the Podere Galampio vineyard on the other side of Le Ripi) come from more conventional plantings, at 4,000 vines/hectare. Little is conventional here: the cellar has been built using artisanal methods avoiding cement.

Tenuta la Poderina

Loc. Poderina, 53020 Castelnuovo Dell'abate, Montalcino	*+39 0577 835737*
lapoderina@tenutedelcerro.it	*Raffaele Pistucchia*
www.lapoderina.it	*[map p. 101]*
	27 ha; 120,000 btl

Tenute del Cerro is the holding company for wine properties of Gruppo Unipol, a huge European insurance company. It has five estates, with four in Tuscany or Umbria, including the flagship property, Fattoria del Cerro, in Montepulciano, and others in Montefalco Sagrantino and Monterufoli. La Poderina is the property in Montalcino, and produces only DOC wines: Rosso, Brunello, the Poggio Abate Riserva, and Moscadello di Montalcino. Rosso and Brunello age in a mix of Slavonian botti and French barriques; the Riserva ages only in barriques. The property also offers accommodation.

Poggio di Sotto

Loc. Poggio Di Sotto, 53024 Castelnuovo Dell'Abate	*+39 5778 35502*
info@poggiodisotto.it	*Claudio Tipa*
www.collemassariwines.it	*[map p. 101]*
	20 ha; 55,000 btl

Piero Palmucci founded the estate in 1989 after researching terroirs in Montalcino. He then worked with the University of Milan to select the best Sangiovese clones from the old vines in the vineyards (some now 50-years old). He sold the domain in 2011 to Claudio Tipa, owner of ColleMassari (see profile) in Montecucco and Grattamacco (see profile) in Bolgheri. Claudio bought another estate in Montalcino in 2016, San Giorgio, also in Castelnuova dell'Abate. Poggio di Sotto covers 48 ha, with 19 ha of olive trees as well as vineyards. Vineyards are in parcels at 200m, 300m, and 450m elevation, overlooking the Orcia river valley. Plantings are exclusively Sangiovese, and there are three cuvées. All age in 30 hl Slavonian oak botti, the Rosso di Montalcino for 24 months, the Brunello for 40 months, and the Riserva (made in the best vintages) for 60 months.

Poggio San Polo

Loc. Podere San Polo di Podernovi, 53024 Montalcino	*+39 0577 835101*
info@poggiosanpolo.com	*Riccardo Fratton*
www.poggiosanpolo.com	*[map p. 101]*
	16 ha; 110,000 btl

The well known Valpolicella producer Allegrini purchased San Polo in 2008 together with an estate at Monteluc belonging to the same owners. San Polo now describes the combined estates. "It was biodynamic, but the vines were dying," says Marilisa Allegrini. "We started over, and have converted it to sustainable." (It has the CasaClima certification.) The San Polo home estate at Podernovi was planted in 1990, and Monteluc more recently at higher vine density. Half of the vineyards are classified for Brunello. The style is between modern and traditional. "If you ask my brother," says Marilisa, "he equates modernist with technology, but we do some modern things and some traditional things." The style is on the lighter side for Montalcino: the light red fruits and tannins of the Rosso are halfway to Brunello, the Brunello has a little more weight, but the house style of elegance, you might almost say delicacy, comes out fully in the Riserva. The Rosso comes from Podernovi and ages in second-year tonneaux, the Brunello is a blend from both vineyards and ages in new tonneaux, while the Riserva aged in mix of new and one-year tonneaux. In addition to the DOCG wines, there are two IGTs: Mezzopane is a Sangiovese-Merlot blend from Monteluc aged in barriques, and Rubio is a monovarietal Sangiovese aged for 12 months in large casks. Allegrini also own Poggio al Tesoro in Bolgheri (see profile). Carlo Ferrini is the consulting oenologist.

Tenuta Le Potazzine

53024 Montalcino	*+39 5778 46168*
tenuta@lepotazzine.it	*Gigliola Giannetti*
www.lepotazzine.com	*[map p. 100]*
	5 ha; 29,000 btl

Gigliola Giannetti started working for Biondi Santi in 1985. She then opened a wine shop in Montalcino in 1987, worked for the Consorzio, and bought her first parcel of land in 1993, when her daughter Viola was born. The winery is located here, at Le Prata, high in the northeast sector, where the winery is located, at around 500m elevation. In 1996, when Sofia was born, she purchased another parcel, is in the southern area at 420m elevation near Sant'Angelo in Colle. (Potazzine describes the great tit, a colorful local bird, and is used as a nickname for children.) Viola and Sofia are now both at the domain. The wines are traditional: blends across vineyards, aged in 30 hl and 50 hl botti of Slavonian oak, with the Rosso di Montalcino aged for 12 months and the Brunello for 42 months. In top years, a Riserva has been made, but only a handful of times. The entry level IGT Toscana, Parus, is Sangiovese aged in stainless steel.

Le Ragnaie

Loc. Le Ragnaie, 53024 Montalcino	*+39 0577 848639*
info@leragnaie.com	*Riccardo Campinoti*
www.leragnaie.com	*[map p. 101]*
	21 ha; 90,000 btl

Riccardo and Jennifer Campinoti purchased the property in 2002 and are building a reputation as a producer of traditional Brunellos. Le Ragnaie has vineyards in three different areas of Montalcino: most of the vineyards are in the home estate, at one of the highest points in the appellation, around 600m; the Petroso vineyard is 1 ha just below the village of Montalcino; and Vigna Fornace is at Castelnuova dell'Abata in the southeast corner. The Rosso comes mostly from Petroso. The Brunello takes the classic approach of blending from all the vineyards. The Brunello V.V. comes only from the Ragnaie estate, while Brunello Fornace comes only from Castellnovo dell'Abata. Wines are aged in 25 hl botti of Slavonian oak for three years. There is also a Chianti Colli Senesi from the Ragnaie estate, also 100% Sangiovese, but aged in French barriques. The farm house on the Ragnaie estate offers accommodation.

Salicutti

Leanza Francesco, 53024 Montalcino	*+39 5778 47003*
leanza@poderesalicutti.it	*Felix & Sabine Eichbauer*
www.poderesalicutti.it	*[map p. 101]*
	4 ha; 18,000 btl

This small estate started in 1990 when Francesco Leanza retired as a chemical engineer and purchased an 11 ha property in Montalcino. He began replanting the vineyards in 1994, starting with the Piaggione plot below the winery and the Teatro plot farther up the hill. Francesco is considered to be a leader of the natural wine movement in Montalcino, and the wines have occasionally had technical problems. The major product is the Piaggione Brunello, which is a blend from Piaggione and Teatro. The Rosso di Montalcino comes from a separate plot above the winery. The Rosso ages in tonneaux of French oak, including 20% new wood, while the Brunello ages in larger casks, mostly of Slavonian oak. The Dopoteatro IGT Toscana comes from Cabernet Sauvignon and Canaiolo. In 2017, Francesco sold the estate to Felix and Sabine Eichbauer of the Tantris restaurant in Munich, which has always taken the wines, but he remains as winemaker for three years.

San Polino

53024 Montalcino	*+39 5778 35775*
vino@sanpolino.it	*Luigi & Katia Nussbaum*
www.sanpolino.it	*[map p. 101]*
	7 ha; 25,000 btl

This is very much a small artisanal domain, the creation of Luigi Fabbro and Katia Nussbaum, who bought the farmstead in the southeast quadrant in 1968. Vines and olive trees had been long grown there The first mention of vines at the property dates from 1581, but most of the vines had been pulled out. There are still 6 olive trees dating from 1581. Luiga and Katia started by planting 2.5 ha. Right from the beginning, the vineyards were cultivated organically. Today there are other vineyards to the north of San Polino, and in the far south of Montalcino, as well as at the farmstead. The Rosso ages for six months in wood, Brunello ages in 35 hl botti of Slavonian oak, the Brunello Helichrysum comes from the highest vineyards (450m) at San Polino, and ages for six months in barriques followed by 3 years in botti of Slavonian and French oak, and the Riserva has similar aging but spends four years in the botti. The style is relatively stern for Brunello: Helichrysum is strongly structured and takes several years to come out of its shell.

Podere Sanlorenzo

Sanlorenzo 280, 53024 Montalcino	*+39 3396 070930*
info@poderesanlorenzo.net	*Luciano Ciolfi*
www.poderesanlorenzo.net	*[map p. 100]*
	7 ha; 18,000 btl

High up in the southwest quadrant of the appellation, above 500m elevation, this small domain has four vineyards on rocky soils of galestro, facing towards Maremma and the Mediterranean. The estate was purchased five generations ago, two generations later vineyards expanded from the original 1 ha, and then another two generations later, current owner Luciano Ciolfi was the first to bottle wine. Vineyards were planted between 1972 and 2018, all Sangiovese. Rosso di Montalcino comes from the youngest plantings, and ages in barriques and tonneaux. The Brunello (about half of production) and the Riserva age in 30-35 hl botti. There is also a rosé IGT Toscana.

La Serena

Mantengoli Andrea, 53024 Montalcino	*+39 3288 113302*
info@cantinalaserena.com	*Elisabetta Mantengoli*
www.cantinalaserena.it	*[map p. 101]*
	13 ha; 40,000 btl

The Mantengoli family have owned this 50 ha estate since 1933. Andrea and his brother Marcello took over in 1988, starting with 2,700 bottles of Brunello. They built a new winery, designed by Marcello, who is an architect. Andrea runs the domain. The terroir is on a limestone base, to the east of the town, at about 400m elevation. The Rosso di Montalcino comes from the lower slopes, while Brunello comes from higher up. The Riserva Gemini is a selection from the oldest vines. Rosso ages in a mix of tonneau and French barriques, Brunello ages in 10% barriques and 90% 20hl botti, and the Riserva starts in barriques for malolactic fermentation, and after a year moves to 20hl and 40hl botti.

Tenuta di Sesta	
Loc. Sesta, 53024 Castelnuovo Dell'Abate	*+39 0577 835612*
tenutadisesta@tenutadisesta.it	*Giovanni Ciacci*
www.tenutadisesta.it	*[map p. 101]*
	31 ha; 150,000 btl

Giovanni Ciacci founded the winery in 1995, and continues as winemaker, with his children Andrea and Francesca now taking over the business side. The estate of 200 ha includes 20 ha of vineyards for Brunello and Rosso di Montalcino, and another 11 ha in Sant'Antimo. The rest is devoted to olive trees and grain production. The approach is traditionalist, with the Rosso and Brunello aged in botti. The Rosso gives a good preview of the Brunello, which is quite complex aromatically. In addition to the Rosso, Brunello, and Brunello Riserva, there is a single vineyard Riserva from the Duelacci plot, coming from the eastern side in cooler years, and the western side in warmer years. The back label says Duelacci Est or Duelacci Ovest. Camponovo is an entry-level IGT Toscana based on a Chianti-like blend of 90% Sangiovese with 10% Colorino, aged in stainless steel. Poggio d'Arna is an IGT Toscana of 40% Sangiovese, 30% each of Cabernet Franc and Merlot, aged in barriques followed by botti.

Tassi	
via P Strozzi 1-3, 53024 Montalcino	*+39 0577 846147*
info@tassimontalcino.com	*Fabbio Tassi*
www.tassimontalcino.com	*[map p. 101]*
	8 ha; 20,000 btl

Fabio Tassi is something of an entrepreneur, with a wine shop, the Enoteca la Fortezza, showcasing the local wines in Montalcino, a restaurant, Locanda Franci, just across the street (with accommodation above), and the winery that has his name on the edge of town. The vineyards are on a single slope in Castelnuovo dell'Abata, at the southeast. Aging policy is to increase the size of the cask going up the hierarchy, so Rosso ages in 500 liter barrels, Brunello in 700 liter barrels, and the Selezione Franci in Slavonian botti. Two IGTs have unusual blends: Colsilium is equal parts of Sangiovese, Cabernet Sauvignon, and Petit Verdot, while Aquabona is equal parts of Cabernet Sauvignon and Petit Verdot.

Terralsole	
Villa Collina d'Oro 160/a, 53024 Montalcino	*+39 0577 835764*
info@terralsole.com	*Mario Bollag*
www.terralsole.com	*[map p. 101]*
	12 ha; 55,000 btl

Mario Bollag had a chequered career until he decided to become a winemaker. He created Il Palazzi in 1982, but sold it and then established Terralsole in 1996. The Pian Bossolino Vineyard around the winery is at 420m, overlooking Castelnuvo dell'Abate.

The Fonte Lattaia vineyard is located lower down, around 250,between Castelnuvo dell'Abate Sant'Angelo. The style is modern, with wines aged in 600 liter tonneaux of French oak. Intensity increases from the Rosso to the Brunello, and then to the single-vineyard wines from Pian Bassolino and the rich Fonte Lattaia. Pasticcio is a full-force super-Tuscan, a blend of Cabernet Franc and Merlot with some Sangiovese.

Tiezzi

Loc. Soccorso, 53024 Montalcino	*+39 3286 673884*
info@tiezzivini.com	*Enzo Tiezzi*
www.tiezzivini.it	*[map p. 101]*
	6 ha; 27,000 btl

Enzo Tiezzi played a distinguished role in the history of Brunello di Montalcino. He started at Poggia alle Mura and in 1973 moved to run the Col d'Orcia and Argiano estates, which had just been purchased by the Cinzano family. He obtained a Ph. D. for a study that projected the future of Montalcino. As President of the Consorzio, he was responsible for the introduction of Rosso di Montalcino. He left Col d'Orcia in 1989 to found his own estate, starting with the Soccorso vineyard just outside the town of Montalcino. This vineyard was originally the property of Riccardo Paccagnini, who was the first producer to put Brunello on a label, in the nineteenth century. Subsequently Enzo added the Cigaleta and Cerrino plots in the northeast sector. Vines are exclusively Sangiovese and make up just over half of the 10 ha estate. Production is traditional, with wines aged in 10-40 hl botti of Slavonian oak. The Rosso di Montalcino is declassified from the Brunello (Poggio Cerrino), essentially by limiting aging to 18 months instead of 44 months. The Vigna Soccorso Brunello comes only from Soccorso and a Riserva is made from the vineyard in top vintages.

Villa i Cipressi

Loc. Villa i Cipressi, 53024 Montalcino	*+39 0577 848640*
info@villacipressi.it	*Dario Ciacci*
www.villacipressi.it	*[map p. 101]*
	4 ha; 20,000 btl

This family estate started by making honey, and then expanded in the 1990s when Hubert Ciacci decided to produce wine and olive oil. His sons have now taken over, with Federico in charge of winemaking and production of honey, while Dario manages the vineyards. The winery is underground. One small vineyard is around the winery, just southeast of Montalcino, and there are 2 ha farther southeast at Castelnuova dell'Abate and 1.5 ha at Tavarnalle in the southwest. The IGT Toscana includes other varieties as well as 90% Sangiovese, and ages briefly in wood. Rosso and Brunello di Montalcino age 60% in barriques and 40% in 10hl and 30hl botti, Rosso for 6 months, Brunello for 24 months, and the Zebras Brunello (only in top years) for 36 months.

Bolgheri

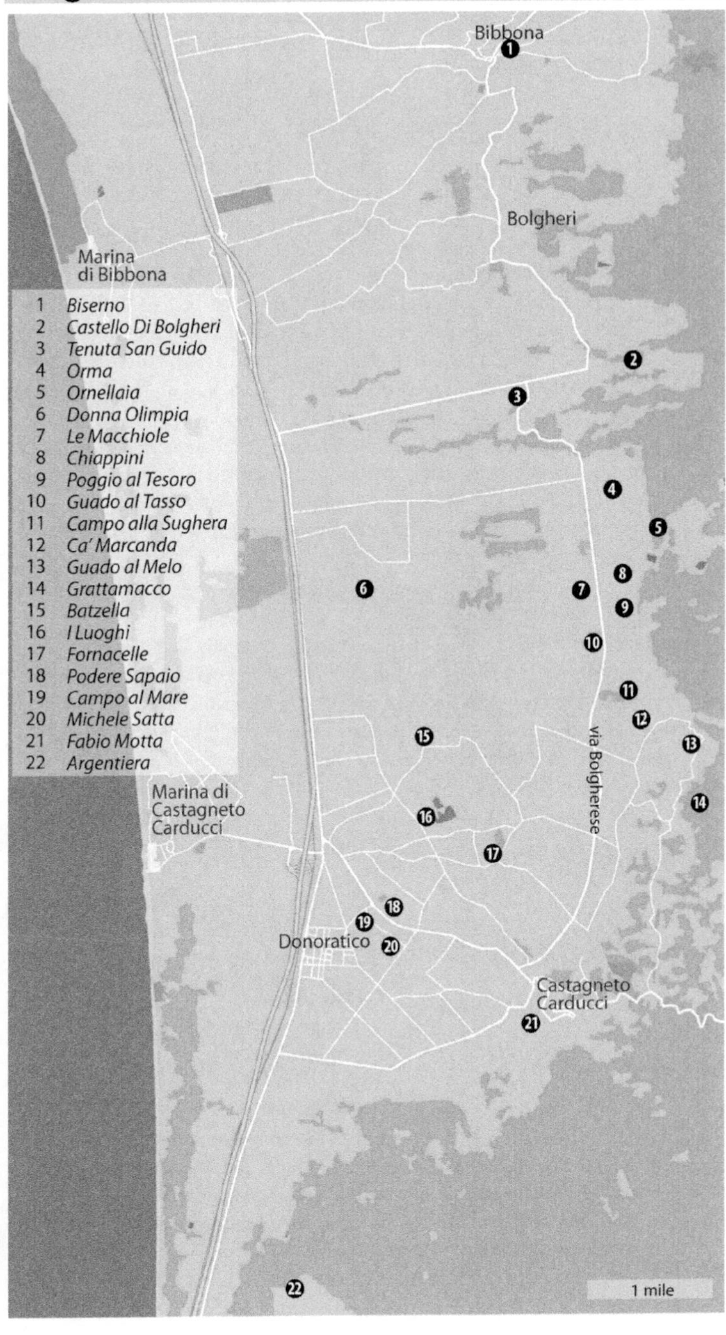
Bibbona
Bolgheri
Marina di Bibbona
1 Biserno
2 Castello Di Bolgheri
3 Tenuta San Guido
4 Orma
5 Ornellaia
6 Donna Olimpia
7 Le Macchiole
8 Chiappini
9 Poggio al Tesoro
10 Guado al Tasso
11 Campo alla Sughera
12 Ca' Marcanda
13 Guado al Melo
14 Grattamacco
15 Batzella
16 I Luoghi
17 Fornacelle
18 Podere Sapaio
19 Campo al Mare
20 Michele Satta
21 Fabio Motta
22 Argentiera
Marina di Castagneto Carducci
via Bolgherese
Donoratico
Castagneto Carducci
1 mile

Batzella *

Località Badia 227, 57022 Castagneto Carducci	*+39 3393 975888*
info@batzella.com	*Khanh Nguyen and Franco Batzella*
www.batzella.com	*[map p. 145]*
8 ha; 55,000 btl	*Bolgheri Superiore, Tam*

Batzella is a boutique operation. I'm not sure if it is the smallest producer in Bolgheri, but it must be one of the smallest. Khanh Nguyen and Franco Batzella worked at the World Bank until they decided to retire early and do something different. Initially they decided to start in Montalcino. "Since no one knew us and we were starting without any reputation, we thought we should start somewhere that had a reputation," says Khanh, who makes the wines. They bought and planted an estate in Montalcino, and started selling the grapes, but then 8 ha became available in Bolgheri, and they decided this was more attractive because of the way the region was expanding. They have 1 ha of Cabernet Franc, 1 ha Syrah, 1 ha white varieties, and 5 ha Cabernet Sauvignon, planted with 6 different clones. The first year of production was 2003.

There are three levels of wine: a Bolgheri Superiore, a Bolgheri, and an entry-level wine. Yields are slightly lower for Tâm, a blend of 60% Cabernet Sauvignon with 40% Cabernet Franc, which is the top of the line Bolgheri Superiore and spends two years in barriques, than for the Bolgheri DOC Peàn, which has 70% Cabernet Sauvignon and 30% Cabernet Franc, and spends one year in barriques. This is really an artisan operation, in semi-permanent surroundings because of problems obtaining a construction permit, which has finally come through. "It proves you don't need a cathedral to make good wine," says Franco.

Ca' Marcanda **

Loc. Santa Teresa 272, 57022 Castagneto Carducci	*+39 0565 763809*
info@camarcanda.com	*Gaia Gaja*
	[map p. 145]
120 ha; 450,000 btl	*Bolgheri Superiore, Camarcanda*

Angelo Gaja is a force of nature—and not one to do things by halves. Famous for his Barbaresco (and Barolo), where his single-vineyard wines are at the top of the hierarchy, he expanded into Montalcino by acquiring the Pieve Santa Restituta vineyards in 1994. Having decided he wanted also to make wine in Bolgheri, he conducted a long and patient search until he identified the best terroirs. "It was difficult when I came here because there was no historical record, all the new vineyards were planted in land that was not vineyards before. Although I am not a Burgundian, land is important for me, so I investigated. There was research done in 1987 to discover whether there was land similar to

Sassicaia. They transferred the research to a big map, with a harlequin of color codes. I asked a friend, a producer, to look at it with me. I asked him, what is the color of Sassicaia's land, he showed me the yellow, and there was yellow also at Ornellaia and Guado al Tasso."

Angelo set out to buy the land from another yellow patch, and after a lengthy wooing process, he was able to purchase the vineyards in 1996. "I visited seventeen times, making many different proposals to rent the land from two brothers, and my wife said, 'You are losing time, these are Ca'Marcanda people' (this means endless negotiations without ever signing a deal). But the eighteenth time their sister was with the two brothers, I had not met her before, she said that renting did not make sense, so why don't we sell it to Mr. Gaja?"

Ca'Marcanda became the name of the winery. There were some small plots of Vermentino and Sangiovese, but most of the land was given over to other crops or was unplanted. "So what to plant? I know the area has an avocation for Cabernet, I tasted the wine of Sassicaia, but I didn't like to make a wine that would be a copy of Sassicaia. So we decided on our own blend, it's a Bordeaux blend but in the mind of the artisan I would like to make a wine that follows *our* ideas, that speaks the Tuscan language." Planting started in 1997. "Every year we planted 7-8 ha, in 2010 we reached 100 ha," says Angelo. "We plan a maximum of 120 ha," he says, explaining that this is more or less the limit he sees for artisan production.

A striking new winery has been built, largely underground. There are three wines. Promis is a blend of Merlot and Syrah, with a little Sangiovese; Magari is half Merlot with a quarter each of Cabernet Sauvignon and Cabernet Franc; and Camarcanda is half Merlot with 40% Cabernet Sauvignon and 10% Cabernet Franc. Production is around 25,000 cases of Promis, 8,000 of Magari, and 2,500 of Camarcanda. The wines typify Bolgheri in their combination of underlying structure with superficial lushness; Promis is always the most forward, " Magari is the flagship of the winery that best matches food," says Angelo, and Camarcanda is the most elegant and structured, with an impression that it has more than the actual 40% of Cabernet Sauvignon.

Campo alla Sughera *

SP Bolgherese, 57022 Castagneto Carduccii	*+39 0565 766936*
info@campoallasughera.com	*Elisabeth Finkbeiner*
www.campoallasughera.com	*[map p. 145]*
17 ha; 110,000 btl	*Bolgheri Superiore, Arnione*

The Knauf family fortune comes from construction; Knauf is now a multinational company that dominates the market for drywalls. The family owns 70 ha of vineyards in the Mosel and Franconia (where it originated), and came to the Bolgheri area because they have a plant for producing plasterboard nearby. They founded Campo alla Sughera in 1998, when the land had only olive and cork trees and tomatoes. (The name means the field of the cork trees.) The first vintage was 2001.

The major wine in terms of volume (about two thirds of production) is Adèo, an entry-level blend of the more fruit-forward lots of Cabernet Sauvignon with Merlot, aged in 20% new oak. It has upfront fruits and is immediately attractive.

The flagship wine is Arnione. Until 2005, Arnione was a blend of 50% Cabernet Sauvignon with the rest divided between Merlot and Petit Verdot; then another vineyard (across the main road) was added, and Cabernet Franc was included. Now it's 40% Cabernet Sauvignon with equal amounts of each of the other three varieties. "This has brought more refinement," says Elisabeth Finkbeiner, who has been managing the estate since 2016. Arnione ages mostly in new oak, spends two years in the bottle before release; "we want to release it when it begins to be ready," Elisabeth says. On release, it might fairly be described as full-force Bolgheri: rich, chocolaty, and quite aromatic. It takes about a decade before it shows signs of development, but even then the main impression remains juicy.

Two special cuvées go in opposite directions. Anima d'Arnione was produced as a limited edition of 1,500 magnums in 2016. It has 85% Cabernet Sauvignon and 15% Merlot from the best parcels. It makes sophisticated impression with greater precision than Arnione. More restrained, it goes for elegance rather than power. It's undecided whether there will be future vintages. The eponymous Campo alla Sughera is an IGT Toscana from 70% Petit Verdot and 30% Cabernet Franc, made since 2006 but not in every vintage. Spicy with powerful aromatics, it really needs time to come around.

The white Arioso is Vermentino; about 10% of production, it is vinified in stainless steel and has that characteristic touch of salinity of the variety in Bolgheri.

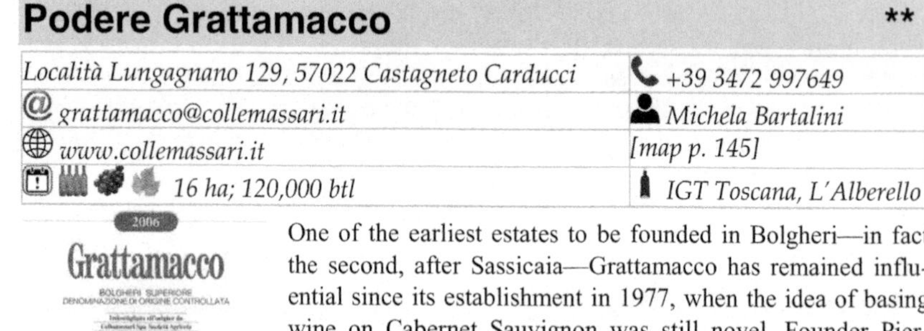

Podere Grattamacco **

Località Lungagnano 129, 57022 Castagneto Carducci	*+39 3472 997649*
grattamacco@collemassari.it	*Michela Bartalini*
www.collemassari.it	*[map p. 145]*
16 ha; 120,000 btl	*IGT Toscana, L'Alberello*

One of the earliest estates to be founded in Bolgheri—in fact the second, after Sassicaia—Grattamacco has remained influential since its establishment in 1977, when the idea of basing wine on Cabernet Sauvignon was still novel. Founder Piermario Meletti Cavallari ran the estate for a quarter century until he sold it in 2002 to Claudia Tipa's ColleMassari (see profile). ColleMassari Wine Estates (with its headquarters in Montecucco) also own Poggio di Sotto (see profile) and San Giorgio in Montalcino. Piermario Meletti Cavallari continued to live at Grattamacco, but now makes wine on Elba.

Grattamacco is located between Bolgheri and Castagneto Carducci, on an elevation of about 100m, basically on a plain that gets steady breezes. About half of the 34 ha estate is planted with vineyards or olive groves; the rest is uncultivated Mediterranean shrubs. The flagship wine is the Bolgheri Superiore Grattamacco, a blend of 65% Cabernet Sauvignon, 20% Merlot, and 15% Sangiovese (which in this windy location avoids the problems of humidity that occur elsewhere in Bolgheri. It ages for 18 months in barriques. The Bolgheri Rosso is a second wine, 50% Cabernet Sauvignon, 20% each of Cabernet Franc and Merlot, and 10% Sangiovese aged for 10 months in barriques. L'Alberello comes from a 2 ha plot planted with 70% Cabernet Sauvignon, 25% Cabernet Franc, and 5% Petit Verdot; the name reflects the unusual training of the vines very high in the alberello style. It ages in barriques for 18 months. The reds are quite structured, in the juicy Bolgheri style. There is also a white from Vermentino. The winemaker today is Lucca Marone, aided by consulting enologist Maurizio Castelli.

Guado al Melo *

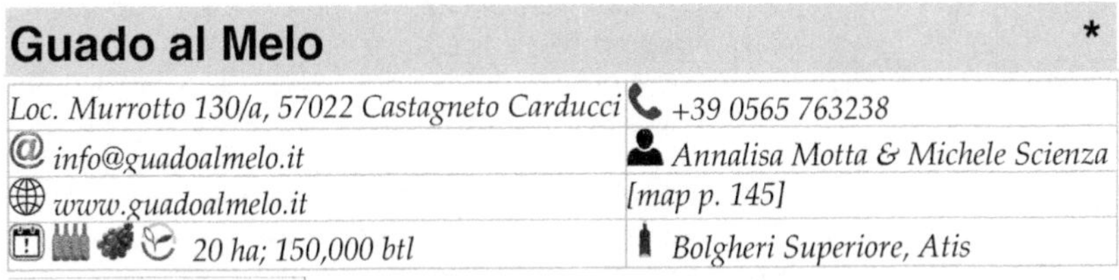

Loc. Murrotto 130/a, 57022 Castagneto Carducci	*+39 0565 763238*
info@guadoalmelo.it	*Annalisa Motta & Michele Scienza*
www.guadoalmelo.it	*[map p. 145]*
20 ha; 150,000 btl	*Bolgheri Superiore, Atis*

"My family is from Trentino," says Michele Scienza. "My father Attilio and I decided to move to Bolgheri, and we've been here since 1998. My father was a Professor of Viticulture at the University of Milan, and he had made a study of soils in Bolgheri in 1994-1996. In 1999 we planted the first vineyard, and in 2003 we built the cellar."

About half a mile to the east of the main wine route, the bunker-like winery is deceptively built into the hillside. It's on one level, with the entry hall forming a spacious tasting room, and the vinification facility to the right and the aging cellar to the left. It's an education to visit the tasting room, as the academic background shows in the information panels all around, which describe the region, winemaking, and the history of wine in Italy. "This is not only a cellar where we produce wine, we want to explain the culture that lies behind wine," says Michele. It feels more like a museum round the back where you can see Attilio's library of several thousand books.

The two whites are l'Airone, 100% Vermentino, and Criseo, a blend of five varieties (dominated by Vermentino) from a single vineyard that are cofermented. "I come from Trentino, my heritage is that I must make good white wine," Michele says. l'Airone has that saline character particular to white Bolgheri; Criseo is more powerful and complex.

The entry-level red is Bacco in Toscana, a blend of 60% Sangiovese and 40% Syrah, that makes a pleasant wine for easy drinking. Rute is the Bolgheri DOC, a blend of 80% Cabernet Sauvignon and 20% Merlot that is effectively the second wine to the flagship Atis, a blend of 80% Cabernet Sauvignon with 10% each of Cabernet Franc and Merlot. The style is restrained, and can be a little stern at first; these are food wines.

Jassarte is an unusual cuvée from 30 varieties grown in a single vineyard, and blended in equal amounts. "The wine must be a picture of the vineyard, similar to pre-phylloxera wines," Michele says. It develops quite slowly. Atis and Jassarte are produced only in the best years. Antillo, which was a blend of 50% Sangiovese with Cabernet Sauvignon and Merlot, is no longer produced. All the reds age in barrique, "but only 10% new oak because I don't want the wood to cover the wine."

Guado al Tasso **

SP Bolgherese Km. 3.9, 57024 Bolgheri	*+39 0565 749735*
guadoaltasso@antinori.it	*Marco Ferrarese*
www.guadoaltasso.it	*[map p. 145]*
320 ha; 1,700,000 btl	*Bolgheri Superiore, Guado al Tasso*

Guado al Tasso is part of Antinori's Florentine Empire, which has estates all over Tuscany and Umbria, including several in Chianti, and in Montalcino and Orvieto. Antinori's most important super-Tuscans are Tignanello (Sangiovese based but historically the first wine to blend in Cabernet Sauvignon), Solaia (Cabernet based, coming from the Tignanello estate in Chianti), and Guado al Tasso (the super-Tuscan from Bolgheri). Some of the production at Guado al Tasso goes into the Villa Antinori IGT Toscana.

Guado al Tasso is a vast estate of 1,000 ha, stretching two miles from the Via Bolgherese to the coast road. The visitor entrance is being moved to Via Bolgherese, where there will be a new wine shop and a restaurant. Guado al Tasso itself is made in the old cellar, as well as the Merlot (Cont'Ugo) and the Cabernet Sauvignon (Matarochio). There is a new winery close to the coast for Il Bruciato—which started as a second label, but is now the majority of production—and the Vermentino and Rosé, which make up most of the rest. Guado al Tasso is only 100,000 bottles, and production of the varietals is very small. The approach to terroir is quite Bordelais: Cabernet Sauvignon, Cabernet Franc, and Merlot are planted with increasing proportions of clay. The estate includes 200 ha of cereal (some of this is used to feed their pigs) and 1,000 olive trees.

"The styles of Il Bruciato and Guado al Tasso are different so each has its own identity," says winemaker Marco Ferrarese. "Originally they had the same blend, but now Il Bruciato has Syrah, and Guado al Tasso has Cabernet Franc." Both have around 60% Cabernet Sauvignon, with Merlot as the second variety. Sometimes Guado al Tasso has a little Petit Verdot. "The Syrah makes Il Brucciato more forward; Cabernet Franc gives Guado al Tasso more elegance and longevity."

Il Bruciato offers appealing aromatics for drinking immediately. Guado Al Tasso varies between warm vintages, where it shows the soft plushness that typifies Bolgheri, to cooler vintages where Cabernet character comes out more directly, but it always has a pleasing sense of restraint. Matarochio is the most precise, very fine, but not as varied. Cont'Ugo is an exuberant expression of Merlot. Guado al Tasso is the most sophisticated of the top wines, which all use new oak (Il Bruciatio has no new oak). The Vermentino is produced in stainless steel and is lively with attractive aromatics.

Le Macchiole **

Via Bolgherese 189/a, 57022 Bolgheri	*+39 0565 766092*
info@lemacchiole.it	*Cinzia Merli & Elia & Mattia Campolmi*
www.lemacchiole.it	*[map p. 145]*
30 ha; 185,000 btl	*IGT Toscana, Paleo Rosso*

This estate has an unusual origin, as it is indigenous to Bolgheri, instead of being formed by outsiders. One of the first wineries in Bolgheri, it was founded when Eugenio Campolmi extended his experience producing wine for his father's restaurant into purchasing a vineyard and producing wine commercially. "In 1983 my parents bought the first piece of land—where the winery is now—and planted some vineyards.

Father experimented with many Tuscan and Bordeaux varieties because he wanted to make red wine," says Mattia Campolmi. The first wine was produced in 1987. After Eugenio's death in 2002, it continued to be run by his wife, Cinzia Merli, until she handed it on to their sons, Mattia and Elia Campolmi.

The original vineyard was 4 ha and now has the oldest vines. There's another 4 ha at the winery, which is more or less surrounded by Guado al Tasso. There are now also five other plots (including one outside the Bolgheri DOC). "In each area we planted almost all the varieties we produce. In each harvest we separate each variety from each vineyard. So each wine is a blend from several vineyards," Elia says. "It's the philosophy of Le Macchiole to experiment with everything," he adds.

The winery found its focus on producing monovarietal super-Tuscans from international varieties. "We produce Bolgheri DOC only for the entry-level, the IGT wines are the upper crust," Mattia says. The Bolgheri Rosso is a blend of about 50% Merlot together with Cabernet Franc, Cabernet Sauvignon, and Syrah, and is about three quarters of production. Full of black fruits, it is quite forceful for "entry-level" wine.

"Paleo Rosso is our flagship because it was the first wine our father produced in 1989," Mattia says. "We were known better for Paleo than as Le Macchiole, and they called us the Paleo Rosso winery. It started as a blend of Sangiovese with Cabernet Sauvignon. In 1992 our father started to add Cabernet Franc to the blend, every year he increased it, and in 1998 he regrafted all the Cabernet Sauvignon to Cabernet Franc. In 2001 he released it as a 100% Cabernet Franc." This was revolutionary at the time. The most aromatic of Le Macchiole's varietals, the black fruits show the precision of Cabernet Franc with an overlay of tobacco and oak.

Scrio was introduced as a monovarietal Syrah in 1994. It makes a very fine impression with something of the restraint of the Northern Rhône, but slightly lifted aromatics. Messorio, a monovarietal Merlot, has been a signature wine ever since its introduction in 1994. It offers the typically fresh impression of Merlot in Tuscany. There is also a white, Paleo Bianco (90% Chardonnay and 10% Sauvignon Blanc) These are not wines for instant gratification, but need some time to get out from under the oak and to express themselves.

Tenuta Dell'Ornellaia ***

Via Bolgherese 191, 57020 Bolgheri	*+39 0565 71811*
info@ornellaia.it	*Axel Heinz*
www.ornellaia.com	*[map p. 145]*
112 ha; 950,000 btl	*Bolgheri Superiore, Ornellaia*

Close to the Sassicaia estate, Ornellaia became one of the great names in Bolgheri almost immediately after it produced its first vintage in 1985. It was created by Marchese Lodovico Antinori, younger brother of Marchese Piero Antinori of the wine producer Marchese Antinori. The Mondavi winery of California took a minority interest in the estate in 1999, acquired the entire estate in 2002 and went into partnership with the Frescobaldi family; and then Frescobaldi purchased the estate outright in 2005 after Constellation Brands took over Mondavi.

Ornellaia has two separate vineyards: the home estate around the winery; and the Bellaria vineyard a little to the south (planted between 1992 and 2005). Today four wines are produced. The top two are Ornellaia itself, and the 100% Merlot produced from the Masseto hill. A second wine, La Serre Nuove, was introduced in 1997, and is made by declassifying lots from Ornellaia. "There's a limit to how much great Ornellaia can be made; we do not need to create scarcity as is done in Bordeaux by diverting to the second wine," says winemaker Axel Heinz. Le Volte is more a separate blend (of Sangiovese with Cabernet Sauvignon and Merlot) than a third wine, since it includes purchased grapes.

Ornellaia's varietal composition has changed somewhat over the years. The original intention of a blend of Cabernet Sauvignon with Merlot was somewhat sidetracked when the Merlot from the Masseto hill (which is planted exclusively with Merlot) was diverted into a separate cuvée because it was so good. Merlot increased in the blend after the vineyard at Bellaria (a slightly cooler site exposed more to the sea) was acquired. Having peaked at almost a third of the blend, now it is back down to around a quarter. Cabernet Sauvignon was around 80% for the first decade, then dropped abruptly to 65% with the 1997 vintage, but for the past few years has been only just above half; it's dropped a little recently as the result of a replanting program. Perhaps reflecting the warmer climate, Cabernet Franc has been increasing (5% in the first vintages, 15-20% in recent years) and Petit Verdot has been included since 2003. "The tendency is for warm years to use less Merlot and more Cabernet Franc," Axel explains. The grapes for Ornellaia come roughly half from the home vineyard and half from Bellaria. Ornellaia's level of production has been fairly steady, something over 8,000 cases, although production of La Serre Nuove has increased from 2,500 to 12,500 cases since its inception.

The Masseto hill is 6.6 ha with an elevation of 100m; its special feature is that it has parcels of blue clay (the same terroir as Petrus in Pomerol). "Merlot can soak up water from the soil, that is probably the secret of Merlot at Masseto, and why it isn't jammy and over ripe," Axel explains. Its first vintage was 1987, and in 2019 production moved from the Ornellaia winery to its own new winery. Eleonora Marconi came from Frescobaldi to be the cellarmaster. It's significantly more expensive than Ornellaia.

Tenuta San Guido ***

Loc. Le Capanne n. 27, Bolgheri, 57020 Castagneto Carducci	*+39 0565 762003*
info@sassicaia.com	*Carlo Paoli*
www.sassicaia.com	*[map p. 145]*
103 ha; 800,000 btl	*Bolgheri Sassicaia*

Sassicaia stands alone. It's the only wine in Italy to have its own DOC. "Sassicaia was Vino da Tavola until 1994 when we got the DOC. Until that time the proportion of Cabernet Sauvignon and Cabernet Franc was 85:15, so when we had to decide regulations for the DOC we decided 80% should be Cabernet Sauvignon and the rest could be anything," says the Marquis Incisa. It is no longer the most expensive super-Tuscan, perhaps because it has not moved in the direction of power and extraction, but has remained true to its original objective of an elegant wine in the tradition of Bordeaux's left bank, although naturally more Mediterranean than Atlantic in style. It remains typically 85% Cabernet Sauvignon and 15% Cabernet Franc, with relatively minor adjustments to the proportions in each vintage.

Reflecting on changes over time, the Marquis Incisa says, "There is a little difference (in alcohol levels). Twenty years ago it was difficult to get 12%, today we try keep it as low as possible. People say we are picking the grapes too early. People have been reducing yields because they thought it makes higher quality, but this then makes the wine unbalanced. Sassicaia started at 60 hl/ha, when everything else was generally around 100 hl/ha. Some people went down to 30 hl/ha but this makes it very difficult to contain the alcohol."

The main change has been the move to introduce a second wine. "Until 2000 we made only one wine. We were using 98-100% of our grapes. Since 2000 we have made another wine, and we select. The reason we started making Guidalberto was that we didn't want to increase the production of Sassicaia. The wines with the highest ratings in American journals were all based on Merlot so we thought we must make a wine with Merlot to follow the trend." Guidalberto is 60% Cabernet Sauvignon to 40% Merlot; it comes mostly from specific vineyards, but about 20% comes from grapes declassified from Sassicaia. There is also another wine, Le Diffese, a blend of 55% Cabernet Sauvignon and 45% Sangiovese, "but it's not really a third wine, it's a different wine." Sassicaia and Guidalberto come exclusively from estate grapes, while for Le Diffese the Cabernet Sauvignon comes from estate vineyards and the Sangiovese is purchased. Sassicaia is 85% of production; Guidalberto and Le Diffese are IGT Toscana.

Michele Satta **

Loc. Vigna Al Cavalière 61, 57020 Castagneto Carducci	*+39 0565 773041*
info@michelesatta.com	*Fabio Motta*
www.michelesatta.com	*[map p. 145]*
20 ha; 150,000 btl	*Bolgheri Superiore, I Castagni*

One of the pioneers in Bolgheri, Michele Satta started in 1982 with only 4 ha, "but it wasn't a project, he moved slowly into wine production," said Fabio Motta, his son-in-law, an oenologue who was in charge of marketing until he started his own winery (see profile). Today the home vineyard occupies 25 ha at the southern limit of the Bolgheri region. Its gradual development has been responsible for the higgledy piggledy organization of many varieties across the vineyards. Standing at one spot in the vineyard, I could see Cabernet Sauvignon, Merlot, Syrah, Teroldego, Vermentino, and Viognier. Overall, plantings are 30% Cabernet Sauvignon, 30% Merlot, 20% Sangiovese, 10% Syrah, 10% Teroldego, but I Castagni focuses on 70% Cabernet Sauvignon, 20% Syrah, and 10% Teroldego. "I Castagni started with only Cabernet Sauvignon and Merlot. After Michele decided to make a single-vineyard wine, he decided to add Syrah and Teroldego. Originally when Michele planted the vineyard he felt he must plant Cabernet Sauvignon because the area is in Bolgheri, but he also wanted to plant his favorite grapes, Syrah and Teroldego. Teroldego has rich color and lots of tannins, but is very soft. This was planted rather than Merlot because ripening is very slow. Probably the Syrah will increase in future," says Fabio. Michele has been an enthusiast for Syrah ever since visiting the northern Rhône, and he introduced a varietal Syrah with the 2007 vintage. The small winery is on the edge of the home vineyard. It's quite unassuming, with plans to build a second storey with a tasting room, but in true Alice in Wonderland fashion, this has been stuck in the bureaucracy because of fears that carbon dioxide (notably heavier than air) might rise up and kill the patrons. In the meantime, Michele continues to make wine in a traditional manner; no modern gimmicks here.

Poggio al Tesoro *

Via del Fosso 33, Donoratico, 57022 Castagneto Carducci	*+39 0565 773051*
info@poggioaltesoro.it	*Lorenzo Fortini*
www.poggioaltesoro.it	*[map p. 145]*
	Bolgheri Superiore, Sondraia
68 ha; 410,000 btl	*Bolgheri Superiore, Solasole*

Poggio al Tesoro is a project of Allegrini, one of the best and largest producers in Valpolicella, who expanded into Bolgheri in 2002 (and into Montalcino by purchasing San Polo in 2008: see profile). The estate has three vineyards, Via Bolgherese, Le Grottine, and Le Sondraia. The style is typically rich. "Poggio al Tesoro always harvests very late," says Marilisa Allegrini.

The entry-level wine is Il Seggio, a blend of 40% Merlot, 30% Cabernet Sauvignon, 20% Cabernet Franc, and 10% Petit Verdot, aged in French oak with a third new wood. The signature wine is Sondraia, about two thirds Cabernet Sauvignon with 25% Merlot and 10% Cabernet Franc, matured in an equal mix of new and one-year barriques. It gives an impression of having more Cabernet Franc than it really does, but apparently this is due to the more structured character of Merlot in this location. Both show a relatively forward style, with the typical softness of Bolgheri, but there is more structure and stuffing to Sondraia.

Dedicato a Walter, named for Walter Allegrini, is a 100% Cabernet Franc that brings out a full, chocolaty expression of varietal character. Medittera is Syrah with some Merlot and Cabernet Sauvignon.

The white wine, Solosole, was part of the start of a trend to grow Vermentino in Bolgheri. "I didn't want to make the standard Italian white. It comes from a special clone originating in Corsica," says Marilisa. Far from the often amorphous character of the variety, it conveys fresh and herbal impressions with depth on the palate.

Profiles of Important Estates

Tenuta Argentiera

Via Aurelia 412/a, Località I Pianali, 57022 Donoratico	*+39 0565 0565774581*
enoteca@argentiera.eu	*Leonardo Raspini*
www.argentiera.eu	*[map p. 145]*
	80 ha; 480,000 btl

Brothers Corrado and Marcello Fratini established Tenuta Argentiera in 1999 at the southern border of the appellation in what used to be part of the Donaratico estate, several miles away from the main concentration of wineries in Bolgheri. Ownership changed when they sold a controlling stake in 2016 to Stanislaus Turnauer, an Austrian industrialist, who has full control as of 2019. The focus is on Bordeaux varieties. The Argentiera cuvée is the top wine, a classic Bordeaux blend with 40% each of Cabernet Sauvignon and Merlot, and 20% Cabernet Franc. Villa Donaratico is the second wine, not as smooth, and has 10% Petit Verdot together with the other Bordeaux varieties. Aged in steel, the third wine, Poggio ai Ginepri is a Bordeaux blend with all the varieties, and makes a rustic impression. The wines tend to be somewhat forceful and lack the plushness usually found in Bolgheri; only Argentiera itself can lay claim to elegance. The Cru series are monovarietals including Cabernet Sauvignon, Cabernet Franc, and Merlot, each named after a member of the Fratini family. Because tannins become progressively smoother going up the series from the third and second wines, the top wines curiously seem ready to drink sooner than the second or third wines. The olive oil is smoother than the wines. There is also a white blend of Vermentino and Sauvignon Blanc. Visits start at the tasting room on the main road, and continue at the winery on the hills above, with a panoramic view over the Mediterranean, but the €40 fee for visiting and tasting is exorbitant.

Campo al Mare

Via del Fosso 31, 57022 Donoratico	*+39 0558 59811*
folonari@tenutefolonari.com	*Roberto Potentini & Raffaele Orlandini*
www.tenuteambrogioegiovannifolonari.com	*[map p. 145]*
	30 ha; 180,000 btl

Campo al Mare is the Bolgheri winery of the Folonari family, who also own Nozzole in Chianti (see profile), La Fuga in Montalcino, and wineries in Montepulciano and Maremma. The general approach is modern, emphasizing fruit, and relying on new oak. The flagship Bolgheri is a Bordeaux blend, with 60% Merlot, 20% Cabernet Sauvignon, 15% Cabernet Franc, and 5% Petit Verdot. Under Bolgheri Superiore, Baia al Vento is 90% Merlot. Both age in 500 liter barriques, with 50% new and 50% 1-year oak for Baia al Vento. There are also a rosé and a Vermentino.

Castello Di Bolgheri

Loc. Bolgheri, Sda Lauretta 7, 57020 Castagneto Carducci	*+39 0565 762110*
info@castellodibolgheri.eu	*Federico Zileri Dal Verme*
www.castellodibolgheri.eu	*[map p. 145]*
	50 ha; 80,000 btl

The Castello di Bolgheri was part of the vast estate of Counts of Gherardesca in the sixteenth century. It is still owned by their descendants, the Zileri Dal Verme family. Federico Zileri Dal Verme became President of the Consorzio in 2013. The castle dates from the fifteenth century, and its wine cellar was built in 1796 in the town. The Castello has 130 ha of land in the northern part of Bolgheri, and in 1997 planted vineyards with what has become the typical mix of Bolgheri, Cabernet Sauvignon, Cabernet Franc, Merlot, Syrah, and Petit Verdot. The Bolgheri Rosso Varvàra is a Bordeaux blend of 60% Cabernet Sauvignon, 20% Merlot, 15% Cabernet Franc, and 5% Petit Verdot, aged in barriques for 12 months. The Bolgheri Superiore is a similar blend, sometimes with more Cabernet Sauvignon, selected from the best lots.

Azienda Agricola Chiappini

SP Via Bolgherese 189/c, 57022 Bolgheri	*+39 0565 765201*
info@giovannichiappini.it	*Giovanni Chiappini*
www.giovannichiappini.it	*[map p. 145]*
	15 ha; 80,000 btl

The Chiappini family were farmers in the Marche who moved to Bolgheri in the 1950s. Giovanni moved into viticulture after 1978. Half of the estate is planted, with the typical varieties of the area, interspersed with olive trees. The Bolgheri Superiore, Guado de' Gemoli, is 70% Cabernet Sauvignon with 15% each of Merlot and Cabernet Franc, aged for 18 months in barriques, with 15% new oak and the rest 1-2-year. There are two Bolgheri Rosso: Felciaino is 50% Cabernet Sauvignon, 40% Merlot, and 10% Sangiovese, aged in used barriques, and ages in used barriques; Ferruggini is 50% Sangiovese, 30% Cabernet Sauvignon, and 20% Syrah, aged in stainless steel. The white Bolgheri is Le Grottine, 100% Vermentino aged in stainless steel. The Lienà line of varietals is IGT Toscana, made only in top years, from Merlot, Cabernet Sauvignon, Cabernet Franc, and Petit Verdot, aged in barriques with some new oak.

Donna Olimpia 1898

Località Migliarini 142, 57020 Bolgheri	*+39 0302 279601*
hospitality@donnaolimpia1898.it	*Guido Folonari*
www.donnaolimpia1898.it	*[map p. 145]*
	45 ha; 250,000 btl

Guide Folonari comes from one of Italy's most successful wine families, which owned Ruffino in Chianti. After the breakup of the family, one branch of the family owned several estates under the holding of Tenute Folonari (see profile). Guido started three wineries: l'Illuminata in Barolo, Tenuta San Giorgio in Brunello di Montalcino, and Donna Olimpia in Bolgheri, founded in 2001. The project was based on a collaboration into research on clones and rootstocks with Attilio Scienza of the University of Milan. Under Bolgheri DOC, the Donna Olimpia 1898 red is Cabernet Sauvignon, Merlot, Petit Verdot, and Cabernet Franc, aged in new and 1-year barriques for 12 months, the rosé comes from Merlot and Cabernet Franc, and the white is Vermentino, Viognier, and Petit Manseng, aged on the lees in stainless steel with frequent battonage. Millepassi is Bolgheri Superiore, selected from the best lots of Cabernet Sauvignon, Merlot, and Petit Verdot, given the same aging as the red Bolgheri. Targeto is an IGT Toscana from the same varieties as the Bolgheri red, aged similarly in new and 1-year barriques, but only for 4-6 months. Obizzo is a white IGT Toscana, 100% Vermentino, aged for 5 months in stainless steel. Orizzonte is described as a super-Tuscan, and comes from 100% Petit Verdot.

Fornacelle

Loc. Fornacelle, 232/a, 57022 Castagneto Carducci	*+39 0565 775575*
info@fornacelle.it	*Famiglia Billi-Battistoni*
www.fornacelle.it	*[map p. 145]*
	9 ha; 35,000 btl

Fornacelle takes its name from the area near Castagneto Carducci where several furnaces used to operate (there are remnants under the cellar). The family estate dates from the end of the nineteenth century when Giulio Batistoni was a tenant farmer. Two generations Vincenzino Billi (son-in-law of Giulio's granddaughter) started a farm of for fruit and vegetables. Stefano Billi took over in 1996, planted vineyards and renovated the farm and cellars. The Bolgheri Superiore, Guarda Boschi, is 40% Merlot and 30% of each Cabernet, aged for 15 months in barriques with a third each of new, 1-year, and 2-year. The Bolgheri Rosso, Zizzolo (named for the vineyard), is 60% Merlot and 40% Cabernet Sauvignon, aged for 6 months in 2-year barriques. The white Zizzolo is Vermentino, vinified in stainless steel. The Artistic collection, identified by paintings on the labels has four varietal cuvées. The reds ferment and then age in barriques. The Bolgheri Superiore, Foglio38, is 100% Cabernet Franc, vinified in new oak; IGT Toscana Erminia is 100% Merlot. The two whites are 100% Sémillon (fermented and aged in barrique) and Fiano (aged in stainless steel).

I Luoghi

Loc. Campo al Capriolo 201, 57022 Castagneto Carducci	*+39 0565 777379*
info@iluoghi.it	*Stefano Granata*
www.iluoghi.it	*[map p. 145]*
	5 ha; 15,000 btl

Stefano and Paola Granata created this tiny property in 2000. Stefano was an electrical engineer before he decided on a change of career to winemaking. They produce two wines. The major wine is Podere Ritorti, a Bolgheri DOC, which is 80% Cabernet Sauvignon blended with Cabernet Franc, Merlot, and Syrah; production is about 12,000 bottles, and the wine ages in barriques of French oak for 14 months. Campo al Fico is a Bolgheri Superiore, 80% Cabernet Sauvignon and 20% Cabernet Franc; aged in new barriques, production is about 3,000 bottles. The wines tend to have a strong tannic structure.

Fabio Motta

loc le Fornacelle 232/c, 57022 Castagneto Carducci	*+39 3461 403750*
info@mottafabio.it	*Fabio Motta*
www.mottafabio.it	*[map p. 145]*
	6 ha; 30,000 btl

After five years working at Michele Satta, his father-in-law's property, Fabio Motto established his own winery in 2009. The main vineyard. Le Pievi, is in Castagneto Carducci, and produces the Bolgheri red, a blend of half Merlot with a quarter each of Cabernet Sauvignon and Sangiovese, aged in 2- and 3-year barriques. A smaller vineyard just to the north in Le Fornacelle produces a white based on Vermentino and Viognier. Another small vineyard. Le Gonnare, purchased in 2012, has clay-rich soil, and is the source for the Bolgheri Superiore, a blend of 85% Merlot and 15% Syrah, aged in barriques with one third new oak.

Orma

Via Bolgherese, 57020 Bolgheri	*+39 0575 477857*
info@ormabolgheri.it	*Antonio Moretti*
www.tenutasetteponti.it	*[map p. 145]*
	6 ha; 50,000 btl

One of the smaller estates in Bolgheri, next to Ornellaia, Orma was bought in the mid 1990s by Antonio Moretti, who owns Tenuta Sette Ponti in his native Arezzo, and Feudo Maccari in Sicily. The terroir is clay soil rich in pebbles. The vineyard was planted in 1999, and the first vintage was 2005. Orma is the grand vin, IGT Toscana from a classic blend of 50% Merlot, 30% Cabernet Sauvignon, and 5% Cabernet Franc. Passa di Orma is the second wine, a Bolgheri DOC blend of 40% Merlot, 35% Cabernet Sauvignon, and 25% Cabernet Franc, introduced in 2015. Orma ages for a year in barriques, while Pass di Orma ages for 6 months. There are no visits or tastings here, but the wines can be tasted at Tenuta Sette Ponti.

Podere Sapaio

Loc. Lo Scopaio 212, 57022 Castagneto Carducci	*+39 0438 430440*
info@sapaio.it	*Massimo Piccin*
www.sapaio.it	*[map p. 145]*
	25 ha; 100,000 btl

Originally from the Veneto, a graduate who worked in the family construction business, Massimo Piccin changed career and purchased the 40 ha estate in 1999; it was virgin land, and he planted the vineyards in 2000. Soils are clay and sandy loam: plantings are the four major black Bordeaux varieties. The estate produces two wines: Sapaio is a Bolgheri Superiore from 70% Cabernet Sauvignon, 10% Cabernet Franc, and 20% Petit Verdot, aged in barriques for 18 months. The second wine, Volpolo, is Bolgheri Rosso and comes from 70% Cabernet Sauvignon, with 15% each of Merlot and Petit Verdot. It ages for 16 months in a mix of barriques and tonneaux. Carlo Ferrini is the consulting oenologue.

Tenuta di Biserno

Palazzo Gardini, Piazza Gramsci 9, 57020 Bibbona	*+39 0586 671099*
info@biserno.it	*Helena Lindberg*
www.biserno.com	*[map p. 145]*
	46 ha; 160,000 btl

Located a couple of miles north of Bolgheri on the road to Bibbona, this is the project Lodovici Antinori started after he sold Ornellaia (see profile) in 2001. It's a joint project with his brother Piero, the Marchese Antinori, and Umberto Mannoni, who owned the site. Lodovico had found it in 1994, when he was planning to expand Ornellaia, but it became a separate project. The soils are the type known as Bolgheri Conglomerate, a combination of silt, clay, and calcareous rocks. Vineyards were planted between 2001 and 2005 with Bordeaux varieties, predominantly Cabernet Franc, but also Cabernet Sauvignon, Merlot, Petit Verdot, and Syrah. Michael Rolland from Bordeaux consults. Il Pino is the cuvée from the younger vines at Biserno, aged for 12 months in barriques, and the grand vin is called simply Biserno, aged for 15 months in 90% new barriques. The price almost doubles going to the Lodovico cuvée, made in small amounts only in top years, typically 95% Cabernet Franc with 5% Petit Verdot. Two cuvées are made from another estate just to the southwest of Biserno, Tenuta Campo di Sasso: Insoglio del Cinghiale is mostly Syrah, and Occhione is a blend of Vermentino and Viognier.

Maremma

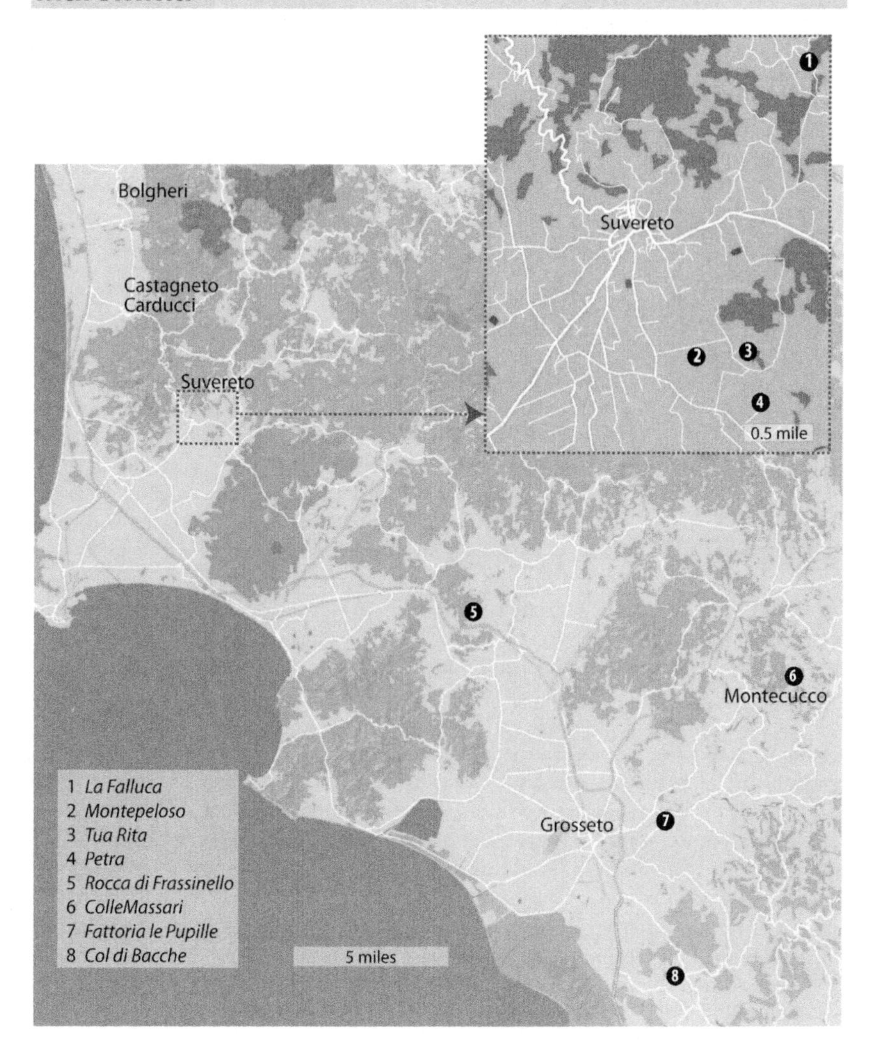

Bolgheri
Castagneto Carducci
Suvereto
Suvereto
0.5 mile
Montecucco
Grosseto
1 La Falluca
2 Montepeloso
3 Tua Rita
4 Petra
5 Rocca di Frassinello
6 ColleMassari
7 Fattoria le Pupille
8 Col di Bacche
5 miles

Montepeloso **

Loc. Montepeloso 82, 57028 Suvereto	*+39 0565 828180*
contact@montepeloso.it	*Fabio Chiarelotto*
www.montepeloso.it	*[map p. 159]*
17 ha; 100,000 btl	*IGT Toscana, Gabbro*

Fabio Chiarelotto grew up in Switzerland; Suvereto is his mother's native place. He purchased Montepeloso in 1995, starting with 9 ha on the Montepeloso hill and then added another 5 ha on the facing Fontanella hill. Things have turned out a little differently from what he expected. "When I bought the estate the wine was mainly Sangiovese, with some Cabernet and white varieties. My idea was to make an Italian wine, I wanted to shape an Italian Tuscan blend, I wanted to get away from Sangiovese pumped up with Merlot." But the wine that has made Montepeloso famous is Cabernet Sauvignon.

"When we purchased the winery and tasted the separate Cabernet lots, we were impressed by how complete the Cabernet was. So I felt that since there was no real history here, I would start with Cabernet, get a reputation, and then work on the Italian project." He makes four wines: the Gabbro Cabernet Sauvignon, Nardo, which is mostly Sangiovese, the Eneo Sangiovese-based blend, and the entry-level A Quo. The blends in Nardo and Eneo have been moving towards the Italian project, to blend Montepulciano, Sangiovese, Alicante, and Marselan (a cross of Cabernet Sauvignon with Grenache). Gabbro, the top wine, spends 18 months in oak (85-90% new). "I tried a little Cabernet Franc in early vintages but I preferred 100% Cabernet Sauvignon; it is such a great variety when it is ripe that it doesn't need anything else, it's a complete variety."

The wine started out with Cabernet Sauvignon from the Montepeloso hill, but as the new plantings at the Fontanella vineyard have come on line, they have formed an increasing proportion of the blend. Whether it's because of the difference in exposure (southwest at Montepeloso as opposed to west at Fontanella) or the age of the vines (old at Montepeloso but only a few years old at Fontanella), barrel samples show a richer wine from Montepeloso, although the blend is more complex.

Fabio is considering an old vines selection from Montepeloso (but the issue of course is the effect of taking this out of the Gabbro.) I asked about stylistic objectives and reference points? "A reference point for sure is the old style California Cabernet, Ridge Montebello or Heitz Martha's Vineyard, it goes in a direction I can see here, not as an imitation but as an expression of Cabernet. So the reference points are California Cabernets from the period when they were elegant, before they became brutal." It's ironic that Fabio's intention was (and still is) to produce a great wine from indigenous varieties; his first great success has been with a 100% Cabernet Sauvignon, but the search for elegance continues. Estate grapes provide 85% of sources, the rest are purchased.

Fattoria le Pupille *

Piagge del Maiano 92/a, loc. Istia d'Ombrone, 58100 Grosseto	*+39 0564 409517*
info@fattorialepupille.it	*Elisabetta Geppetti*
www.elisabettageppetti.com	*[map p. 159]*
85 ha; 450,000 btl	*Morellino di Scansano*

This part of Maremma has always been agricultural, but Elisabetta Geppetti was a pioneer in establishing vineyards for quality wine after she took over the family winery, only 2 ha at the time, in 1985, when she was only 20. The winery started in a farmhouse, but with success and expansion a new winery was built. The farmhouse remains at the heart of the estate, and is surrounded by 12 ha of vineyards. In 2002, the vineyards were expanded by buying the 43 ha Bozzino estate on a neighboring hill. The estate now covers 420 hectares, and includes 20 ha of olive trees as well as the vineyards.

There is one dry white wine, Poggio Argentato, a blend of Gewürztraminer and Sauvignon Blanc: it is very aromatic and perfumed. The same varieties, together with Sémillon, are used for the botrytized sweet wine, Solalto. The entry-level red is the Morellino di Scansano; the first wine to be produced at the property, it's an unusual blend of Sangiovese with Alicante and Ciliegiolo. Driven by red fruits, it can be stern rather than obvious. A monovarietal Syrah, first produced in 2015, is fermented in amphora, and plays to the ripe, nutty side of Syrah.

The two top wines come from single vineyards in the original area: Saffredi is a Bordeaux blend aged in barriques with 75% new wood, and Poggio Valente is 100% Sangiovese aged in tonneaux of 500 or 600 liter. Poggio Valente is relatively restrained for the region, and tends to show the fruity rather than the savory side of Sangiovese. It ages slowly, just beginning to move in a tertiary direction after a decade.

Saffredi is the most famous cuvée, one of the early super-Tuscans, first produced in 1987. Saffredi started as a pure Cabernet Sauvignon, but is now a blend of 60% Cabernet Sauvignon, 30% Merlot, and 10% Petit Verdot. Recent years show the full range of vintage variation. The 2017 is soft and less obviously structured than other vintages, while 2016 is quite stern and the most Bordeaux-like, showing structure before its fruits. The 2015 is aromatic and almost perfumed, with more of a plush Bolgheri-like expression. The 2014 is the most elegant of the decade, refined and classy, a bit in the direction of Margaux.

Tua Rita **

Loc. Notri 81, 57028 Suvereto	*+39 0565 829237*
info@tuarita.it	*Stefano Frascolla*
www.tuarita.it	*[map p. 159]*
51 ha; 350,000 btl	*IGT Toscana, Giusto di Notri*

Tua Rita has been a fantastic success story, reaching cult status within a few years of its first release. The estate was founded in 1984 when Rita Tua and her husband Virgilio

Bisti planted Cabernet Sauvignon and Merlot in Suvereto. The first vintage was released in 1992. The vineyards are on the low-lying hills overlooking the town of Suvereto. Extended in 2002, the cellar is built underground to allow for gravity feed.

Giuso di Notri, a Bordeaux blend of Cabernet Sauvignon, Merlot, and Cabernet Franc, is the signature wine named for the first vineyard that was planted; the style Is international, but it has unusual elegance for the region. Redigaffi, a 100%% Merlot whose first vintage was 1994 with only two barriques, became the cult wine by the end of the decade. Matured in new French barriques, this has a full force style. Perlato del Bosco is a monovarietal Sangiovese (until 2011 it also contained Cabernet Sauvignon). Per Sempre is a monovarietal Syrah, and can be quite nutty in style; another Syrah, Keir, introduced with the 2016 vintage, has the novelty of aging in amphora, and has an elegant, fresh style. Rosso dei Notri is effectively a second wine from the young vines, and is a blend of all the varieties; aged in stainless steel, it's intended for easy drinking. There are also two white wines.

The second generation, in the form of daughter Simena and son-in-law Stefano Frascolla, has been running the estate since Virgilio's death in 2010. In an expansion in 2015, they rented Poggio Argentiera in Grosseto.

Profiles of Important Estates

ColleMassari

Loc Poggi del Sasso, Cinigiano 58044	*+39 0564 990496*
collemassari.spa@legalmail.it	*Claudio Tipa*
www.collemassariwines.it	*[map p. 159]*
	110 ha; 500,000 btl

This was the first domain in the ColleMassari wine estates, which also include Grattamacco (see profile) in Bolgheri, and Poggio di Sotto (see profile) and San Giorgio (both in Montalcino). Claudio Tipa, who is now president of the Montecucco Consorzio, purchased the fortified hamlet of Castello ColleMassari in 1999, and the first vintage was in 2000. The winery is located at an elevation of 320m in the foothills of Monte Amiata, about 24 miles northeast of Grosseto. The wide range starts with a rosé (70% Sangiovese), and two whites, Melacce (100% Vermentino aged in stainless steel and intended as an aperitif) and Irisse (85% Vermentino, 15% Greccheto, aged in barrique). Rigoleto is the entry-level red (70% Sangiovese, aged in a mix of barriques and large casks). The estate gets into higher gear with the flagship ColleMassari Riserva (80% Sangiovese aged in 40 hl casks, and 10% each of Ciliegiolo and Cabernet Sauvignon, aged in 500-liter tonneaux of French oak). Poggio Lombrone is 100% Sangiovese from old vines in the best plot, aged in 40 hl oak casks. All the wines are Montecucco DOC.

Col Di Bacche

Strada Di Cupi, 58051 Montiano Magliano In Toscana	*+39 0564 589538*
info@coldibacche.com	*Alberto Carnasciali*
www.coldibacche.com	*[map p. 159]*
	14 ha; 80,000 btl

Alberto Carnasciali and his wife Franca, bought 15 hectares a few miles south of Grosseto, about 5 miles from the coast. They planted vineyards in 1998 on virgin land on a hill with sandy and calcareous soil, facing southeast, at elevations from 170-260m. They are in the center of Morellino di Scansano, and half the vineyard is planted with varieties for the DOCG, the other half with Merlot and Cabernet Sauvignon for IGT Toscana. The Morellino di Scansano follows the appellation guidelines with 85% Sangiovese plus other varieties, and ages in stainless steel. It accounts for more than half of all production. Rovente is the Morellino Riserva, 90% Sangiovese and 10% Syrah; it ages in French barriques, including new oak. Cuvées in IGT Toscana go to extremes of local versus international varieties. Poggio alle Viole is a selection of the best Sangiovese, aged for 15 months in barriques. Cuperino is almost exclusively Merlot, with 2-4% Cabernet Sauvignon, aged in new and older barriques for 12 months. Campo Amarene is a blend of Sangiovese, Merlot, Cabernet Sauvignon, and Syrah, aged in 2-3-year barriques for 12 months. The white IGT Toscana is Vermentino, and there is also a passito from Sangiovese and grappa.

La Fralluca

Loc. Barbiconi, 153, 57028 Suvereto	*+39 0565 829076*
info@lafralluca.com	*Luca Recine & Francesca Bellini*
www.lafralluca.com	*[map p. 159]*
	10 ha; 45,000 btl

La Fralluca was a change of career for Francesca Bellini and Luca Recine who were in fashion in Milan when they decided in 1998 to make wine instead. Three years later they bought land in Suvereto, ten miles from the coast, and started a renovation. The name of the estate is a combination of their names. They planted vineyards in 2005 and 2006, on three adjacent hills within the estate, offering a variety of exposures, and the winery was completed in 2009. Soils are albarese (calcareous clay) and the climate is hot, but with strong diurnal variation. Varietal IGT wines include Cabernet Franc, Syrah, Alicante, Vermentino, and Viognier. The varietal Sangiovese is DOC Suvereto. Fillide is the only blend: Sangiovese, Syrah, and Alicante.

Rocca di Frassinello

Loc. Giuncarico, 58023 Gavorrano	*+39 0566 88400*
visite@roccadifrassinello.it	*Paolo Panerai*
www.roccadifrassinello.it	*[map p. 159]*
	90 ha; 400,000 btl

This is an example of a successful producer of Chianti Classico (Castellare de Castellina: see profile) expanding into Maremma, in this case in collaboration with Château Lafite Rothschild of Bordeaux. Terroir was selected that's similar to Chianti Classico, but of course there's the important difference that temperatures at about 5°C higher, so harvest is 3-4 weeks earlier. The estate was assembled by combining five small farms, with a total area of 500 ha. Renzo Piano designed the winery. The flagship wine, Rocca di Frassinello, is 60% Sangiovese with 20% each of Cabernet Sauvignon and Merlot, and ages in 80% new barriques. La Sughera di Frassinello is effectively a second wine, 50% Sangiovese with 25% each of Cabernet Sauvignon and Merlot, and ages in 50% new barriques. Baffonera is 100% Merlot from a plot just below the winery; aged in 100% new barriques, the aim is to challenge Ornellaia's Masseto from Bolgheri. Ornello is a variant that includes some Syrah. Poggia alla Guardia, and the Vigne Alte version, are entry-level wines aged in concrete.

Petra

Loc. San Lorenzo Alto 131, 57028 Suvereto	*+39 0565 845308*
info@petrawine.it	*Mario Botta*
www.petrawine.it	*[map p. 159]*
	100 ha; 350,000 btl

Coming from the construction industry in the 1970s, Vittorio Moretti founded Bellavista in Franciacorta, and subsequently started other wineries, Contadi Castaldi, also in Franciacorta, and La Badiola in Maremma. Petra was founded in 1997, with a striking winery designed into the hillside by Swiss architect Mario Botta. Vittorio's oenologist daughter, Francesca is in charge. A wide range of wines is based on Cabernet Sauvignon, Merlot, Syrah, and Sangiovese, with both blends and monovarietals. A second range of wines, the entry-level Belvento, was added in 2015.

IGT Toscana

Profiles of Leading Estates

Bibi Graetz ***

Piazza Mino, 37 Fiesole	*+39 0555 97222*
info@bibigraetz.com	*Bibi Graetz*
www.bibigraetz.com	*[map p. 41]*
	IGT Toscana, Testamatta
70 ha; 500,000 btl	*IGT Toscana, Bugia*

Bibi Graetz has a penchant for making wine in unusual places—high up in the hills of Fiesole, overlooking Florence, and on Giglio, a steep and rocky island off the coast of Maremma. Well outside the famous areas, the winery in Fiesole is there because "I was born here. My grandfather bought the house and land, did some farming and made some wine that was sold in bulk. My father planted a 2 ha vineyard here in the 1960s."

Bibi started making wine in 2000, and sources grapes from vineyards all over the area, "like a stripe running through the whole area of Chianti," Bibi says. The approach is the antithesis of the increasing worldwide focus on single vineyards; the wines are blends from multiple sources. "I was in love with old vineyards, so it didn't make any sense to buy land and plant, so I looked for old vineyards. I have long term contracts; we manage vineyards but don't own land. So it doesn't make sense for us to make a single-vineyard wine. Our idea is more like a super-Tuscan than a Burgundy concept."

The two major reds, Testamatta and Colore, are labeled as IGT Toscana. Testamatta comes from seven plots and is 100% Sangiovese. Its vivid label reflects the family background in art: Bibi's father is an artist, and so was Bibi before he turned to winemaking. Colore is a selection of the best lots, from the oldest vineyards, and is about a third each of Canaiolo, Colorino, and Sangiovese. The vineyard plots used for Testamatta are usually the same each year; there is a little variation in the Sangiovese used for Colore as it always has the best barrels. "Colore has a little new oak, we look for the lots with more structure, so it has a bit more volume."

Tasting barrel samples from the individual vineyards, it becomes clear that Bibi is in love not only with old vineyards, but also with high altitude vineyards; all except one are above 300m. They vary from the cool climate impressions of a plot at high elevation above Greve in Chianti, to the more powerfully structured expression of a south-facing vineyard south of Siena. Variations in oak also contribute, although there is no new oak in Testamatta. In the early years, the wines went into 100% new oak, under the advice of an oenologist, but this changed after 2005. "I don't work with an oenologist any more because I like to do my thing." Today Bibi's view is that, "for Testamatta it is important not to use new oak, we wouldn't have the fruit coming forward. The uniqueness of Testamatta is that we don't impose a style, you don't have the oak, you just have the impression of the grapes coming out." Indeed there is wide vintage variation: 2016 will be a powerful vintage, but 2015 is infinitely elegant.

The white wines all come from Giglio. "It's basically a rock in the middle of the sea, it's a pretty arid climate—it never rains!" Bibi says. "Vineyards go from sea level to 300m. We are planting one at 550m. You can do a big white wine in Giglio, it's not so easy to find a big white from Tuscany." Bibi's whites have their own character. Aside from the entry-level wine, Scopeta, the whites are all 100% Ansonica. Chiozzolo is an orange wine, fermented on skins for 7 days and aged in new oak. Bugia is more conventional, with 90% aged in stainless steel and 10% in wood. In 2016, Bibi produced a white Testamatta for the first time, just 700 bottles. "For Testamatta I took the best parcels, there's no skin contact but it's fermented and aged in 100% new oak. Here I think you go towards a big white wine." The common feature, whether coming from the grapes or from skin contact or oak maturation, is a sense of extract and texture to the palate, almost a sense of austerity to restrain the fruits. These are definitely wines with personality.

Making wine in three places, Bibi is a busy fellow. In addition to the reds of Fiesole and the whites of Giglio, there are entry-level wines, part of a negociant activity under the Casamatta name, made in rented space at a larger winery. "Our winery is not big enough to do entry-level wine," Bibi explains. It has been difficult to visit the winery, because it's basically a small group of buildings extending from the family house. But this may change as Bibi is thinking about moving into larger space, which would relieve the cramped conditions at the winery, and allow there to be a tasting room. It's not just wine that ferments here: there is a constant whirl of ideas. In the air at the moment are the possibilities of introducing a single-vineyard wine or a second wine to Testamatta. This must surely be one of the liveliest wineries in Tuscany.

Profiles of Important Estates

Caiarossa

loc. Serra all' Olio 59, 56046 Riparbella (pi)	*+39 0586 699016*
info@caiarossa.it	*Eric Albada Jelgersma*
www.caiarossa.com	
	31 ha; 115,000 btl

The winery was founded in 1998, with organic vineyards and a cellar built on Feng Shui principles. (More practically, it is built into the hillside for gravity-feed operation.) It's located a few miles north of Bolgheri, in an area where wine was usually made just for local consumption. The property was acquired in 2004 by Eric Albada Jelgersma, who owns Châteaux Giscours and du Tertre in Margaux. Soils are very varied. There's a surprisingly wide range of plantings, and the wines are IGT Toscana. (Sangiovese is the only Italian grape variety.) Caiarossa is a selection of the best lots, with a blend of Merlot, Cabernet Franc, Cabernet Sauvignon, Syrah, Sangiovese, Petit Verdot, and Alicante, aged in a mix of tonneaux and barriques with 30% new oak. The proportions of grape varieties vary widely from year to year. Pergolaia is 90% Sangiovese, with some Cabernet Franc, Cabernet Sauvignon and Merlot, and ages in old tonneaux. Aria is a blend of Cabernet Franc, Merlot, Syrah, and Cabernet Sauvignon, aged in barriques and tonneaux with 15% new oak. Starting in 2009, Essenzia has been made only in top vintages, and there's no commitment to any specific blend: in different vintages it's been Syrah and Alicante, Cabernet Sauvignon and Alicante, or Cabernet Franc. The white is a blend of 70% Viognier and 30% Chardonnay, from the chalkier areas, barrel-fermented, and then aged in barriques and tonneaux.

Index of Estates by Rating

Index of Organic and Biodynamic Estates

Index of Estates by Appellation

Sassodisole
La Serena
Tenuta di Sesta
Tenuta Silvio Nardi
Talenti
Tassi
Terralsole
Tiezzi
Uccelliera
Val di Suga
Valdicava
Villa i Cipressi

Chianti Classico

Castello d'Albola
Castello Di Ama
Marchesi Antinori
Tenuta di Arceno
Badia A Coltibuono
Tenuta di Bibbiano
Podere le Boncie
Castello di Bossi
La Brancaia
Villa Cafaggio
Cantalici
Azienda Agricola Caparsa
Tenuta di Carleone
Fattoria Carpineta Fontalpino
Fattoria Casaloste
Casavecchia Alla Piazza
Tenuta Casenuove
Castell'in Villa
Castellare Di Castellina
La Castellina di Tommaso Bojola
Castello Della Paneretta
Fattoria Castelvecchio
Famiglia Cecchi
Fattoria di Cinciano
Collazzi
Fattoria Di Fèlsina
Castello Di Fonterutoli
Fontodi
Castello di Gabbiano
Gagliole
Castelli Del Grevepesa
I Fabbri di Susanna Grassi
I Sodi
Isole E Olena
Istine
La Sala
Lamole di Lamole
Azienda Agricola Lanciola
Le Cinciole
Villa Le Corti
Tenuta di Lilliano
Livernano
Le Miccine
Il Molino Di Grace
Castello Di Monsanto
Monte Bernardi
Monteraponi
MonteVertine
Fattoria Nittardi
Tenuta di Nozzole
Panzanello
Fattoria Poggerino
Podere Poggio Scalette
Poggio Torselli
Castello Di Querceto
Querceto di Castellina
Querciabella
Castello di Radda
Castello Dei Rampolla
Barone Ricasoli
Riecine
Rocca Delle Macìe
Rocca di Castagnoli
Rocca di Montegrossi
Ruffino
Borgo Salcetino
Tenuta di Perano
San Felice
Fattoria San Giusto a Rentennano
Savignola Paolina
Tenuta Tignanello
Tolaini
Val Delle Corti
Vallepicciola
Castello di Verrazzano
Castello Vicchiomaggio
Villa Calcinaia
Vignamaggio
Fattoria di Viticcio
Castello Di Volpaia

Chianti Rufina

Marchesi de Frescobaldi

IGT Toscana

Caiarossa

Bibi Graetz

Maremma

Rocca di Frassinello

Montecucco

ColleMassari

Morellino Di Scansano

Col Di Bacche

Fattoria le Pupille

Suvereto

La Fralluca

Montepeloso

Petra

Tua Rita

Vino Nobile Di Montepulciano

Avignonesi

Podere Le Bèrne

Bindella

Boscarelli

La Braccesca

Fattoria del Cerro

Cantine Dei

Palazzo Vecchio

Poliziano

Salcheto

Tenuta Valdipiatta

Tenuta Trerose

Index of Estates by Name

Printed in Great Britain
by Amazon

73625742R00108